Paddling the
Boundary Waters and
Voyageurs National Park

Help Us Keep This Guide Up to Date

Every effort has been made by the authors and editors to make this guide as accurate and useful as possible. However, many things can change after a guide is published—trails are rerouted, regulations change, techniques evolve, facilities come under new management, etc.

We would love to hear from you concerning your experiences with this guide and how you feel it could be improved and kept up to date. While we may not be able to respond to all comments and suggestions, we'll take them to heart and we'll also make certain to share them with the authors. Please send your comments and suggestions to the following address:

The Globe Pequot Press
Reader Response/Editorial Department
P.O. Box 480
Guilford, CT 06437

Or you may e-mail us at:

editorial@GlobePequot.com

Thanks for your input, and happy travels!

A FALCON GUIDE®

Paddling the Boundary Waters and Voyageurs National Park

James Churchill

FALCONGUIDE®

GUILFORD, CONNECTICUT
HELENA, MONTANA
AN IMPRINT OF THE GLOBE PEQUOT PRESS

Copyright © 2003 by The Globe Pequot Press

Text design: Amy Bransfield
Overview map: Topaz © The Globe Pequot Press
Route maps: Mary Ballachino © The Globe Pequot Press
Base maps provided by myTopo.com
All interior photos are by the author except where noted.

Library of Congress Cataloging-in-Publication Data

Churchill, James E., 1934–2002
    Paddling the boundary waters and Voyageurs National Park / James Churchill.
       p. cm.
    ISBN 0-7627-1148-5
     1. Canoes and canoeing—Minnesota—Voyageurs National Park—Guidebooks. 2. Canoes and canoeing—Minnesota—Boundary Waters Canoe Area—Guidebooks. 3. Voyageurs National Park (Minn.)—Guidebooks. 4. Boundary Waters Canoe Area (Minn.)—Guidebooks. I. Title.

GV776.M62 C58 2002
797.1'22'09776—dc21   2002069244

Manufactured in the United States of America
First Edition/Second Printing

CONTENTS

Fernberg Road Region

State Highway 1/Sawbill Trail and Caribou Trail Region

Gunflint Trail Region

Voyageurs National Park

Sadly, James Churchill passed away before the publication of this book. His daughter Jolain has asked that his book be dedicated to the following: Her mother, Joan, who helped James do research for this book and followed him as they traced the path the Voyageurs used centuries ago. She stood by him during their forty-seven years of marriage and always allowed him to follow his dream. Also, to his fishing partners—son Jim Jr., brother Gene, and Stuart and Jim P.—for the many hours they spent with James on the water. Finally, this book is dedicated to James's parents and his sister Janet, who were called home before him, for the contributions they made to his life.

Acknowledgments

This guide could not have been written but for the dozens of people who offered advice, pored over the text, and corrected my mistakes.

I particularly want to thank Terry Eggum, Assistant Ranger, Superior National Forest, for the hours he spent on trip descriptions. Nancy Pius from the Superior National Forest also helped with in depth information.

After Jeff Serena gathered the components, Josh Rosenberg, Associate Editor at Globe Pequot, worked very hard to bring this capricious project to the finish line, as did Pamela DeRusso. Patricia Meyers deserves special mention for her uncanny ability to spot an inconsistency.

I would also like to acknowledge the enthusiastic paddlers that we met out in the Boundary Waters Canoe Area Wilderness. They ranged in age from infants carried in their mother's arms to one who had been paddling for six decades and showed no signs of giving up. Some had good advice on paddling, camping, or cooking, or where the best fishing could be found. All were good company and helpful. Indeed, the people who journey deep into unspoiled wilderness are a special breed and I feel privileged to know some of them.

Joan Churchill deserves mention for her willingness to keep trying, come what may.

MAP LEGEND

Canoe route	——————
Portage	····················
USA–Canada Border	▬▬ ▬ ▬▬
Parking	🅟
Parking—Multiple Lots	🅟 6
Entry Point	㊹ 🅔
Campsites	•
Forest Service Roads	—[351]—
State Highway	—(26)—
Interstate	—(53)—
County Road	—(777)—
BWCAW Boundary	– – – – –
Put In/Take Out	↔
Water	⬭

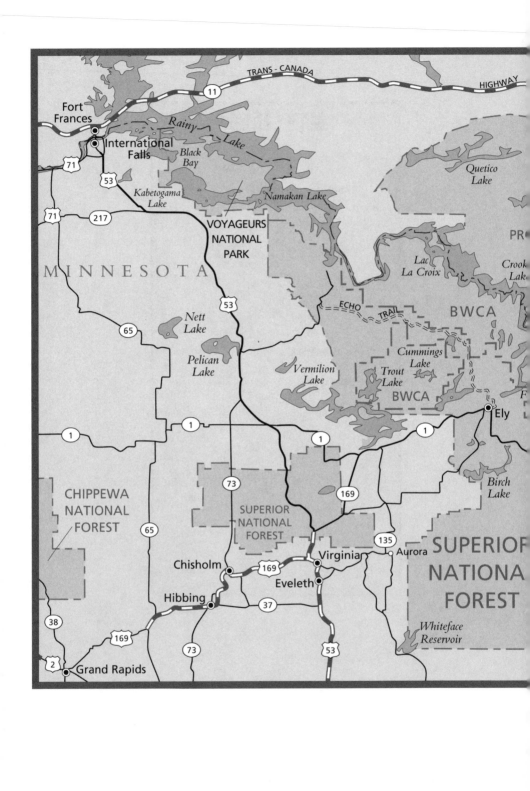

How to Use This Guide

Paddling the Boundary Waters and Voyageurs National Park was written to help wilderness paddlers find a route in the Boundary Waters (BWCAW) or Voyageurs National Park that would gratify their personal mission. Some paddlers are seeking solitude in an unspoiled wilderness setting, and others are primarily interested in the fishing and wildlife sightings. A few want to test their canoeing skills and stamina during a long, rugged trip. Most want some measure of all.

I have carefully selected the routes that I believe will be the most satisfying. Each trip has been proven by me—or by Forest Service officials or guides—to be worthy of consideration. Motors are allowed in the park, but in the BWCAW most lakes are paddle only, although motors are permitted on part of some routes. There is no quota on trips in the park, but a quota is set for each entry point in the BWCAW. A complex arrangement of lottery and reservation requirements is in place to regulate the trips. Some entry points fill early, others seldom are filled. Some flexibility in a departure date will probably be required for the most popular entry points. See the appendix for more information.

Each trip entry in this book begins with capsulized information meant to be read at a glance to help determine if the trip might meet expectations. The information includes:

Entry point: The starting point for the route, this number is assigned by the USDA Forest Service, and appears on the section locator map. There are no entry point numbers in Voyageurs National Park, so none are listed in that section.

Character: A short description of the lake or river and what makes it worthy of consideration.

Length: The distance of the trip in miles.

Average run time: The time it takes to paddle the run at an average pace. In the BWCAW paddle time is figured at 2.0 mph; portaging time is calculated at 0.33 mph. This varies widely depending on wind direction, speed, and difficulty of portages. Most groups can average 8 miles per day on most trips.

Class: Where rivers are involved, the difficulty level of the water is based on the opinions of Forest Service officials, since none of the rivers have been officially classified according to the International Scale of River Difficulty. The ratings range from I to V; the higher the number, the more difficult the run. A very slow current is classified as quiet.

Skill level: Beginner, Intermediate, or Expert, based largely on difficulty and perceived hazard. The remoteness of a particular stretch is also taken into consideration. The different levels of paddling skills are an approximation. Only the parameters for the Beginner level are detailed below, since the Intermediate and Expert levels do not apply to routes in this guide.

Beginner: Knows the basic strokes and can handle craft competently in smooth water. Knows how to bring the boat to shore safely in fast current, can negotiate sharp turns in fast current, can avoid strainers and others obstacles and understands the difficulties of the stream to be floated. A beginner is not a person who is picking up a paddle for the first time. Novices should get some practice on a lake before taking their first trip. Optimal flow and average gradient are not known for the BWCAW rivers and are not included.

Hazards: Any risks that require attention.

Maps: A list of the detailed maps needed for navigation. The maps included in the book are designed to give a general idea of the water route. They are meant to be used for trip planning, not as navigational tools. See the appendix for navigational map sources.

The paddling: Narrative detailing the trip itself.

Access: Provides directions for motoring to a developed or carry-in canoe landing. Some accesses are located on a separate but connected lake, stream or river, from the entry point.

Shuttle: Tells how to reunite the trip vehicle and the canoe at the end of the trip. Two vehicles can be used, or an outfitter can be hired to provide the shuttle. Walking or cycling are options. Most trips return to the starting point.

Camping: Lists the nearest public campground to the entry point. Often private campgrounds are available also.

Food, gas, lodging: Lists nearby communities where these essentials can be obtained.

For more information: Gives the names of offices or agencies that can provide greater detail and may be able to answer questions that are not answered in this book.

Safety

Although the most dangerous part of a canoe trip, by far, is the trip from home to the entry point, there are some risks associated with paddling into the wilderness. Severe weather, physical exertion, rough water, rapids, and accidents on portages or in camp can produce an emergency situation. Medical help is a long ways away. In the event of a serious accident where the victim can't be moved, make the victim as comfortable as possible and send ablebodied paddlers for help immediately. Send more than one canoe, if available. Also, start a signal fire and partially smother it with green leaves or grass to produce a dense smoke signal. A series of three signals, whether audible or visible, is the standard SOS signal.

If a circling airplane eventually appears, get out into the lake and paddle in tight circles or wave a brightly colored cloth tied to a canoe paddle to signal for help. After the authorities are contacted, a determination is made whether evacuation by motorized vehicle or airplane is necessary. The victim will be billed for any such evacuation. A set of rules for staying safe follows.

1. Leave word of where you are going and when you will return with Forest Service officials or a friend. A permit covers this, but stick to an itinerary. The Forest Service does

not initiate searches immediately, if a party does not return on schedule. This will have to be done by family or friends by notifying the county sheriff's department. See the appendix for contact information.

2. Don't shoot rapids. This is a high-risk venture for most paddlers and bringing a damaged canoe out of the BWCAW is expensive. Canoes have been disabled and people hurt or drowned because they were trying to avoid a portage by paddling down rapids.

3. Don't canoe in a lightning storm. A canoe on a lake is likely the highest point on the lake. Land the canoe immediately. If caught in a location where landing the canoe is impossible, stay near the shore but about three canoe lengths away from the bank.

After landing, remember lightning will tend to hit a tree or other high point rather than a person if the object is five times as high as the person and the horizontal distance from the person to the object is about half the object's height. But avoid the tallest trees; they are lightning rods for any nearby strikes. Don't lean on wet ropes, tree trunks or sit on wet rocks or tree roots during a storm. If skin begins to tingle or hair stand on end, squat low to the ground, with head between knees.

4. Always wear a life jacket, even if you can swim and even in shallow water. Stay with a capsized canoe. It won't sink.

5. Boil or treat all water. Use a filter or chemical designed to remove *Giardia Lamblia* or "Beaver Fever." Ingesting this parasite can cause severe illness and even death if untreated. Bringing water to a full boil will also kill this parasite.

6. Carry a first aid kit and know how to use it. Learn CPR.

7. Use common sense in all situations. Don't take unnecessary chances to save time.

Forest Fires

Fire danger in the BWCAW is at an all-time high due to the July 4, 1999, windstorm that flattened trees over a good portion of the area. Fires can start that could quickly burn across swamps and jump lakes and rivers. If a major fire starts, it is likely that some visitors are going to be trapped by flames. If trapped on a sizeable lake quickly make an anchor by taping a heavy rock to an anchor rope. Abandon camp gear or place it in the water along the shoreline. Keep the rain fly (or other large cloth) to cover up with. Paddle to the middle of the lake, find a depth where the anchor rope will reach the bottom—with about one-third of its length to spare—and anchor there. Cover up completely with the wet rain fly or at least cover the face with a wet cloth. Wait until the fire passes by. If trapped on a small lake or river, turn the canoe over in shallow water and get under it. Again, cover the face with a wet cloth. The air under the canoe will be much cooler than the superheated air accompanying the fire. Wait until the fire has completely gone by.

The air could be full of burning sparks for awhile after the main fire goes by. Don't attempt to travel across the fire corridor for at least twenty-four hours. By then search planes will probably be flying overhead. Get out in a clearing or well out on the lake and wave a bright cloth, or signal with a mirror or reflector made from aluminum foil.

A *derecho* (Spanish for "straight") windstorm is an extremely violent windstorm with straight winds caused by a complex of thunderstorms configured in a certain pattern. On July 4, 1999, a derecho developed along a stationary boundary from north-central South Dakota northeast to International Falls, Minnesota, and east from there to Thunder Bay, Ontario, Canada. It was generated by a complex of thunderstorms in South Dakota and moved easterly at about 90 mph. Damage occurred in Fargo, North Dakota, and then the storm moved into north-central Minnesota, snapping off trees and downing power lines in five Minnesota counties. The storm seemed to get more powerful as it moved along. Winds roared between 80 and 100 mph into the BWCAW, where it caused massive destruction in an area 30 miles long and 5 miles wide. Trees were leaned over or broken off in a 350,000-acre area. In some sections all of the trees were downed. The most destruction occurred in a corridor starting at Moose Lake near Ely and heading northeast through the Kekekabic Lake area all the way to the Gunflint Trail. About 800 campsites and 80 miles of portages were damaged.

Several hundred campers were out in the BWCAW when this happened. It was extremely fortunate that the storm occurred during the day. If it had been night, some campers would have been asleep in their tents when trees fell on them. Fortunately, no one was killed, but thirty to thirty-five people were injured, some seriously. Hundreds were stranded. Forest Service crews and volunteers quickly began sawing trees out of portage trails so campers could get out. Some of the injured had to be removed by helicopter. By the end of the season most of the portages were opened, and campers were allowed to go back out again.

Now, however, in some places, the downed trees are piled three times as high as a tall man. This wood is drying out and creating a potential for dangerous forest fires. Campfires are restricted or forbidden in the most impacted areas, and the potential for injury to campers climbing among the downed trees or cutting them up for fuel is great. Any tree that is leaning over or is in a pile is probably under tension and if cut could whiplash and injure or kill anyone nearby. At present, officials are deciding what can be done about the danger. Suggestions range from mechanically removing the hazards to setting them afire in a prescribed burn to doing nothing at all and letting nature take its course.

It will be several decades before nature heals the destruction, but on the positive side, the hills, the lakes, and the rivers are still there. Fishing and wildlife viewing is still as rewarding as ever. Most of the portages and campsites are open. Moose, deer, bear, and small mammals as well as most birds will benefit from increased growth of green plants and underbrush. In short, most of the BWCAW is still there and it will keep getting better.

Planning the Trip

First, decide what you expect from a trip to the BWCAW and Voyageurs National Park. Do you enjoy fishing? Fishing can be fabulous, and the best tasting fish—anywhere—are found in the BWCAW. Do you enjoy base camping? Some campsites are very rewarding, and many entry points offer convenient access to base camping opportunities. Sightseeing? Topographical and lake scenery, pictographs and waterfalls are found in the BWCAW. Viewing or taking wildlife photographs? Wildlife is about and usually nonwary. Traveling as far as you can? There is almost no end to the canoe routes in this area.

Next, decide how many will be in your party, when you want to go, and how long you want to stay. Most BWCAW groups camp for four days, but get together and hash this out ahead of time. Well ahead of your departure date contact the appropriate U.S. Forest Service office (see the appendix for ranger station information) or commercial outfitter, tell them what you want to do, and apply for a permit. There is a fee for camping in the BWCAW and a fee for a reservation for a permit. After deciding on an area, acquire the necessary maps (see appendix).

Now assemble the outfit and develop skills that will smooth the trip. If necessary, learn to paddle, carry a canoe, set up camp, and find and stay on a route. Everyone should have a working knowledge of compass reading and map reading. These two items are a necessary part of an unguided trip into the BWCAW and Voyageurs National Park.

Portages can be the most stressful part of the trip. Decide who is going to carry the canoe, the food, and the rest of the gear. Often the canoe is the heaviest part of the gear. Canoe carriers can prepare for the task by carrying the canoe at home to build muscles and confidence. Pack the Duluth Packs at home to see what can be carried in each pack. Weigh them, too. Except for base camping, try to keep the weight of each pack at forty pounds or less.

When the big day comes, arrive at the right time, get the permit, and head for the entry point. When it's time to portage, move steadily. Don't block the passage with a canoe or gear so that the next group cannot get started using the portage. Also, when other groups are portaging ahead, don't crowd them. Sit in the canoes and wait for them to clear the area. It is most convenient to camp at designated campsites. They are equipped with a fire grate, a privy, and tent pads. Off-site camping is illegal and punishable by a fine. Canoe and camp quietly. Try not to disturb other campers.

Visitors have literally hundreds of outfitters to chose from that will rent any or all equipment and supply the food needed. They will also help plan the trip and obtain permits and reservations. See the appendix for further information.

Assembling the Outfit

Volumes have been written on the proper clothing to wear in the BWCAW, but the choice isn't really that complicated. Clothing need not be expensive or elaborate. Tight fitting clothing should be avoided, and flimsy footwear will not be satisfactory. Otherwise, most gear commonly used for outdoor pursuits will do the job. Two sets of footwear are convenient to have: high-top, waterproof boots for portaging and lightweight sneakers or sandals for wearing around camp. Ten- to fourteen-inch-high leather boots treated with waterproofing material are a good choice; some people wear rubber boots at portages. To avoid ankle injuries though, footwear used for portaging should have ankle support. Many of the portage paths are rough and strewn with rocks and roots. Lightweight sneakers are more comfortable around camp and while paddling on a hot day. They also minimize the impact at the campsite.

In summer one sturdy, long-sleeved, loose fitting shirt and one pair of sturdy, loose-fitting trousers—besides one pair of lightweight walking shorts and T-shirt—are almost mandatory. The shorts and T-shirt can be worn for swimming, as a change of underwear, as pajamas, or when the other clothing is being washed. A baseball style cap is functional, but a hat with a brim on all sides that can be adjusted to protect the ears and neck is most appropriate. Don't take a hat with an oversized brim, though; if you carry the canoe, you can't wear the hat. Sunglasses are very nice to have along for bright days and for heading into the afternoon sun.

Long underwear is appropriate for all seasons in the BWCAW. One wool sweater or sweatshirt should be brought along, also. Most paddlers take a stocking cap and gloves along for cool days. Lightweight, two-piece rain gear is almost a necessity. It will keep the paddler dry and also function as windbreaker on cool days. The jacket should have a hood and the bib needs strong suspenders; elastic waists are acceptable, too.

This is the basic wardrobe needed. Beyond this list take whatever is necessary for confidence and comfort in season, but remember it all has to be carried over each portage.

Tents

There is a wide variety of tents made for backpacking and canoe camping. Some are A-frame design and some are dome shaped. A-frame tents will shed rain better and are easier to set up. Dome tents have more useable room but are heavier, need more poles and are more difficult to set up. Get the best, lightweight tent that you can afford and be sure it is large enough for comfort while waiting out a windy day or rainstorm. Figure about 30 square feet per camper. A four-person tent with 50 to 60 square feet of floor space is a good choice for two people. It should have a rain fly and sewn seams. The floor should be of the bathtub design. The windows should be screened with fine mesh netting. It should have two doors. Aluminum poles are stronger than fiberglass. Tent and poles should not weigh over ten pounds; six to seven pounds is better. The Eureka Timberline model meets these specifications, as do several other models. If in doubt, rent a tent from an outfitter and try it out. Outfitters have valuable opinions on the best models, based on long experience.

A plastic tarp used for a ground cloth is advantageous to have. It will be most helpful if placed on the floor inside the tent, except then it will not keep the bottom of the tent clean. A rain tarp is well worth packing in; a 10 x 12 plastic tarp is a good size. Tie 8-foot ropes to each corner and leave them in place for a quick set up. Keep the tarp in a convenient location. Set it up first when pitching camp in rain and darkness; it will provide a protected haven for the gear and campers while the priorities are sorted out.

Every camper will want a comfortable sleeping bag and pad. A down bag is light and warm and can be crushed into a very small package. Down bags must be kept completely dry, though, and they are expensive to buy. They have a very long life, though, and can be kept dry with proper packing. Synthetic material bags are an option, also. A summer weight, synthetic fill bag might be warm enough, but it is heavier and bulkier than down. If it should happen to get wet it will dry quite well and retain some warmth. They are relatively inexpensive, but most have a short life. The sleeping bag should be compressed into a stuff sack and then placed inside a heavyweight plastic bag that can be sealed before being placed in the Duluth Pack.

A sleeping pad can be a roll of foam or it can be a self-inflating model; either is satisfactory. Plastic or rubber pads should be fitted with a cloth sack for comfort, warmth, and ease of cleaning.

Canoe packs such as Duluth Packs and Granite Gear have evolved to the point where they are almost perfect for the serious canoe camper. They are expensive, however. Economical versions are widely available, though, and some people even pack their gear in two or three heavy-duty plastic bags placed inside one another.

Canoes

There are hundreds of models of canoes made by dozens of manufacturers. Where frequent portages must be made, as in the BWCAW, Kevlar material is an advantage because it is lightweight. Kevlar canoes can be damaged, though, by contacting rocks or stumps. They are also the most expensive canoe. Royalex canoes are a little heavier, but more rugged. Fiberglass is heaviest of all, but rugged and economical. Lightweight aluminum is useable also, and some wood and canvas canoes are in use in the BWCAW, as are cedar strip models.

To my mind, the choice is simple: Buy a Kevlar canoe if you can afford it, and load and unload from the water and stay mostly on lakes where few rocks or hidden obstructions are found. Otherwise, buy a Royalex canoe. My third choice is fiberglass, followed by aluminum.

Fishing

A Minnesota fishing license is required to fish in the BWCAW and Voyageurs National Park. Licenses are available from sport stores and canoe outfitters, as well as from the Minnesota Department of Natural Resources. All canoes must be registered, either in the home state or in Minnesota (see appendix). Anglers who fish in Canada need an Ontario license. Motorboats are allowed in Voyageurs National Park, but please consult park rangers for information on horsepower restrictions.

Fishing in the BWCAW is not much different than fishing in other places. Walleyes can be taken most readily on live bait such as minnows in the spring and fall and leeches or night crawlers the rest of the time. Live bait is best presented with leadhead jigs or with a hook and split shot combination. Plastic tails will sometimes enhance or substitute for live bait when jigging.

Hard body, minnow-imitating baits such as Rapalas are second best. Northern pike will hit buzzbaits, spinners, spoons, hard body baits, and live bait. Smallmouth bass can be taken on live bait or with the artificial baits already described. Lake trout are usually taken on spinners in the early spring or with spoons or heavy jigs tipped with cut bait when they go deep in summer. A few lakes have stream trout; spinners, flies, and live bait will take these fish.

A proven fishing outfit consists of a two-piece, rugged, medium-action spinning rod of the Rhino Rod class and a well-made reel. Use the strongest line available in six pound diameter size to save snagged lures. Two dozen ⅛ ounce jigs—orange and chartreuse—twenty-five #2 Aberdeen hooks, and a package of assorted split shot are needed. Also take a dozen assorted artificial lures for walleyes, bass, and northern pike. These lures should include at least one #8 black and silver or crayfish color shaprap. Three daredevil-type spoons, three assorted in-line spinners, and one buzzbait are well worth their weight. Some small spinners can be taken for stream trout fishing. This is the basic outfit. Take personal favorites, also. Most fishing lures are light in weight, and a few extra will not diminish the enjoyment of the trip. A net is not necessary but nice to have along.

Other Items

Compass: A Brunton sportsman or a classic model is a good choice.

Maps: McKenzie, Fisher, or United States Geological Survey (USGS) topographical maps (see appendix).

Rope: 50 to 100 feet of ¼-inch nylon rope, in addition to the tent and tarp tie downs.

First-aid kit in a waterproof container

Camera and film

Folding saw: Needed for wood cutting and possible portage clean out. Don't hang it from a tree limb. It can blow out and injure someone and it is easy to forget when breaking camp.

Repair kit: Duct tape, a multipurpose tool of the Leatherman type, epoxy, repair kit for eyeglasses, needle and thread, sharpening stone for knives.

Sponge or towel: For bailing out canoe and cleaning it.

Pocket knife and sheath knife

Compact flashlight (with spare batteries)

Cigarette lighter and stick matches in a waterproof container: For starting campfires and lighting the stove.

One large candle: For starting fires and illumination.

Gasoline cooking stove and gasoline: One gallon of fuel is enough for one four-day trip.

Introduction to the Boundary Waters

The Boundary Waters Canoe Area Wilderness (BWCAW) lies in northeastern Minnesota and stretches for nearly 150 miles along the international border between Canada and the United States. It covers 1,098,057 acres of some of the most scenic land, lakes, rivers, and streams in the world. This is a land made for canoes: 1,200 miles of canoe routes lead the paddler among 2,000 lakes dotting 1,400 square miles of wilderness. No one is allowed to live in the BWCAW, and there are no man-made structures. It is the second largest unit of the National Wilderness Preservation System and has the largest virgin forests remaining east of the Rocky Mountains. At present it is visited by over 200,000 people a year.

History

Some pictographs on lakeside cliffs apparently tell of a more ancient people, but the Sioux were reported to be very early inhabitants of this region. It is not known how long they lived in the territory, but in the mid- or late 1600s the Sioux were replaced by the Chippewa, also called the Ojibway. During the seventeenth and eighteenth centuries the Chippewa were in control of what is now the BWCAW. The first white man known to travel through the BWCAW region was the fur trader Jacques de Noyons. He returned in 1732 to establish fur trading posts on the border lakes.

This began the era of the fur trade, which soon became the most important commerce in the New World. This activity was so profitable that it returned a twentyfold increase to the fur trader. At the heart of the fur trade were the Voyageurs: short, powerful French-Canadian boatmen who would start out from Montreal or nearby regions in a 25-foot birchbark canoe carrying goods to trade with the Indians in return for luxurious pelts of beaver, otter, mink, and muskrat. The Voyageurs were some of the most colorful people in history and were reputed to have paddled seventeen to eighteen hours per day and carry 180 to 270 pounds per man per carry over the portages.

The French dominated the fur trade until they lost Canada to the English in the French and Indian War in 1760. English and Scottish traders replaced the French, but the fur trade was declining due to a scarcity of beaver and changing clothing fashions in Europe. By the end of the seventeenth century the trade had almost disappeared.

It is no accident that the international United States–Canadian border was established along the same Voyageurs highway that the fur traders used. After disputing the borderline for years, the United States and Canada finally compromised and settled on the Voyageurs's route in the Webster-Ashburton Treaty of 1842. It established that "all the water communications and all the usual portages shall be free and open to the use of the citizens and subjects of both countries."

During the late 1800s settlers, including farmers, loggers, and miners, moved into the area. Shortly thereafter railroads were built, which stimulated logging and mining activities

Canoeing the Boundary Waters.

and also threatened to devastate this pristine area. Fortunately, far-sighted leaders began a movement that eventually saved the area from development. In 1909 the Superior National Forest was established, and in 1926 1,000 acres were set aside as a primitive wilderness area. In 1939 the wilderness area was redesignated as The Superior Roadless Primitive Area and enlarged to include over 1,000,000 acres. This was further defined by the BWCAW Bill of 1978, which included 1,098,057 acres. This bill also prohibits logging, restricts mining, and limits the use of motorboats to 24 percent of the water. Consequently, the 2,500 lakes of the BWCAW don't look much different now than they did when the first white man paddled into the interior of the region.

Geology

The BWCAW is underlain with the Canadian Shield, a vast rock area, billions of years old, that covers about 2 million square miles of Canada and the Lake Superior region. There is generally only a thin layer of glacial deposits over the shield, and in the BWCAW the bedrock is exposed in many places.

The abundance of lakes in the BWCAW is the result of erosion and four major glaciers that dammed up valleys and scraped basins out of less resistant rock deposited between harder rock deposits. Scratches and gouges in the solid rock, piles of polished boulders, and an occasional gigantic boulder set down in an unlikely place are further signs of glacial activity.

The lake basins give some indication of the type of bedrock they were formed on. Some are long and narrow and are aligned east and west. These are either underlain with coarse igneous rock or Rove Slate formations. Rove Slate formation lakes are often bordered by 300- to 400-foot cliffs. Where the bedrock is granite, lakes are formed in the eroded cracks in the rock. These lakes have bays and arms reaching in different directions. Lakes underlain by Ely Greenstone rock have shallow basins.

The Laurentian Divide wanders haphazardly through the eastern BWCAW, generally heading south from North Lake to Sawbill Lake. North of the divide, all waters flow to the Arctic Ocean through Rainy River, Winnepeg River, and Nelson River to Hudson Bay. South of the divide, all waters flow to the Atlantic Ocean through Lake Superior and the Saint Lawrence River. The most famous of the Laurentian Divide portages is the Height of Land portage between North Lake and South Lake in the Arrowhead region. The 480-rod portage from Zenith Lake to Lujenida Lake in the Gunflint region is the most stressful portage crossing the divide.

Climate

The weather in the BWCAW can vary greatly from east to west because of Lake Superior and, in a more subtle way, the Laurentian Divide. Generally speaking, there is more sunshine in the western region and more fog, rain, and changeable weather in the eastern region. The opposite can occur, however, and often does. Average temperature in May is 51°, average for June 60°; July, 66°; August, 63°; and September, 53°.

The ice is usually melted from the lakes by May 5; the trees are usually leafed-out by May 15. Right after ice-out is often a pleasant time to enter the BWCAW. The water level is high enough to minimize portaging, insects are not out yet, and lake trout, walleye, and northern pike are often biting well. Birds and animals are active and easily spotted. Access roads and portages can be soft and muddy, however. It can get cold, and a rare snowstorm could occur.

June is warmer and it is the best time for fishing, but biting insects are abundant and rainfall is frequent. July through mid-August is the most comfortable time for camping, swimming, and paddling, but except for smallmouth bass, the fish aren't usually biting as well. Water levels have fallen and some routes become impassable. From mid-August through September, insects have almost disappeared, fish are again biting well, colored leaves appear, and people are scarce. Moose sightings and wolf howling are at peak levels. It can rain, freeze, or even snow during this period, however. After September 30, no reservations are required. Early October can be very rewarding, but check ahead before committing to a long trip: The lakes might be frozen over.

Wildlife

Mammals

The beaver which brought the fur traders here in the first place, although once almost exterminated, now have returned to what is probably more than their original abundance.

Beaver seem to be almost everywhere. Beaver houses, peeled sticks, mud scent mounds, and dams are almost continually in sight. Beaver dams have created ponds where aquatic plants and animals flourish. When the dams are abandoned, the pond basin, combined with the tree felling the beavers did, has opened up clearings called "beaver meadows" where grassy plants flourish and provide food for a variety of large and small creatures.

Moose are common in the BWCAW in swampy, low-land areas. Probably the greatest concentration of moose is found in the Isabella River region and the lakes west of Crab Lake, but they are widely scattered and some are found almost anywhere there are marshy areas. Moose avoid lakes and river with rocky bottoms and shorelines. Most people believe a canoe trip is a success if they see a moose or two, and sightings of twenty or more are not unheard of. Whitetail deer are sometimes seen in the eastern and mid sections of the BWCAW, although the Echo Trail region in the western section probably has the greatest concentration.

Timber wolves live here also and their night howls are guaranteed to bring chills of pleasure to the heart of anyone who respects the outdoors. They assemble in packs of from two to twelve animals and live by killing moose, deer, and beaver, along with a variety of small animals.

Wolves can cover 40 miles in a night and can run several miles at a rate of 30 to 35 mph. There are four separate wolf packs living in the BWCAW. Most are found near the moose herds in the Clear Lake, Bald Eagle, Gabbro Lakes, and Isabella River areas. Coyotes, also, live in the BWCAW.

Black bears are common and widely distributed, and they cause the most concern to campers. Bears have learned that campers have food and will approach campsites to try and find it. Probably the best way to avoid having food supplies raided by bears is to hang supplies on a rope strung between two trees. This rigging should be at least 10 feet high and 6 feet away from the trunk of the trees or from any heavy limbs that might support a bear. They can swim between islands and will swim out into a lake and attempt to climb into an anchored canoe where food is secreted if they can smell it. They might wreck the canoe doing this.

Many campers hide their food in tight, odor-proof containers placed well away from the campsite. No one, to my knowledge, has ever lost food when they did this. Black bears are not considered dangerous but should be treated with respect and kept at a distance. In all fairness, I believe more food is lost to small mammals and rodents than bears. I personally don't know anyone who has ever lost food to a bear in the BWCAW. The following rules are generally heeded by campers in the BWCAW. If everyone followed them, bears would probably stop visiting campsites because there would be no reward for doing so.

1. Never store food in your tent.

2. When away from camp and at night, hang your food 10 feet high and 6 feet away from the tree.

3. When you leave camp, tie your tent flaps open so a bear can get in the tent to satisfy its curiosity without ripping the entrance.

4. Keep a clean campsite. Completely burn all garbage and food scraps.

5. An island campsite is not immune to bear visits. They are ready swimmers.

6. Never get between a mother bear and her cubs. Female bears are protective of their cubs.

7. If a bear wanders into your campsite, try yelling or banging on pots or pans to scare it away. Don't corner or charge it.

8. If the bear doesn't readily leave, spray it with Capsaicin (pepper spray), if available, or move to a distant campsite.

9. Realize that serious bear encounters are very rare. Many campers have visited the BWCAW for decades without a single bear encounter.

Smaller mammals common to the BWCAW region are eastern chipmunk, red squirrel, woodchuck, muskrat, snowshoe hare, red fox, pine marten, fisher, otter, and lynx.

Birds

There are about 240 species of birds living in the park. Probably the most famous is our national symbol, the bald eagle. An extremely large bird, a female bald eagle can have an 8-foot wingspan; males are smaller but can have a 7-foot wingspan. Breeding pairs live in the BWCAW, as do many immature eagles. Most nesting eagles frequent the bluffs and cliffs along the United States–Canadian border. They also nest in the tall white pines along the Kawishiwi River and in the Cummings Lake region south of Echo Trail. Turkey vultures and osprey are present and can be mistaken for an eagle at a distance. Note that vultures have a red head and osprey have a more streamlined wing configuration than eagles and a white underside. Stay at least 0.25 mile away from large raptor nests.

Loons are common on most lakes. They probably generate the most interest in bird watching because they are highly visible and vocal. Loons should be enjoyed from a distance. They might abandon their nest or chicks if agitated by being chased or shouted at. Ruffed grouse, several species of woodpeckers, blue and gray jays, chickadees, redwing blackbirds, yellow warblers, broadwing hawks, owls, crows, and ravens are also indigenous to the area.

Herring gulls and great blue herons are frequently seen, as are cormorants and several species of ducks such as mallards, mergansers, common goldeneye, American widgeon, scaup, and ring necked ducks. Bluewing teal, canvasback, bufflehead, and black duck live in or migrate through the park. The largest bird that visits the region is the whistling swan, a white bird with an imposing wing span. Don't approach the rookeries of gulls, cormorants, or herons. They might abandon or injure their chicks.

Over 300 plant species can be found in the BWCAW. White pine, red pine, white and black spruce, fir, tamarack, cedar, and jack pine are common. Extensive stands of paper birch and quaking aspen are found in some sections. Wildflowers are plentiful. Pond lilies, marsh marigolds, wild iris, and white calla flowers grow in wet areas, while lady's slipper, wild roses, columbines, devil's paintbrush, and oxeye daisies thrive on drier soil.

Many species of wild berries supply a treat to paddlers. Strawberries, blueberries, dewberries, blackberries, raspberries, huckleberries, thimbleberries, juneberries, lowbush cranberries, and wintergreen plants produce berries in season. Patches of wild rice grow in some wetlands.

Reptiles

There are five kinds of reptiles and twelve types of amphibians living in the area. Reptiles include the snapping turtle, painted turtle, ringneck snake, red-belly snake, and common garter snake. Amphibians include the blue-spotted salamander, tiger salamander, red-backed salamander, eastern newt, American toad, gray tree frog, spring peeper, western chorus frog, green frog, northern leopard frog, mink frog, and wood frog.

Camping

Camping is a necessary and enjoyable part of traveling in the Boundary Waters. Fortunately, there is a plentiful supply of campsites; most lakes have at least one and large ones have several. They usually consist of a fire ring, tent pads, and privy set in a cleared area. It is illegal to camp outside of a designated campsite, so it is prudent to start looking for one early in the day. Sites located off the regular travel routes are often more secluded, quieter, and cleaner than the others; some are only used a few times a season. It is often worth the effort to seek these out. Experienced BWCAW travelers often start paddling by 6:00 A.M. and stop by noon or as soon after as a good campsite is located. This leaves plenty of time to set up camp and relax or fish for awhile before the evening meal and bedtime.

Stay as quiet as the surroundings dictate. Most campers are there for a rest from the hustle, bustle, and noise of their regular lives. Loud talking, shouting, scraping a metal canoe across a rock, or loud radios can spoil someone's wilderness experience. Try to minimize the visual impact of your campsite, also. Bright-colored tents can be set back from the lakeshore if a pad is available, and bright-colored gear can be hidden from the lakeshore. It is prudent, however, to have at least one bright-colored object in the unlikely event that an emergency develops and signaling for help becomes necessary.

A campfire is a pleasant and useful part of canoe camping. At the heart of a campfire is good, dry wood. Almost all dry wood found in the BWCAW will burn well. The best campfire material comes from wood that is not lying directly on the damp ground. Dead snags held off the ground by limbs usually will burn well. To avoid injury, use only small leaning snags; paper birch is the exception. Birchbark is waterproof and will not allow the wood to dry out. The bark, however, will burn well and is a good fire starter. It must be gathered from dead trees; green trees must not be cut and make very poor firewood anyway.

The best wood is usually all used up near the campsites. When it becomes time to think about camping, start looking for choice firewood along the shore. Stop and load up some to take along, if space permits, or remember where you saw it, so you can quickly return after unloading the canoe at the campsite. Many campsites, though, do have some good wood within walking distance. Store dry wood under a tarp to keep it from rain and dew.

Wood not lying on the ground will probably burn even if it has been raining and the wood looks and feels damp. Cut it into short pieces and shave away the outside to expose the dry interior. Once a good, hot fire is burning, wood can be piled on the fire without splitting, as the outside will dry quickly. Fire-starting materials (including those needed to get a blaze started under difficult conditions) are sold in camper's supply outlets.

Campfires are always a potential hazard if left unattended. Be sure to put the fire out with water whenever it is left for an extended period—even when going fishing or exploring. At present, campfires are not allowed in some sections of the eastern BWCAW where the July 4, 1999, windstorm has created a hazard. This is probably temporary, and the restriction will be eased shortly.

Be sure to leave a clean campsite. The zero-impact concept means that the next camper should have a clean, sanitary site to enjoy. Garbage and fish entrails should be fed to seagulls or buried in a shallow hole 150 feet from the lake. Clean the fish before getting back to camp, place the chopped up fish entrails on a highly visible rock, and seagulls will usually clean them up. Don't use the latrine for dumping food. Bears might demolish the latrine to get the food.

Burn anything that is left in a hot fire, or pack it out. Sift the ashes of the dead campfire for man-made material that didn't burn; aluminum foil requires a very hot fire for incineration and probably will have to be carried out. The few items that won't burn can be easily carried out in a garbage bag. Police the area around camp for twist ties, cigarette butts, package labels, or anything man-made. This is a self-serving policy, also: Pocketknives, coins, jewelry, and wristwatches are often left behind by campers.

Dishes should not be washed in the lake. Wash dishes in a cooking pot, well back from the shore. Bathe with a container of water and soap. Walk back away from the lake, soap down, then rinse off, thereby leaving all soap well away from the water. Dump soapy water at least 150 feet from the lake.

A "bear barrel" or bucket makes a dandy clothes-washing device. Put the clothes in the barrel with soap and warm water. Use a canoe paddle to plunge the clothes up and down; or, use an outspread hand and arm to plunge the clothes up and down for a few minutes. It is surprising how fast clothes will get clean this way. Rinse them the same way. Some paddlers clean their clothes by placing them in a heavy plastic bag with soap and water. They seal the top, set the bag on the ground—top upward—grasp the neck of the bag, and plunge it up and down until the clothes are clean. All soapy wash water must be disposed at least 150 feet from the lake. Some campers wash socks and handkerchiefs without soap by dragging them with a piece of fish line behind the moving canoe. Wash shirts and pants without soap by wearing them while swimming.

Try not to enlarge the size of the campsite beyond what is already established. In the case of a large party, try to find two close sites. Some campsites have been enlarged so much that they have been abandoned.

The Echo Trail (County Road 116) starts at the junction of County Road 88 and State Highway 169, about 3 road miles west of Ely. It extends westerly for about 50 miles to County Road 24 near Echo Lake. The trail is hard-surfaced for the first few miles but eventually becomes a gravel road. It is hilly, narrow, and winding. Deer, moose, logging trucks, pickup trucks, and automobiles can appear suddenly on sharp curves. It is also a very scenic route. Drive slowly, avoid mishaps, and have time to enjoy the wooded surroundings.

Twelve entry points can be reached directly from the Echo Trail. Entry point #1, Trout Lake (also listed in this section), is the exception. It is accessed from Vermilion Lake, reachable from State Highway 1/169 and County Road 77 west of Ely.

The entry points on the north side of Echo Trail lead the paddler through some unspoiled territory where rivers and pristine lakes offer fishing and waterfalls. They provide fairly quick access to the U.S.–Canada border and some enormous border lakes. The entry points south of Echo Trail quickly lead to solitude and wild territory where wildlife abounds. Some trips reach busy lakes outside the BWCAW border, such as Burntside Lake and Vermilion Lake. Pictograph sites are available. The trips are listed in numerical order to their entry point numbers.

The bustling town of Ely probably has more supplies for canoeists than any other town in the world. Outfitters, guides, equipment, lodging, hot showers, and many other amenities are readily available.

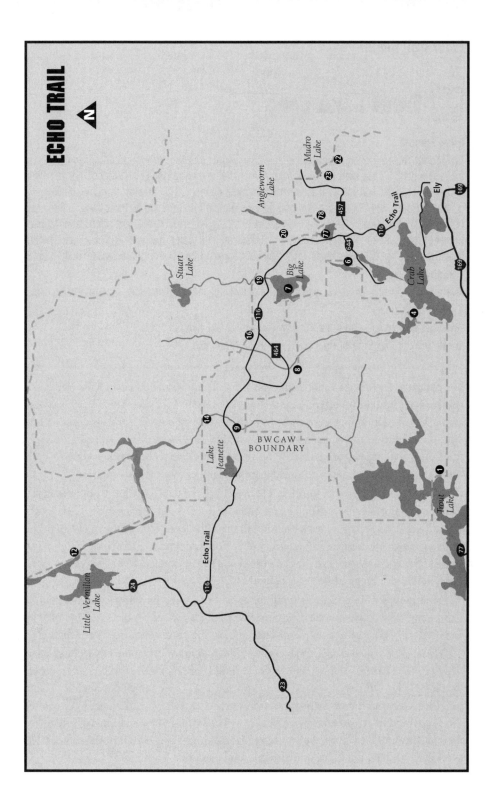

Trout Lake Loop

Entry Point: 1

Character: This rugged trip starts out easy with a lengthy paddle across part of Vermilion Lake and through gigantic Trout Lake to Little Trout Lake. After a long portage you'll encounter the Little Indian Sioux River, and follow it to a series of lakes connected by creeks, rivers, or challenging portages. Finally, only Pine Lake and one portage remain to return you to Trout Lake. Fishing can be productive on several lakes, and moose, deer, and smaller mammals are often seen. Most of the lakes are picturesque wilderness gems with clean blue water and wooded shorelines. The put in and the take out will probably be crowded, but between those points people will be quite scarce.

Length: 48 miles.

Average run time: 5 to 8 days, with fishing, sightseeing, and possible windy days on the big lakes.

Skill level: Beginner.

Hazards: Wind, waves, and motorboat wakes on the big lakes.

Maps: USGS: Sioux Pine Island, Chad Lake, Little Crab Lake.

The paddling: Launch the canoe at the public landing on Vermilion Lake's Moccasin Point, and head north to the 60-rod portage to Trout Lake. Trout Lake covers almost 10,000 acres and is 98 feet deep in one place. Lake trout, walleye, northern pike, and smallmouth bass can be caught from its waters. Motorboats are allowed, however, and some groups might want to escape by proceeding directly up the east shoreline to the creek leading to Little Trout Lake. Find a campsite and spend a restful night. Tomorrow is a rough day.

Little Trout Lake covers 147 acres, is 56 feet deep, and has lake trout to offer the angler. Paddle to the northeast corner of the lake, and find the 376-rod portage to the Little Indian Sioux River. This portage may be muddy, but it is fairly level. Turn to the right (south) on the river and paddle upstream. A rapids must be portaged; there are several shorter portages as well. Beaver dams may also present obstacles. The last portage, from the river to Otter Lake, is 120 rods long in low-water periods.

Most groups will be ready to camp for at least one night on Otter Lake or adjoining Cummings Lake. It has a dozen campsites. Cummings Lake sprawls over 1,139 acres, is 46 feet deep, and has northern pike, smallmouth bass, and panfish waiting to be caught.

Notice on the map that you can portage from Cummings Lake directly to Buck Lake. This 480-rod portage will eliminate several beautiful lakes from the trip but will probably save some time. Otherwise, leave Cummings Lake by a 70-rod portage to Korb Lake, find the Korb River and follow it downstream to Little Crab Lake. Find Lunetta Creek on the northwest section of this lake and follow it to Lunetta Lake. From Lunetta Lake follow Lunetta Creek to Schlamn Lake and camp for the third night. Schlamn Lake covers 100 acres and is shallow but holds northern pike and panfish.

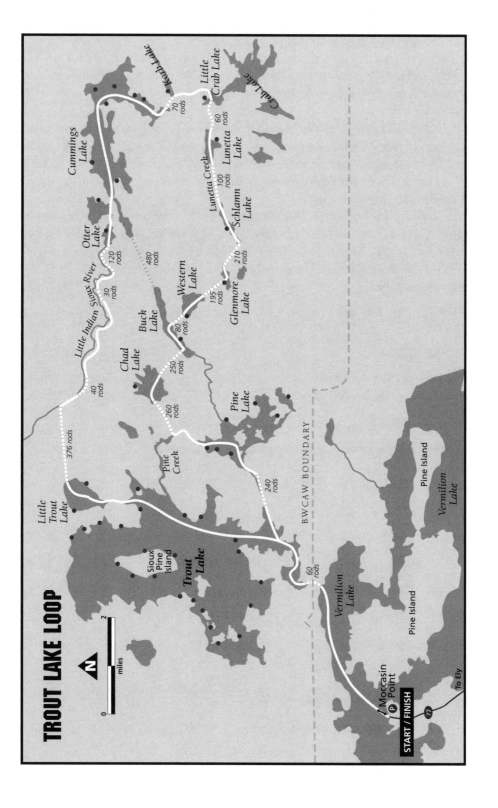

TROUT LAKE LOOP

N

0 miles 2

Little Trout Lake

Sioux Pine Island

Trout Lake

Little Indian Sioux River

376 rods

40 rods

Chad Lake

260 rods

Pine Creek

Buck Lake

30 rods

120 rods

Otter Lake

480 rods

250 rods

80 rods

Western Lake

195 rods

Glenmore Lake

Pine Lake

240 rods

Cummings Lake

Knob Lake

70 rods

Little Crab Lake

60 rods

Crab Lake

Lunetta Creek

100 rods

Lunetta Lake

Schlamm Lake

210 rods

BWCAW BOUNDARY

60 rods

Vermilion Lake

Pine Island

Vermilion Lake

Pine Island

Moccasin Point

P

START / FINISH

77

To Ely

The next day portage 210 rods to Glenmore Lake, 195 rods to Western Lake, 80 rods to Buck Lake, and 250 rods to Chad Lake. After you portage well over 2 miles, the Chad Lake campsite may look inviting. Chad Lake covers 277 acres, is 18 feet deep, and has largemouth bass as well as northern pike and bluegills. Campsites are found on the intervening lakes also.

Leave Chad Lake by a 260-rod portage to Pine Creek. Follow Pine Creek to Pine Lake, portage 240 rods to Trout Lake and from here on follow familiar water to Vermilion Lake and find the take-out point at Moccasin Point. Notice, also, that the long portage from Pine Lake to Trout Lake can be avoided by following Pine Creek directly to Trout Lake instead of paddling to Pine Lake.

In the dry season the Little Indian Sioux River will probably be too low to navigate. This trip should not be attempted then. Alternate routes include exploring Trout Lake or following Vermilion Lake to Trout Lake to Pine Creek to Pine Lake to Trout Lake to Vermilion Lake. Study the map. There are twenty-four campsites on Trout Lake; Pine Lake has nine campsites.

Access: Follow Minnesota Highway 1/169 from Ely west for 26 miles. Turn right on County Road 77 and follow for 12 miles to the public landing on Moccasin Point.

Shuttle: None.

Camping: Pfeifer Lake (USFS park), Tower Sudan State Park, McKinley Park, Tower Park. A fee is charged at all of them.

Food, gas, lodging: Ely.

For more information: La Croix Ranger District (see appendix).

² Crab Lake

Entry point: 4

Character: This short trip starts as a long paddle across busy Burntside Lake to a rugged portage. The Crab Lake portage will bring you to a series of small, remote, and scenic lakes. Solitude should be easy to find. Fishing and camping opportunities abound. This route can return to Burntside Lake without portaging by following Crab Creek. Further, it connects into the Trout Lake Loop trip (see chapter 1) for possible additional adventure.

Length: 19 miles.

Average run time: 3 to 5 days, with fishing and sightseeing.

Skill level: Beginner.

Hazards: Wind, waves, and motorboats on Burntside Lake.

Maps: Shagawa Lake, Crab Lake.

The paddling: Launch the canoe at the public landing on the south shore of Burntside Lake, and paddle about 4 miles west to the 320-rod portage to Crab Lake. It climbs over three slopes and has some muddy conditions, also. The difficulty of this portage keeps traffic to a minimum; consequently it is about the quickest way to find a silent and isolated location anywhere near Burntside Lake.

Burntside Lake is a maze of islands and can be confusing to navigate. There is one route, however, that is easy to find. Study the map. Turn left at the boat landing, and follow the south shoreline until Waters Island is in view on the starboard. Turn northwest here and set a course about halfway between Waters Island and Dollar Island. Continue on this course to the opposite shore. Paddle directly toward the only island in this "channel." It is near the portage. Pass to the portside of this island to find the Crab Lake Portage.

Crab Lake covers 424 acres, is 60 feet deep, and is known as an excellent fishing lake. Walleyes, smallmouth bass, largemouth bass, northern pike, and panfish all live in this water. Further, the lake is configured in a series of narrow arms and so is not adversely affected by wind. Several campsites are available. At least a day could be spent just fishing and sightseeing this lake.

Leave Crab Lake by a 140-rod portage to Clark Lake, which covers 72 acres and is 44 feet deep. Anglers could find northern pike, largemouth bass, or bluegills for shore lunch.

Meat Lake is next on the trip and is a 48-rod portage from Clark Lake. Sprite Lake is a 90-rod portage from Meat Lake, while adjoining Phantom Lake is only a 24-rod portage away. Phantom Lake covers 100 acres and can furnish good fishing for northern pike, but Battle Lake is only a 32-rod portage away and has walleyes, northern pike, largemouth bass, and bluegills living within its 75 acres. It has a campsite and is a good place to camp overnight.

Portage 140 rods to Hassel Lake, which covers 75 acres but offers only marginal fishing for northern pike and bluegill, and then 280 rods to Lunetta Lake. It covers 102 acres and has walleyes, northern pike, smallmouth bass, largemouth bass, and panfish in its 14-

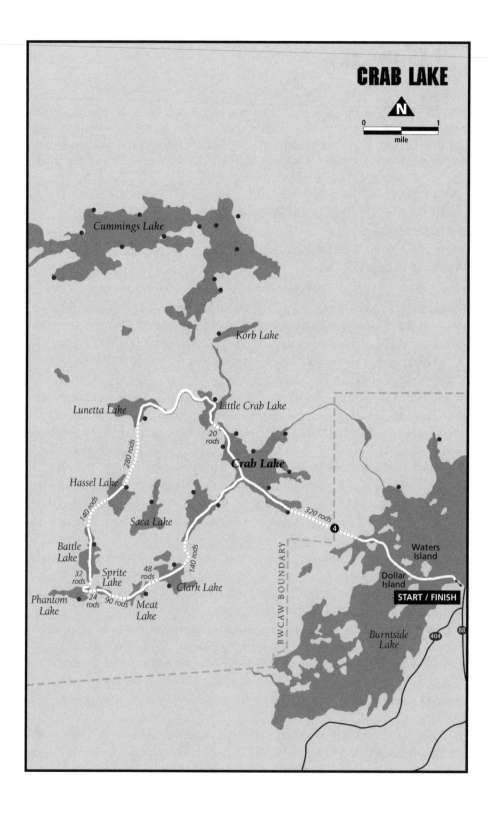

CRAB LAKE

N

0   1
mile

Cummings Lake

Korb Lake

Lunetta Lake

Little Crab Lake

20 rods

280 rods

Crab Lake

Hassel Lake

140 rods

Saca Lake

320 rods

4

Battle Lake

Waters Island

32 rods

Sprite Lake

48 rods

140 rods

Dollar Island

Phantom Lake

24 rods

90 rods

Clark Lake

START / FINISH

Meat Lake

Burntside Lake

BWCAW BOUNDARY

404

88

Canoeing in the Ely area. Photo: Courtesy Minnesota Office of Tourism

foot depths. Lunetta Lake has a campsite if a layover is on the agenda but is important also because it connects into the Trout Lake canoe route. This route will lead to other routes, and almost any canoeing experience available in the western BWCAW.

Follow Lunetta Creek east to Little Crab Lake, portage 20 rods to Crab Lake, and connect into familiar water. Here a decision can be made: Return over the 320-rod portage to Burntside Lake or use Crab Creek to return to Buntside Lake as an alternative to this long portage.

Crab Creek (study the map) leaves Crab Lake at the northeast arm and flows into Burntside Lake about 0.5 mile north of the portage. It has rapids and is not maintained as a canoe route and is apt to have beaver dams and fallen trees as well as thick streamside vegetation to hinder progress. Nevertheless, it is an adventurous way to return to Burntside Lake. The water level in the stream can vary from impassable to easy. Find the outlet, leave the canoe, and scout the banks of the creek to get a perspective of the present conditions before committing to the trip.

Retrace the route to the public landing on Burntside Lake and the take-out point.

Access: Follow Minnesota Highway 1/169 3 miles west from Ely to County Road 88. Drive north on CR 88 for approximately 4.5 miles to the public boat landing on the left side of the road.

Shuttle: None.

Camping: Fenske Lake Campground, Bearhead Lake State Park. Fees are charged.

Food, gas, lodging: Ely.

For more information: Kawishiwi Ranger District (see appendix).

Vermilion Lake to the Little Indian Sioux River

3

Entry point: 12

Character: This is a short, easy trip with few portages. It starts at a large, bustling lake and ends at a quiet river crossing on the Echo Trail. The most spectacular lakes in the western BWCAW are visited on this trip. You'll see scenic waterfalls and possibly moose, deer, and beaver. The fishing can be excellent in spring, early summer, or fall. Motors are allowed on the first part of the trip.

Length: 30 miles.

Average run time: 4 to 6 days, with fishing and sightseeing.

Skill level: Beginner.

Hazards: Wind and motorboats on the large lakes.

Maps: USGS: Crane Lake, Lake Jeanette, Shell Lake.

The paddling: Study the map first, then launch the canoe at the public landing on Crane Lake. This busy lake covers 3,088 acres, is almost 4 miles long, 3 miles wide, and 80 feet deep. It holds walleye, sauger, northern pike, smallmouth bass, crappie, and yellow perch for fishermen. Canoe north to pass west of Baylis Island and just skirt the west edge of Indian Island. Enter the King Williams Narrows, paddle for another 2 miles to Sand Point Lake. Motorboat traffic is often heavy, so an early morning embarkation is advised.

Sand Point Lake is a border lake and the west (American) shoreline is the boundary for Voyageurs National Park. This lake covers 8,869 acres and has walleyes, northern pike, and panfish for the catching. There are several campsites on Sand Point Lake. Turn east here, and follow the east shoreline to pass through the Little Vermilion Narrows into Little Vermilion Lake. This lake is inside the BWCAW; it covers 13,331 acres and is 48 feet deep. Almost every fish found in the BWCAW lives in its water. Motors are allowed, however. There are several campsites available and this is a good place to stop for the first day.

Leave Little Vermilion Lake by paddling up the Loon River. This is a placid river and the current will not be troublesome. The well-known "56" rapids are encountered as the first portage. This is the site of a historic logging camp. The portage is short and, depending on the water conditions, sometimes the canoe can be paddled or poled up through the rapids. However, a short distance upstream Loon Falls will be encountered. Loon Falls drops 29 feet and is worth stopping to enjoy. It requires an 80-rod portage. A marine railroad is maintained here for portaging heavy boats.

Enter Loon Lake after the portage. Loon Lake covers 920 acres and has a maximum depth of 70 feet. It covers 3,101 acres, is 75 feet deep, and has walleyes, northern pike, smallmouth bass, panfish, and rainbow trout living in its clear water. There are several campsites on this lake, but it is also a popular lake. Find a campsite early. Plan on base camping on Loon Lake for at least a day to enjoy the fishing and explore the lake. Beatty Portage into Lac La Croix is interesting to investigate, and an excursion into Lac La Croix will add substance to the trip. Find Beatty Portage by paddling east along the international

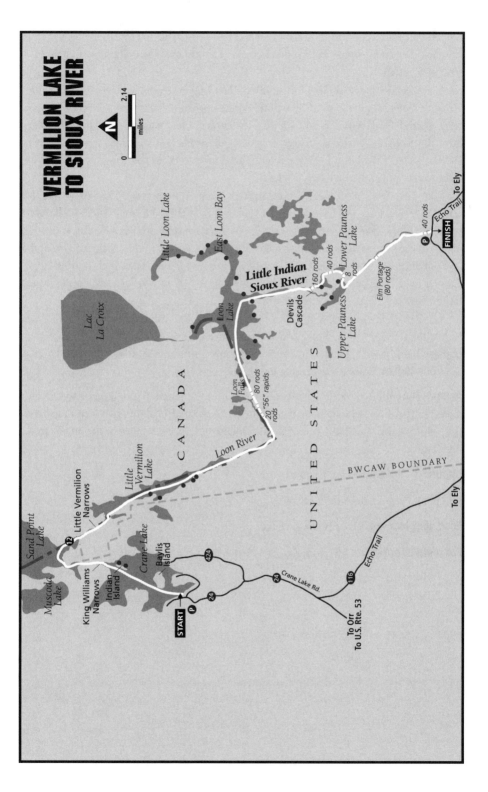

VERMILION LAKE
TO SIOUX RIVER

N

0   2.14
miles

Little Loon Lake

East Loon Bay

Little Indian
Sioux River

Lac
La Croix

CANADA

UNITED STATES

Loon Lake

160 rods

40 rods

Lower Pauness
Lake

8 rods

Devils
Cascade

Upper Pauness
Lake

Elm Portage
(80 rods)

P 40 rods

Echo Trail

To Ely

FINISH

Loon
Falls

80 rods

20 "56" rapids
rods

Loon River

Little
Vermilion
Lake

Little Vermilion
Narrows

Sand Point
Lake

12

Muscoda
Lake

King Williams
Narrows

Indian
Island

Crane Lake

Baylis
Island

BWCAW BOUNDARY

To Ely

424

24 Crane Lake Rd.

116

Echo Trail

START

P

24

To Orr
To U.S. Rte. 53

border. East Loon Bay and Little Loon Lake are also enjoyable to visit. In spring and early summer, the fishing ranges from good to excellent almost anywhere along the shorelines or around the islands.

Leave Loon Lake by finding the mouth of the Little Indian Sioux River (usually abbreviated to Sioux) along the south shoreline. Paddle upstream to the first portage, a 160-rod carry around the Devils Cascade. Devils Cascade is a white-water gorge where the water from the Sioux River drops 75 feet in a series of rapids and waterfalls from the Lower Pauness Lake to the Loon Lake water level. Take time to enjoy the gorge. It is one of the most scenic spots in the western BWCAW.

Lower Pauness Lake is located at the upstream end of the portage. This lake covers 165 acres, is 35 feet deep, and has walleyes and perch. Three campsites are located on the western shore of the lake. This entire area is known to have bear problems. Secret your food pack with care. Leave Lower Pauness Lake by an 8-rod portage in the southwest arm of the lake; an alternate 40-rod portage is located on the west shore. They both lead to Upper Pauness Lake. The upper lake covers 188 acres and is shallow. Walleye and northern pike live in its water. Three campsites are available.

Leave this lake by finding the inlet of the Sioux River on the southern shore of the lake. Paddle the river to 80-rod Elm Portage. The Jeanette Creek waterfall adds interest to this portage. Continue 1.29 miles upstream to the take-out point. A 40-rod portage leads to the Little Indian Sioux River parking lot on the Echo Trail.

Access: Start approximately 2½ miles west of Ely at the junction of County Road 88 and County Road 116 and follow the Echo Trail (County Road 116) 49 miles west to its junction with County Road 24. Turn right and follow CR 24 for 8 miles to the public access on Crane Lake.

Shuttle: 27 miles one way. 2 hours.

Camping: Echo Lake. A fee is charged.

Food, gas, lodging: Orr, Ely, Crane Lake.

For more information: La Croix Ranger District (see appendix).

4 Slim Lake

Entry point: 6

Character: This trip has both lake and river travel and one long portage. Start the trip with an 80-rod portage to Slim Lake. Then head west through two small lakes to a very long portage to Big Rice Lake. Leave by following the Portage River. Stay on the river until it crosses the Echo Trail (County Road 116). Then reverse the route to return to Slim Lake. Options include shuttling back from the trail or portaging to Big Lake and shuttling back from there. This trip connects to other routes. Independence Day storm–impacted area.

Length: 33 miles. River length is estimated.

Average run time: 4 to 6 days.

Class: Quiet, with eight sets of mild rapids.

Skill level: Beginner.

Hazards: Storm-damaged trees (see introduction).

Maps: Angleworm Lake, Lapond Lake, Shagawa Lake.

The paddling: Portage 80 rods to Slim Lake from the road on the west side of the North Arm of Burntside Lake. Slim Lake covers 142 acres, is 40 feet deep, and has northern pike available for fishing. At the south end of the lake, the Slim Lake Hiking Trail leads to a summit that overlooks a considerable portion of the surrounding countryside. It is well worth the time it takes to enjoy it. There is a campsite on Slim Lake and the first day could be spent fishing and sightseeing on this lake.

The second day, portage 52 rods to Rice Lake. This shallow lake has a campsite but few, if any, angling opportunities. Leave it by a 130-rod portage to Hook Lake. It covers 92 acres, has some 13-foot depths, and holds northern pike. A side trip can be taken by portaging 30 rods to Keneu Lake. It covers 37 acres, is 27 feet deep, and also holds northern pike. There are campsites on both lakes. Consider a layover here because the next portage is 540 rods long to Big Rice Lake. Some groups would consider a portage like that to be a day's work in itself.

Big Rice Lake is the premier fishing lake on this trip. It covers 416 acres, is 6 feet deep, and has walleyes, northern pike, smallmouth bass, and panfish in its basin. There is a campsite on the lake. Leave Big Rice Lake by finding the mouth of the Portage River in the lake's most northern arm. The Portage River flows north so the outbound trip will be with the current. A short portage between Big Rice Lake and Lapond Lake will be needed in low-waters period. Otherwise, no other portages are necessary along the whole stretch of the river between Big Rice Lake and the Echo Trail, although some mild rapids are encountered.

Lapond Lake covers 176 acres and is very shallow but contains some northern pike. One campsite is available. The trip can be ended here, going out or coming back, by portaging 150 rods to Big Lake and either hiring one of the outfitters on Big Lake to transport the canoe back to the trip vehicle or having a shuttle vehicle waiting. Or, continue

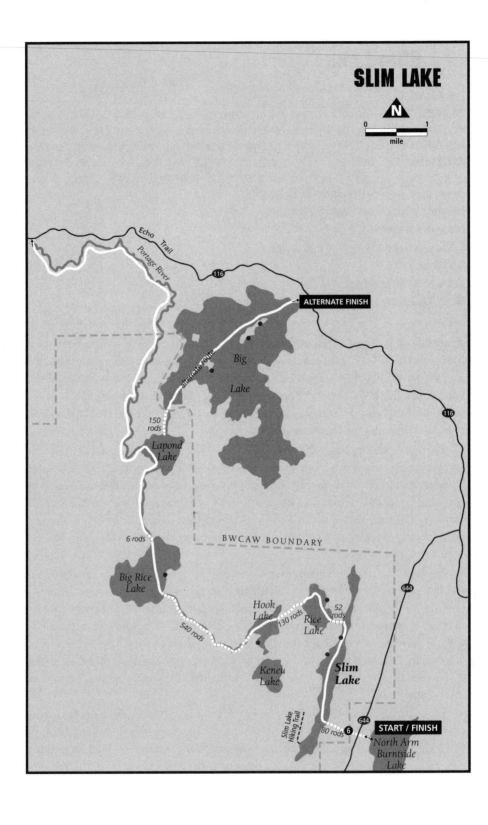

SLIM LAKE

N

0 _____ 1
mile

Echo Trail

Portage River

116

ALTERNATE FINISH

alternate route

Big Lake

150 rods

Lapond Lake

6 rods

BWCAW BOUNDARY

Big Rice Lake

Hook Lake

130 rods

Rice Lake

52 rods

116

644

540 rods

Keneu Lake

Slim Lake

Slim Lake Hiking Trail

80 rods   6

644

START / FINISH

North Arm Burntside Lake

paddling down the Portage River, which gets a little larger and easier to navigate, as it goes north. Take out or turn around at the Echo Trail. A campsite can be found along the Stuart Hiking Trail, which crosses the Portage River about 2 miles upstream from the Echo Trail.

Reverse the route at the Echo Trail and paddle back through Lapond Lake, Big Rice Lake, Hook Lake, and Rice Lake to finally arrive at Slim Lake and the take-out point.

Access: Start approximately 2½ miles west of Ely at the junction of County Road 116 and County Road 88. Follow the Echo Trail (County Road 116) 9 miles west from the junction with County Road 88. Turn left (south) on County Road 644 (North Arm Road) and proceed to the public access to Burntside Lake. The portage to Slim Lake is directly across the road.

Shuttle: 16-mile, one-way shuttle from Echo Trail. Approximately 1 hour. 8-mile, one-way shuttle from Big Lake. Approximately 30 minutes.

Camping: Fenske Lake Campground. A fee is charged.

Food, gas, lodging: Ely.

For more information: Kawishiwi Ranger District (see appendix).

⑤ Big Lake Loop

Entry point: 7 (this trip requires both a #7 entry point permit and #16 entry point permit)

Character: This trip starts at Big Lake and follows a river north to another large lake. Then it picks up a second river and continues north to Lake Agnes. At Lake Agnes it locates a third river and follows it to a fourth river. The trip then proceeds south to Stuart Lake where it transfers to the Stuart River and follows that river south to a long portage back to Big Lake. Five rivers and three lakes are visited. This is a difficult trip, if completed. However, it can be shortened by putting in and taking out on the Echo Trail. The Stuart River is impassable in dry weather. Independence Day storm–affected area.

Length: 39 miles.

Average run time: 5 to 7 days.

Class: Quiet, I, II on different stretches of the rivers.

Skill level: Beginner.

Hazards: Storm-damaged trees (see introduction).

Maps: USGS: Angleworm Lake, Iron Lake, Lake Agnes, Lapond Lake.

The paddling: Launch the canoe at the boat landing on the north shore of Big Lake. Paddle southwest to the creek that leads from Big Lake to the Portage River. If this creek is impassable, find the portage to Lapond Lake and portage 150 rods to the lake. The Portage River flows through Lapond Lake. Find the outlet on the north shore of the lake and proceed downstream on the river. The Portage River is 40 to 50 feet wide in spots and has a steady current. Mild rapids are encountered quite often, but in a normal water flow they do not have to be portaged. The Portage River meanders a considerable amount, but as the crow flies it is about 5 miles from Big Lake to the Echo Trail and about 4 miles from the Echo Trail to Nina Moose Lake. In actual distance it might be twice that far.

There are no Forest Service–maintained campsites on the river. It is prudent to make camping arrangements somewhere along or near the Echo Trail. This part of the trip is outside the BWCAW boundary but within the Superior National Forest, so camping is legal anyplace that does not post otherwise. The gravel pit that lies between the river and the Echo Trail along the Stuart Hiking Trail is utilized by river runners for camping. On this stretch, as along most river corridors, it is sometimes difficult to tell exactly where you are. A hint: When the Echo Trail is close by, traffic can often be heard.

If the group wants to travel fast and hard and the water level is favorable, Nina Moose Lake can be reached the first day. Most won't see this 430-acre lake until the second day, however. Fishing for walleye, northern pike, and smallmouth bass can be quite good, and there are several maintained campsites available. Blueberries are often found in this region in season. Bears have been known to raid food packs on this lake: Take precautions. Head north on the Moose River when it is time to leave. Two sets of rapids, requiring a 70-rod portage and a 96-rod portage, lie between Nina Moose Lake and Lake Agnes.

Lake Agnes covers 1,027 acres, is 30 feet deep, and holds walleye, northern pike, and

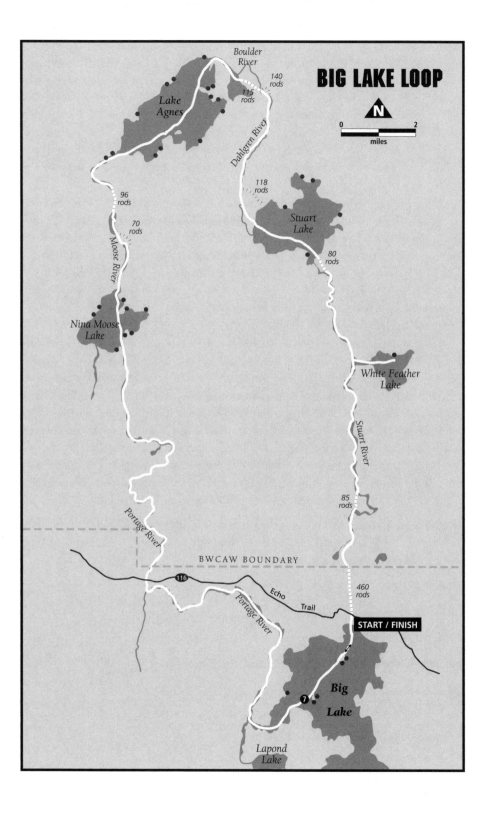

BIG LAKE LOOP

N

0 — 2
miles

Boulder River

140 rods

115 rods

Lake Agnes

Dahlgren River

118 rods

Stuart Lake

80 rods

96 rods

70 rods

Moose River

Nina Moose Lake

White Feather Lake

Stuart River

85 rods

Portage River

BWCAW BOUNDARY

116

Echo Trail

460 rods

Portage River

START / FINISH

7

Big Lake

Lapond Lake

smallmouth bass. There are many campsites, but this is a popular route for travelers heading to Lac La Croix so it is prudent to get a campsite early, if a layover is on the itinerary. Fishing and blueberry picking are added benefits to camping on this lake. Take precautions against bears raiding the food pack (see the introduction for recommended procedures). The largest display of Indian pictographs in the BWCAW, as well as famous Warrior Hill, can be viewed on Lac La Croix about 4 miles north of Lake Agnes. To view these pictographs access the Boulder River by a short portage from the north end of Lake Agnes. Paddle northward to Boulder Bay on Lac La Croix, and continue north to the points of interest. A round-trip can be made from Lake Agnes in one day.

Leave Lake Agnes by following the above-mentioned route to Boulder River, but turn south to find the 140-rod portage to the Dahlgren River. Alternately, portage 115 rods from the northeast bay of Lake Agnes, and then find and follow the Dahlgren River Portage. Study the map to decide which one is most convenient. Paddle south on the Dahlgren River to the vicinity of Stuart Lake and then portage 118 rods to the lake. Stuart Lake covers 804 acres, is 40 feet deep, and has walleye, northern pike, smallmouth bass, large mouth bass, and panfish. It is far better than an average fishing lake and has several campsites, if a layover is on the agenda.

Leave Stuart Lake by an 80-rod portage from the south arm of the lake to the Stuart River. The Stuart River is small and swampy and, depending on the water level, frequent portages might be necessary. The river flows north, but the current isn't hard to overcome. Nevertheless, if your energy level is low by the time you reach White Feather Lake, there is a maintained campsite there. White Feather Lake covers about 100 acres, is shallow, and has northern pike to entertain the angler or feed the hungry. Continue up the Stuart River; it will get narrower until it becomes nearly impassable. First an 85-rod portage is encountered and then the long, 460-rod portage to the Echo Trail parking lot. The trip can end here, as the trip vehicle, if left in the Big Lake parking lot, is only a short distance away. The Stuart River access is well marked with official signs on the Echo Trail.

Access: Start 5½ miles west of Ely at the junction of County Road 88 and the Echo Trail. Drive west on the Echo Trail for 17.3 miles. Turn left (south) on Forest Road 1027 and drive to the north shore of Big Lake.

Shuttle: None.

Camping: Fenske Lake. A fee is charged.

Food, gas, lodging: Ely.

For more information: Kawishiwi Ranger District (see appendix).

Moose River—South

Entry Point: 8

Character: This trip has both river and lake traveling on both large and small lakes. A few of the portages are very long. This is a rugged expedition, if the whole trip is completed. There are several places to take out before the complete trip is finished, however. Fishing opportunities abound; moose, deer, eagles, and waterfowl can be seen; and scenic river corridors and lovely wilderness lakes can be enjoyed. Berry picking can be good, in season. This trip should not be attempted in low-water conditions.

Length: 35 miles.

Average run time: 6 to 8 days, plus any layover days.

Skill level: Beginner.

Hazards: Wind and rough portages.

Maps: USGS: Burntside Lake, Shagawa Lake, Angleworm Lake, Big Moose Lake.

The paddling: Launch the canoe at the Moose River, south access and paddle upriver to find the 160-rod portage to Big Moose Lake. The lake covers 1,116 acres, is 20 feet deep, and has fishing opportunities for northern pike and smallmouth bass. Several campsites are available. Big Moose Lake is a destination in itself for most of the groups that paddle up the river from the access point. But the energetic and adventurous keep going.

Leave Big Moose Lake by a whopping 580-rod portage to Cummings Lake. Although this is a long portage, it is not difficult, as it follows a highland ridge through the surrounding lowlands. The trail would be hard to find, otherwise, because it is used so infrequently. Cummings Lake sprawls over 1,139 acres, is 46 feet deep, and has northern pike, smallmouth bass, and panfish waiting to be caught. More than a dozen campsites are maintained on this lake. An enjoyable side trip can be taken by paddling to the northernmost arm of Cummings Lake.

Leave Cummings Lake by finding the portage to Korb Lake in the easternmost section of Cummings Lake, and portage 70 rods to this 62-acre lake with five common species of BWCAW fish inhabiting its long, narrow basin. Paddle the Korb River to Little Crab Lake when it is time to leave Korb Lake. Look along the south shore of Little Crab Lake to find the 20-rod portage to Crab Lake and negotiate it.

Crab Lake covers 424 acres, is 60 feet deep, and is known as an excellent fishing lake. Walleyes, smallmouth bass, largemouth bass, northern pike, and panfish all live in this water. Further, the lake is configured in a series of narrow arms and is not adversely affected by common wind speeds. Several campsites are available. At least a day could be spent just fishing and sightseeing on this lake.

Leave Crab Lake by the 320-rod portage to Burntside Lake. This portage is not overly difficult, but it climbs over three slopes and has some muddy conditions. There is an alternate route to Burntside Lake, however. Crab Creek (study the map) leaves Crab Lake at the northeast arm and flows into Burntside Lake about 0.5 mile north of the portage. It

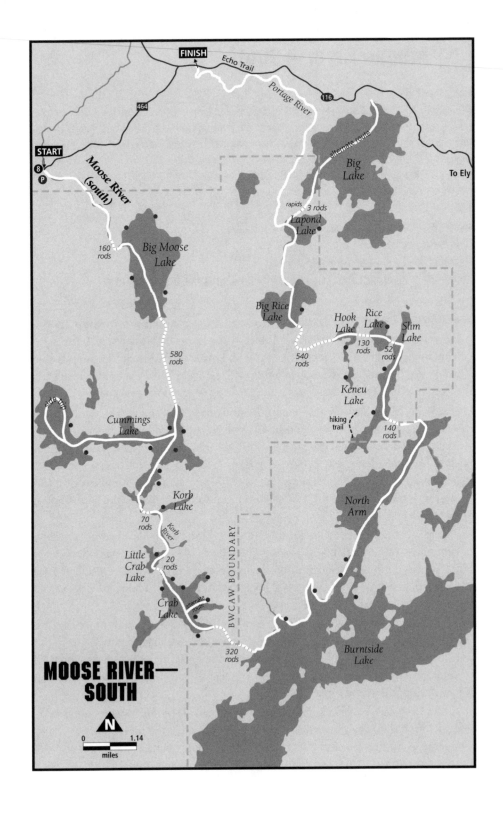

FINISH

Echo Trail

464

START

8
P

Moose River (south)

Portage River

116

To Ely

Big Lake

alternate route

160 rods

Big Moose Lake

rapids   3 rods

Lapond Lake

580 rods

Big Rice Lake

540 rods

Hook Lake

Rice Lake

130 rods

Slim Lake

52 rods

side trip

Cummings Lake

Keneu Lake

hiking trail

140 rods

Korb Lake

70 rods

Korb River

North Arm

Little Crab Lake

20 rods

Crab Lake

alternate route

BWCAW BOUNDARY

320 rods

Burntside Lake

MOOSE RIVER— SOUTH

N

0   1.14

miles

has rapids, is not maintained as a canoe route, and is apt to have beaver dams and fallen trees as well as thick streamside vegetation to hinder progress. Nevertheless, it is an adventurous way to return to Burntside Lake. The water level in the stream can vary from impassable to easy. Find the outlet, leave the canoe, and scout the banks of the creek to get a perspective of the present conditions before committing to the trip.

Burntside Lake is outside the BWCAW boundaries and is a busy, noisy, extremely large, and beautiful island-studded lake. Study the map carefully, and head north up the center of the lake if the motorized boat traffic permits. If traffic is too thick or winds are high, follow the west shoreline to the north arm of the lake. It probably will take all day to negotiate Burntside Lake and find the portage to Slim Lake.

Some campsites are maintained on Burntside Lake, and camping is permitted on the west shoreline. Alternately, the trip can be ended here by paddling about 4.5 miles across the lake to the access point on the east shore. See the Crab Lake trip (chapter 2) for more information. Hire an outfitter to transport you and the gear back to the trip vehicle.

Continue the trip by carrying the canoe and gear about 140 rods from Burntside Lake to Slim Lake. Part of this portage is along a gravel road. Slim Lake covers 142 acres, is 40 feet deep, and has northern pike available for fishing. At the south end of the lake, the Slim Lake Hiking Trail leads to a summit that overlooks a considerable portion of the surrounding countryside. It is worth taking time to enjoy it. There is a campsite on Slim Lake, and a day or more could be spent fishing and sightseeing on this lake.

Then portage 52 rods to Rice Lake. This shallow lake has a campsite but few if any angling opportunities. Leave it by a 130-rod portage to Hook Lake. It covers 92 acres, has some 13 foot depths, and holds northern pike. A side trip can be taken by portaging 30 rods to Keneu Lake. It covers 37 acres, is 27 feet deep, and also holds northern pike. There are campsites on both lakes. Consider a layover here because the next portage is 540 rods to Big Rice Lake. Some groups would consider that portage to be a day's work in itself.

Big Rice Lake is one of the best fishing lakes on this trip. It covers 416 acres, is 6 feet deep, and has walleyes, northern pike, smallmouth bass, and panfish in its basin. There is a campsite on the lake. Leave Big Rice Lake by finding the mouth of the Portage River in the lake's most northern arm. The Portage River flows north, so the outbound trip will be with the current. A short portage will be needed between Big Rice Lake and Lapond Lake in low-water periods. Otherwise, no other portages are necessary along the whole stretch of the river between Big Rice Lake and the Echo Trail, although some mild rapids are encountered.

Lapond Lake covers 176 acres and is very shallow, but contains some northern pike. One campsite is available. The trip can be ended here by portaging 150 rods to Big Lake and either hiring one of the outfitters on Big Lake to transport the canoe back to the trip vehicle or having a shuttle vehicle waiting. Otherwise, continue paddling down the Portage River, which gets a little larger and easier to navigate as it goes north. Take out at the Echo Trail. It will be necessary to walk about 3.75 miles back to the trip vehicle, if you don't have a shuttle waiting.

Access: Start approximately 2½ miles west of Ely at the junction of County Road 88 and the Echo Trail (County Road 116). Follow the Echo Trail about 24 miles west to Forest Road 464. Turn left (south) and follow FR 464 for about 3.5 miles to the Moose River bridge.

Shuttle: About 3.75 miles one way. 20 minutes.

Camping: Fenske Lake Campground, Lake Jeanette Campground. A fee is charged at both.

Food, gas, lodging: Ely.

For more information: Kawishiwi Ranger District (see appendix).

Little Indian Sioux River—South

Entry point: 9

Character: Paddle the Little Indian Sioux River upstream to a loop of scenic lakes that includes huge Trout Lake. Traverse the lakes and then negotiate the river from its headwaters back downstream to the put-in point. Some long portages are needed. Fishing opportunities abound. Moose, deer, and beaver will probably be sighted.

Length: 60 miles.

Average run time: 8 to 10 days, with fishing and sightseeing.

Skill level: Beginner.

Hazards: Fallen trees (see introduction) and wind on Trout Lake.

Maps: Sioux Pine Island, Chad Lake, Bootleg Lake, Shell Lake.

The paddling: Get an early start and launch the canoe on the south side of the Little Indian Sioux River (Sioux) bridge and paddle upstream. Sioux Falls will be encountered about 5 miles downstream. This captivating cascade must be portaged around, and then less than 0.5 mile farther upstream the second portage around a set of rapids must be negotiated. There are no designated campsites along the river. To find a campsite watch for the confluence of the Little Pony River and the Sioux River (the Little Pony River joins the Sioux from the east). Paddle the Little Pony River upstream to Bootleg Lake. If the Little Pony River is not navigable because of low water or windfalls, continue on the Sioux River approximately 6 miles to the 200-rod portage to Bootleg Lake. Bootleg Lake covers 352 acres, is 26 feet deep, and has a good population of smallmouth bass.

Leave Bootleg Lake by the 200-rod portage to the Sioux River, and continue up the river to the 376-rod portage to Little Trout Lake. Just getting to Little Trout Lake may take most of the available energy for one day. Fortunately, there are campsites available. Little Trout Lake covers 147 acres, is 56 feet deep, and has lake trout to offer the angler. Little Trout Lake is connected directly to imposing Trout Lake, which covers almost 10,000 acres and is 98 feet deep in one place. Lake trout, walleye, northern pike, and smallmouth bass can be caught from its waters. Motorboats are allowed; however, it is a beautiful lake. Find a campsite, and spend a day or two of fishing and sightseeing.

Leave Trout Lake by the 240-rod portage to Pine Lake in the southeast corner of Trout Lake. Pine Lake covers 912 acres, is 18 feet deep, and has walleyes, northern pike, and panfish swimming in its depths. It has several campsites. Leave Pine Lake by following Pine Creek to the 260-rod portage to Chad Lake. This lake covers 277 acres, is 18 feet deep, offers two campsites, and has largemouth bass, as well as northern pike and bluegills.

The next portage is a long one: 250 rods from Chad Lake to Buck Lake. Find a campsite on Buck Lake, and get a good night's sleep before tackling tomorrow's 480-rod portage. Buck Lake has walleyes and northern pike swimming in its 228 acres, and a fish dinner is a good possibility.

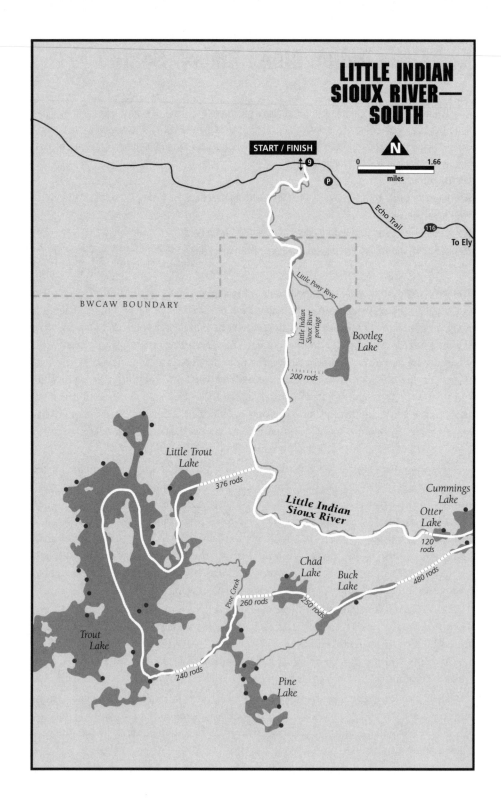

LITTLE INDIAN SIOUX RIVER— SOUTH

N

0   1.66

miles

START / FINISH

9

P

Echo Trail

116

To Ely

Little Pony River

Little Indian Sioux River portage

Bootleg Lake

BWCAW BOUNDARY

200 rods

Little Trout Lake

376 rods

Cummings Lake

Little Indian Sioux River

Otter Lake

120 rods

Pine Creek

Chad Lake

Buck Lake

480 rods

260 rods

250 rods

Trout Lake

240 rods

Pine Lake

Buck Lake to Cummings Lake is the last long portage on this trip—480 rods. If time permits, Cummings Lake can offer good fishing for northern pike, smallmouth bass, and panfish in its 1,139 acres. Many campsites are available. Leave Cummings Lake by paddling directly into Otter Lake and then portaging 120 rods to the headwaters of the Little Indian Sioux River. Thereafter, short portages around rapids are all that interrupt the journey down the Sioux River on the return to the take-out point at the Echo Trail bridge. This could take two days, however, and make it necessary to camp at Bootleg Lake or at an emergency location along the riverbank. The directions for finding Bootleg Lake are covered in previous chapters.

Access: Start approximately 2½ miles west of Ely at the junction of County Road 88 and the Echo Trail (County Road 116). Follow the Echo Trail (CR 116) 31.5 miles west to the Little Indian Sioux River bridge. A small parking lot and put-in point is located south of the bridge.

Shuttle: None.

Camping: Jeanette Lake Campground, Echo Lake Campground. A fee is charged at both.

Food, gas, lodging: Ely.

For more information: Kawishiwi Ranger District (see appendix).

8 Little Indian Sioux River to Portage River Loop

Entry point: 14

Character: Start at the Echo Trail, paddle down one river, visit ten lakes, and return to the Echo Trail by another river. Waterfalls can be viewed, wildlife is abundant, and the fishing could be very good.

Length: 29 miles.

Average run time: 3 to 5 days.

Skill level: Beginner.

Hazards: Storm-damaged trees (see introduction).

Maps: USGS: Shell Lake, Lake Agnes, Lapond Lake.

The paddling: Portage 40 rods from the parking lot on the west side of the Little Indian Sioux River. Launch the canoe in the river and paddle downstream. The first portage will be the 60-rod Elm Portage around a set of rapids. Follow the river into Upper Pauness Lake. The upper lake covers 188 acres and is shallow. Walleye and northern pike live in its water. Three campsites are available.

From Upper Pauness Lake portage to Lower Pauness Lake. Lower Pauness Lake can be reached from a 40-rod portage at midlake or an 8-rod portage to the south arm of the lower lake. Lower Pauness Lake covers 165 acres, is 35 feet deep, and has walleyes and perch. Three campsites are located on the western shore of the lake. This entire area is known to have bear problems. Secret your food pack with care. This is a good place to camp for the first night because the Shell Lakes and Lynx Lake are often crowded. After setting up camp take time to visit one of the most scenic locations in the western BWCAW, Devils Cascade. Here the Sioux River plummets 75 feet in a series of white-water rapids and waterfalls through a granite gorge to the Loon Lake basin. It is located at the north end of the lower lake.

Leave this lake by portaging 216 rods from Lower Pauness Lake to Shell Lake. This portage climbs about 50 feet, but the path is well worn and smooth. Shell Lake covers 525 acres, is 15 feet deep, and has fishing for walleyes, northern pike, rainbow trout, and panfish. Moose are often spotted around this lake. It has ten campsites. Leave this lake by portaging 10 rods to Little Shell Lake, and then portage 8 rods to Lynx Lake.

Lynx Lake covers 282 acres, is 85 feet deep, and has northern pike and walleyes. It has five campsites. Ruby Lake is next on the trip, and it requires a 280-rod portage. It covers 282 acres, is 85 feet deep, and has lake trout and northern pike. There are no legal campsites available, but Hustler Lake, only an 8-rod portage away, has six campsites.

Hustler Lake covers 294 acres, is 74 feet deep, and has only northern pike and bluegill for shore lunch. Leave Hustler Lake by a rugged 240-rod portage to Oyster Lake. The portage trail ascends to almost 150 feet above Oyster Lake. The path is well worn and

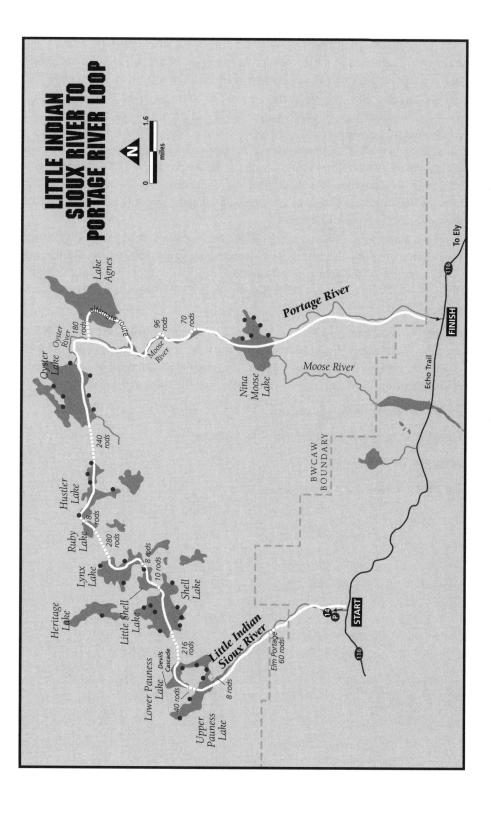

easily followed, though. Oyster Lake is an excellent choice for camping the second night. It covers 772 acres, is 130 feet deep, and has lake trout, northern pike, and smallmouth bass to tempt the angler. There are seven campsites available.

Next morning find the outlet of the Oyster River on the east shore of the lake. In most seasons a 60-rod portage will be required to find navigable water on this river. Paddle downstream to the confluence with the Moose River. Follow the Moose River upstream to Nina Moose Lake. A 96-rod portage and a 70-rod portage are required to bypass two sets of rapids on the Moose River along this stretch. In dry periods, or if the Oyster River is blocked by too many beaver dams or windfalls, an alternate route is found by portaging from the Oyster River 180 rods to Lake Agnes, finding the Moose River outlet, and paddling upstream to Nina Moose Lake.

Paddle through Nina Moose Lake, and find the inlet of the Portage River. Follow the river upstream to Echo Trail and the take-out point. Six sets of rapids will be encountered, but in most seasons the river is easily negotiated. An alternate route is to find the mouth of the Moose River, and paddle upstream to the 160-rod take-out portage to the Echo Trail parking lot.

Access: Start approximately 2½ miles west of Ely at the junction of County Road 88 and the Echo Trail (County Road 116) and follow the Echo Trail (CR 116) west for about 29 miles to the Little Sioux Indian River bridge. Cross the bridge, and turn right on the access road. This well-marked trail leads to a parking lot and the portage trail to the river.

Shuttle: 7.5 miles one way. 30 minutes.

Camping: Jeanette Lake Campground. A fee is charged.

Food, gas, lodging: Ely.

For more information: La Croix Ranger District (see appendix).

Moose River to Lac La Croix

Entry point: 16

Character: Portage from the Moose River north parking lot to the Moose River. Paddle downstream on the river through two lakes. A short trip on another river leads to Lac La Croix. Paddle the length of this gigantic lake, go through big Loon Lake, and find a river to travel south to the Echo Trail again. See waterfalls, pictographs, and Warrior Hill. Wildlife is about and the fishing should be great. Berry picking can be good in season. Motors are allowed on part of the route. Independence Day storm–impacted area.

Length: 50 miles.

Average run time: 6 to 8 days, longer if wind days are needed.

Skill level: Beginner.

Hazards: Wind and motorboat wakes on Lac La Croix and Loon Lake.

Maps: USGS: Shell Lake, Lapond Lake, Lake Agnes, Coleman Island, Takumich Lake, Snow Bay, Lake Jeanette.

The paddling: Portage 160 rods from the Moose River parking lot to the Moose River and head north, downstream. A 20-rod and a 25-rod portage will be encountered before the river flows into Nina Moose Lake. This lake covers 415 acres and is only 6 feet deep. Fishing is fair for walleyes, northern pike, and smallmouth bass. A pure water spring is located on the southwest corner, if drinking water is needed. Scars from a 1971 forest fire are still visible along the west shoreline. Seven campsites are available. This is a good location for the first night campsite. Avoid bear problems by following the procedures—which are outlined in the introduction—for protecting your food supply.

Leave Nina Moose Lake on the Moose River and follow it to Lake Agnes. Two sets of rapids requiring a 70-rod and a 96-rod portage are encountered before the lake is reached. Lake Agnes covers 1,040 acres and is 30 feet deep. It is about 2.5 miles long and has walleye, smallmouth bass, and northern pike. Berry picking can be good in season. There are sixteen campsites, and groups that didn't stop at Nina Moose Lake will no doubt be weary enough to want to camp here. This lake has a history of bears raiding campsites; take the recommended steps to avoid losing the food supply.

Leave Lake Agnes in the northernmost bay by portaging 24 rods to the Boulder River. Paddle across the river and find the 65-rod portage that leads to the Boulder Bay section of Lac La Croix. This gigantic lake is 25 miles long, 7 miles wide in one place, covers 34,070 acres, and is 180 feet deep. It has 250 islands ranging from tiny dots of land to Coleman Island, which covers about 8 square miles. Walleye, northern pike, lake trout, smallmouth bass, and rainbow trout are available for the catching. High winds can come up suddenly on this big lake. Always stay close enough to a shoreline to land quickly if it becomes necessary. Most groups can paddle the length of Lac La Croix in three days unless the wind is unusually fierce. Motors are allowed on the Canadian side of the lake—it is apt to be buzzing with boat motors and even airplanes.

MOOSE RIVER TO LAC LA CROIX

N

0   1.12
miles

CANADA

Lac La Croix

alternate route

Twenty-seven
Island

Twenty-five
Island

*Snow
Bay*

Lac La Croix

Coleman
Island

UNITED STATES

Fish Stake Narrows

pictographs
Warrior Hill

*Little Loon
Lake*

pictured rocks

Beatty Portage
(50 rods)

*East Loon
Bay*

*Boulder
River*

24
rods

*Loon
Lake*

*Cascade
Lake*

96
rods

*Lake
Agnes*

160 rods

*Upper
Pauness
Lake*

*Lower
Pauness
Lake*

**Moose
River**

*Little Indian
Sioux River*

Elm Portage
(80 rods)

70 rods

BWCAW BOUNDARY

25
rods

START

16
P

Nina Moose Lake

25
rods

160
rods

*Portage
River*

40 rods

14
P

FINISH

116

Echo Trail

Echo Trail

After embarking to the southeast end of Lac La Croix, visit Warrior Hill on the Canadian side of the lake. This hill reportedly was a testing ground for Indian warriors, who ran from the lake's edge to the summit of the hill. About a mile farther north, the largest display of old Indian pictographs in the Quetico–Superior region can be located on the west shore of Canada's Irving Island. Be sure to have permission from the Canadian authorities before crossing the border. See the introduction for more information on obtaining permits. After viewing these two points of interest, continue north to Fish Stake Narrows, and turn west through the narrows. Paddle west to pass on the south side of the first, large, unnamed island, and then turn northwest to pass between Coleman Island and the mainland. Campsites are available in this region, and the fishing can be quite good.

Head west the next morning, and set a course to pass between Twenty-Seven Island and the American shoreline. Continue on this route, following the international border as it bends abruptly south. From Snow Bay, west, motors are allowed on the American side also. Find a campsite in the vicinity of Sandbar Island. Get a good night's sleep; the next day will be eventful. The next morning, after about 3 miles of paddling, Beatty Portage—between Lac La Croix and Loon Lake—will be encountered. About 0.25 mile north of the portage, on the east shore, pictographs are displayed on a cliff face. It is not known how old this display is or even what people made them or what the strange symbols mean. They are very intriguing.

Negotiate the 50-rod portage into Loon Lake. A marine railway is located here for use in transporting large motorboats around the portage. Loon Lake covers 3,101 acres, has a maximum depth of 70 feet, and has walleyes, northern pike, smallmouth bass, panfish, and rainbow trout living in its clear water. There are several campsites on this popular lake. If time permits, paddle to the west end of Loon Lake and find scenic Loon Falls. It has a 29-foot drop and is worth taking time to enjoy.

Leave Loon Lake by finding the mouth of the Little Indian Sioux River along the south shoreline. Paddle upstream to the first portage, a 160-rod carry around Devils Cascade. Devils Cascade is a white-water gorge where the water from the Sioux River drops 75 feet in a series of rapids and waterfalls from the Lower Pauness Lake to the Loon Lake water level. Take time to enjoy the gorge. It is one of the most scenic spots in the western BWCAW.

Lower Pauness Lake is located at the upstream end of the portage. This lake covers 165 acres, is 35 feet deep, and has walleyes and perch. Three campsites are located on the western shore of the lake. This entire area is known to have bear problems. Secret your food pack with care. Leave Lower Pauness Lake by an 8-rod portage in the southwest arm of the lake; an alternate, 40-rod portage is located on the west shore. They both lead to Upper Pauness Lake. The upper lake covers 188 acres and is shallow. Walleye and northern pike live in its water. Three campsites are available.

Leave Upper Pauness Lake by finding the inlet of the Sioux River on the southern shore of the lake. Paddle up the river to 80-rod Elm Portage. The Jeanette Creek waterfall adds interest to this portage. Continue 1.29 miles upstream to the take-out point. A 40-rod portage leads to the Little Indian Sioux River parking lot on the Echo Trail.

Access: Start at the intersection of County Road 88 and the Echo Trail (County Road 116) and drive about 24 miles west on the Echo Trail to the Moose River bridge. Turn right and drive about 1 mile to the parking lot.

Shuttle: 7.5 miles one way. 30 minutes.

Camping: Fenske Lake Campground, Lake Jeanette Campground. A fee is charged at both.

Food, gas, lodging: Ely.

For more information: La Croix Ranger District (see appendix).

Stuart River to Iron Lake Loop

Entry point: 19

Character: Portage north from the Echo Trail to the headwaters of the Stuart River and paddle downriver through an isolated and pristine region to Stuart Lake. Continue northeast through a series of lakes to huge Iron Lake. Base camp on this lake and enjoy two waterfalls and the fishing for an extended period; then turn back south and return by a loop through small lakes. Eventually the trip leads back to the Stuart River and the put-in point. Moose and deer are found along the river. Fishing for walleye, bass, and northern pike can be good. Even when water levels are high, this is a rugged route. Do not even attempt this trip during the dry season. Consult with the Forest Service before starting.

Length: 28 miles.

Average run time: 4 to 6 days, with fishing and sightseeing.

Skill level: Beginner.

Hazards: Wind on Stuart Lake and Iron Lake.

Maps: Lake Agnes, Angleworm Lake, Iron Lake.

The paddling: Find the Stuart River Portage on the north side of the Echo Trail, and portage 470 rods to the headwaters of this swampy little river. The trail slopes downhill but isn't used much and could be blocked by windfalls. After reaching the river paddle a short distance to the next 85-rod portage. Continue downstream to the outlet to White Feather Lake. There are no campsites along the river. White Feather Lake has one campsite and many groups will be ready to stop here for the first night. White Feather Lake covers 108 acres, is 6 feet deep, and has northern pike for the catching. The next campsites are located at Stuart Lake, which will require 146 rods of portaging and almost 3 miles of paddling.

Leave White Feather Lake and continue downstream to Stuart Lake. At the northeast corner of Stuart Lake, a 315-rod portage extends northeast to Fox Lake. This long portage is followed by an 80-rod portage from Fox Lake to Rush Lake. Rush Lake covers 119 acres, is 10 feet deep, and has northern pike, walleye, smallmouth bass, and rainbow trout for the angler. There is a campsite available. Continue by an 87-rod portage from the north shore of this lake to Dark Lake. Dark Lake covers 38 acres but has no fishing. Access beautiful Iron Lake by a 72-rod portage from Dark Lake. Try to get the campsite on Peterson Bay so you'll be centrally located. If time permits, plan on staying at least two days; three would be better. It will take at least this long to properly enjoy what this lake has to offer.

Iron Lake is a boundary line lake. It covers 2,300 acres, including about twenty-nine islands; it is 60 feet deep and has walleye, northern pike, and smallmouth bass holding along the rugged shorelines. There are nine campsites. Two picturesque waterfalls can be enjoyed. Rebecca Falls, which has a drop of 23 feet, is located in Canada, just north of Four-Mile Island. Before entering Canadian territory be sure to have permission or a border-crossing permit. See the introduction for more information. Curtain Falls can be found at the east end of the lake on the international border between Iron Lake and Crooked Lake. It has a

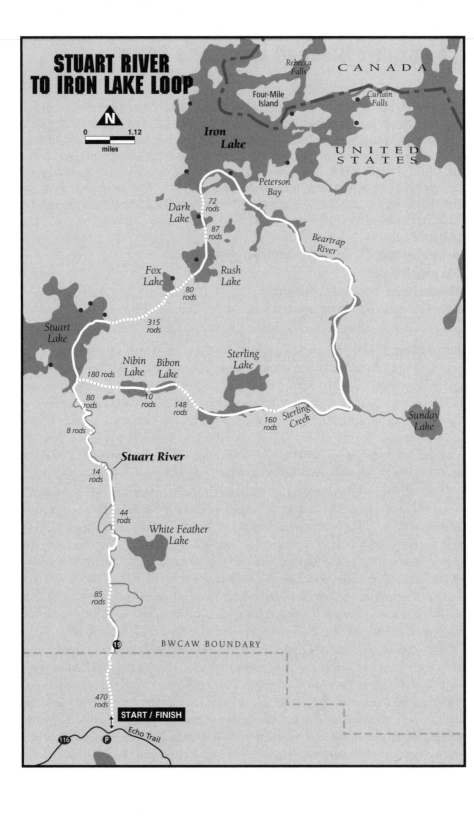

STUART RIVER
TO IRON LAKE LOOP

N

0   1.12
miles

Rebecca Falls

C A N A D A

Four-Mile Island

Curtain Falls

Iron Lake

U N I T E D
S T A T E S

Peterson Bay

72 rods

87 rods

Dark Lake

Beartrap River

Fox Lake

Rush Lake

80 rods

315 rods

Stuart Lake

Sterling Lake

Nibin Lake

Bibon Lake

180 rods

10 rods

148 rods

80 rods

160 rods

Sterling Creek

Sunday Lake

8 rods

14 rods

Stuart River

44 rods

White Feather Lake

85 rods

19

B W C A W B O U N D A R Y

470 rods

START / FINISH

116

P

Echo Trail

drop of about 29 feet. A beautiful lunch site is located on a rock outcropping adjacent to the falls. A day could be spent exploring each waterfall, with time left over to collect some succulent fish fillets.

Leave Iron Lake by finding the mouth of the Beartrap River at the southeast part of Peterson Bay. Paddle up the Beartrap River to Sterling Creek. A 65-rod portage will be encountered shortly after leaving the bay, followed by a 20-rod portage just downstream from the mouth of Sterling Creek. With an adequate flow in Sterling Creek, a loaded canoe can be paddled within 160 rods of Sterling Lake. Portage to Sterling Lake. This lake is configured in a series of narrow arms; it covers 180 acres, possibly has no fish, but does have one campsite. Next portage 148 rods to Bibon Lake, negotiate the 10-rod portage to Nibin Lake, and then a 180-rod portage to Stuart Lake will deliver you to familiar water.

Stuart Lake is a good location for an overnight stop before attempting the return trip to the take-out point. This lake covers 804 acres, is 40 feet deep, and has smallmouth and largemouth bass, walleye, northern pike, and panfish to tempt the angler. It has five campsites.

Get an early start to finish the trip the next day. It will require 611 rods of portaging besides about 5 miles of paddling to reach the Echo Trail. Consider stopping at White Feather Lake if your energy level is low or the hour is late.

Access: From the junction of County Road 88 and the Echo Trail (County Road 116), travel 18 miles west on the Echo Trail to the Stuart River Portage located across the road from the Big Lake access.

Shuttle: None.

Camping: Fenske Lake Campground. A fee is charged.

Food, gas, lodging: Ely.

For more information: Kawishiwi Ranger District (see appendix).

Angleworm Lake to Basswood Lake Loop

Entry point: 20

Character: Two of the longest portages in the BWCAW are negotiated on this trip. Several beautiful, small lakes are utilized, and the largest lake in the BWCAW is visited. Two rivers form part of the journey. Pictographs, galloping white water, waterfalls, and the international border add interest. The fishing can be tremendous, and wildlife is about. The trip can be shortened or modified by utilizing parts of the Mudro Lake or the South Hegman Lake route. This route is so rugged that advance reservations will seldom be needed.

Length: 33 miles.

Average run time: 5 to 7 days.

Class: Horse River, Class I; Basswood River, Class II–VI. Running rapids in the BWCAW is not recommended.

Skill level: Beginner.

Hazards: Wind on Basswood Lake and white-water rapids on the Basswood River. The upper Basswood River is very dangerous.

Maps: USGS: Angleworm Lake, Fourtown Lake, Basswood Lake West.

The paddling: The portage from the Echo Trail to Angleworm Lake will take one day for most groups. Generally, the portage follows the Angleworm Lake Hiking Trail, but pay careful attention to the forks in the trail at the 2-mile point. Do not turn on either intersecting trail. Continue straight ahead. About 80 rods past the intersection, a short trail leads to the water. There are three campsites near the put-in point. Plan on resting and enjoying scenic Angleworm Lake for the rest of the day.

Angleworm Lake is ringed by high, rocky cliffs, and stands of huge white and red pine grow along its shores. It is one of the most scenic lakes in the western BWCAW. Configured as long and narrow, it covers 148 acres, is 11 feet deep, and has good walleye and northern pike fishing. There are seven campsites available, but hikers on the Angleworm Lake Hiking Trail have access to them also. Get one early if staying over. Leave Angleworm Lake by portaging 40 rods to Home Lake. This lake covers 85 acres, has some 24-foot-deep water, and gives shelter to walleye and northern pike. Two campsites are available.

Portage 240 rods from Home Lake to Gull Lake. Gull Lake covers 196 acres, is 13 feet deep, and offers northern pike and sunfish to the angler. There are three campsites available. Leave Gull Lake by a 30-rod portage to Gun Lake. Gun Lake is an accommodating lake for overnight camping. It covers 358 acres, is 57 feet deep, and has walleye, northern pike, smallmouth bass, and panfish in its depths. Five campsites are spread around the lake.

The route to Fourtown Lake goes through Fairy and Boot Lakes. Fourtown Lake covers 1,305 acres and has a maximum depth of 25 feet. Fourtown Lake can offer good fishing for walleye, northern pike, and smallmouth bass. There are thirteen campsites available, but because this is a very popular lake, they might fill early.

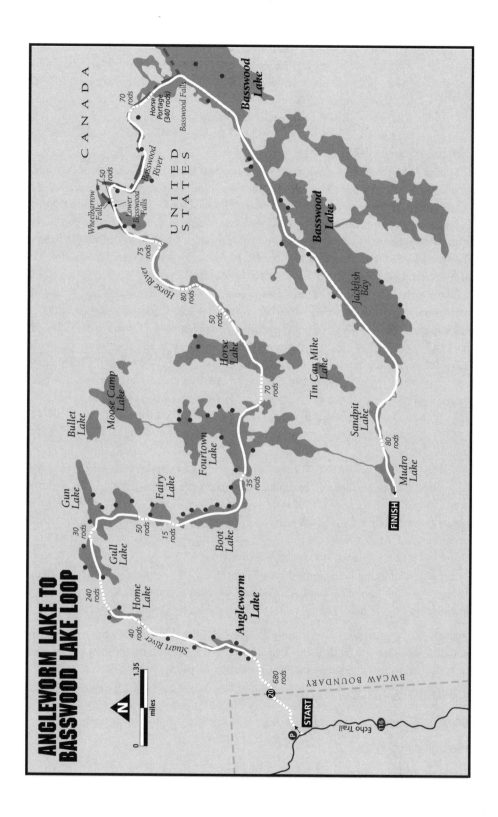

ANGLEWORM LAKE TO BASSWOOD LAKE LOOP

N

0 miles 1.35

CANADA

UNITED STATES

Basswood Lake

Basswood Lake

Horse Portage (340 rods)

Basswood Falls

70 rods

Wheelbarrow Falls

50 rods

Lower Basswood Falls

Basswood River

75 rods

80 rods

Horse River

50 rods

Horse Lake

70 rods

Jackfish Bay

Moose Camp Lake

Bullet Lake

Fourtown Lake

Tin Can Mike Lake

Sandpit Lake

Gun Lake

30 rods

Gull Lake

Fairy Lake

50 rods

15 rods

35 rods

Boot Lake

80 rods

Mudro Lake

FINISH

240 rods

Home Lake

40 rods

Stuart River

Angleworm Lake

680 rods

20

START

P

BWCAW BOUNDARY

Echo Trail

116

Find the portage to Horse Lake, near midlake on the east shore. A 10-rod and a 70-rod portage will probably be needed in times of average water levels. Cross Horse Lake, and find the outlet for the Horse River on the east shore. Some groups may want to overnight on Horse Lake. About 8 miles will have been covered this day, and there are no more campsites until the Basswood River is reached. Except when the water level is high, over a 0.5 mile of portages lie ahead, along with 5 miles of paddling before the next campsites are encountered on the Basswood River.

Horse Lake covers 724 acres, is 25 feet deep, and has good fishing for walleye and northern pike. Leave Horse Lake, and paddle down the Horse River to its mouth on the Basswood River. Turn east and paddle about 0.75 mile upriver to Wheelbarrow Falls. Excellent fishing for smallmouth bass and walleyes is found in this area, and five campsites are in close proximity. Camp overnight, and enjoy fishing, or paddle downstream to Lower Basswood Falls. Here, an enchanting display of cascading water drops 12 feet. See the Mudro Lake Loop trip (chapter 12) for more information.

At Wheelbarrow Falls the Basswood River plunges 12 feet in a stair-step falls. A 50-rod portage, the Wheelbarrow Portage, reaches around the falls. Continue upstream about 2 miles to the Horse Portage. A 70-rod portage is located between Wheelbarrow Falls and the Horse Portage; however, it bypasses a Class III rapids. Horse Portage is on the south bank. It bypasses the most dangerous rapids and Basswood Falls. Both the Wheelbarrow Portage and the Horse Portage are shortcuts across northern loops of the river as well as bypasses for dangerous water. Horse Portage is 340 rods long and ends on Basswood Lake. Take time to enjoy Basswood Falls at the outlet from Basswood Lake. Here water falls 15 feet over a ledge of granite. The pool below the falls was a favorite spearing location for Indians.

Basswood Lake covers 14,610 acres, has some 111-foot depths, and offers fishing for lake trout, walleyes, smallmouth bass, and northern pike. It is about 17 miles long and has over 150 islands. It is probably the most heavily used lake in the BWCAW. After embarking on Basswood Lake, bend south into Jackfish Bay, and find a campsite at the upper end of the bay. Rest up and enjoy the fishing. Be very careful to stay close to land on this lake. Wind can pick up suddenly and create life-threatening waves.

The next morning head south through Jackfish Bay to the portage to Sandpit Lake. Portage from this lake to Mudro Lake, and find the take-out point on the west end. Have a vehicle waiting, or make arrangements to be picked up by a commercial service.

Access: Start at the junction of County Road 88 and the Echo Trail (County Road 116) and drive 13 miles west on the Echo Trail. The marked trailhead is on the right (north) side of Echo Trail. A small parking lot is located nearby. The portage follows the hiking trail.

Shuttle: 8 miles one way. About 25 minutes.

Camping: Fenske Lake Campground. A fee is charged.

Food, gas, lodging: Ely.

For more information: Kawishiwi Ranger District (see appendix).

Basswood Lake. Photo: Courtesy Minnesota Office of Tourism

Mudro Lake Loop

Entry points: 22, 23

Character: Put in at Mudro Lake and paddle down the Horse River to the Basswood River. Follow the Basswood River to Crooked Lake, turn south at Friday Bay, and negotiate a series of small lakes back to the put-in point. View enchanting waterfalls and ancient pictographs. The fishing can be terrific for walleyes, smallmouth bass, northern pike, lake trout, and splake.

Length: 35 miles.

Average run time: 4 to 8 days, with fishing and sightseeing.

Class: Horse River, Class I–II; Basswood River, Class III–V. It is recommended that all rapids above a Class I rating be portaged in the BWCAW.

Skill level: Beginner.

Hazards: Wind on Crooked Lake and waterfalls and rapids on the rivers.

Maps: USGS: Fourtown Lake, Basswood Lake, Jackfish Lake, Friday Bay.

The paddling: See "Access" later in this chapter for the complicated access to Mudro Lake. This lake covers 80 acres, has a maximum depth of 76 feet, and holds lake trout, walleyes, northern pike, and smallmouth bass; it has one campsite. From Mudro Lake portage 80 rods to Sandpit Lake, which covers 65 acres, is 53 feet deep, and can yield walleyes, northern pike, and panfish. One campsite is at hand. The next portage is 160 rods to Tin Can Mike Lake. This lake covers 142 acres, is 29 feet deep, and offers fishing for the succulent and comely splake (lake trout/brook trout cross) as well as for bluegills. Three campsites are located here.

Continue by portaging 90 rods to Horse Lake. This lake covers 724 acres, is 25 feet deep, and can offer walleye, northern pike, and bluegill for shore lunch. Seven campsites are available. With over 1 mile of portaging and 6 miles of paddling behind you, you may want to stop over here before tackling the Horse River. The Horse River has no campsites. Except when the water level is high, over 0.5 mile of portages and 5 miles of paddling lie ahead before the next campsites are encountered on the Basswood River.

Leave Horse Lake and paddle down the Horse River to its mouth on the Basswood River. If time permits, consider a side trip. Travel about 0.75 mile upriver to the scenic Wheelbarrow Falls, where the river cascades over a 12-foot drop. View the falls, then return to the original route, and paddle downstream from the Horse River mouth to Lower Basswood Falls. Here is another enchanting display of cascading water that drops 12 feet. The falls require a 12-rod portage. Excellent fishing for smallmouth bass and walleyes is found in this area, and five campsites are in close proximity.

Continue down the Basswood River to Crooked Lake. A display of Indian paintings is found along the west shore of the Basswood River, about a mile downstream from Lower Basswood Falls. Several fine campsites, including the historic Table Rock campsite where the voyageurs often stopped, are located near here.

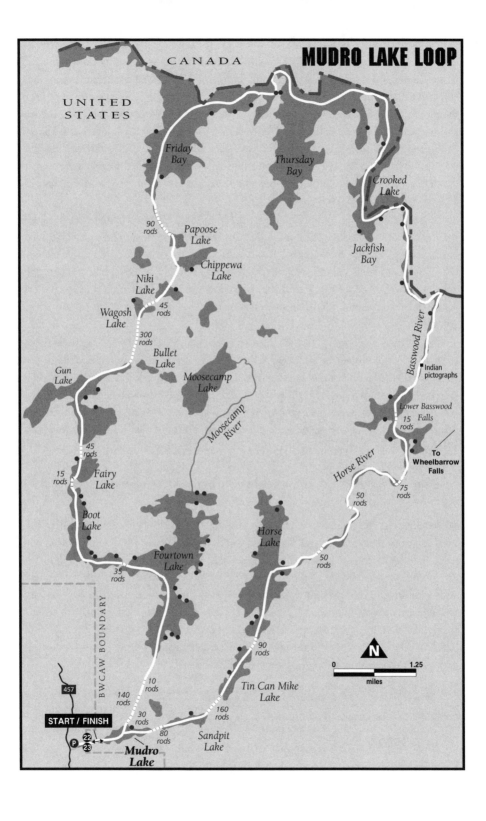

CANADA

UNITED STATES

MUDRO LAKE LOOP

Friday Bay

Thursday Bay

Crooked Lake

Jackfish Bay

90 rods

Papoose Lake

Chippewa Lake

Niki Lake

Basswood River

45 rods

Wagosh Lake

300 rods

Bullet Lake

Moosecamp Lake

Indian pictographs

Lower Basswood Falls

15 rods

Gun Lake

Moosecamp River

To Wheelbarrow Falls

45 rods

Horse River

15 rods

Fairy Lake

50 rods

75 rods

Boot Lake

Horse Lake

50 rods

35 rods

Fourtown Lake

BWCAW BOUNDARY

90 rods

10 rods

457

Tin Can Mike Lake

140 rods

30 rods

160 rods

START / FINISH

80 rods

Sandpit Lake

P 22
   23

Mudro Lake

N

0   1.25
miles

Crooked Lake is a 10,904-acre lake with some 165-foot-deep water. It is about 16 miles long and spreads to 5 miles wide. Crooked Lake offers excellent fishing for smallmouth bass, walleye, and northern pike; the sandy beaches invite sunbathers; and the many bays and rocky shorelines intrigue sightseers. It will take most groups two days to travel from the mouth of the Horse River to Friday Bay. Another day could be spent enjoying the lake and paddling to the west end of the lake to view Curtain Falls at the inlet to Iron Lake. It has a drop of about 29 feet. A beautiful lunch site is located on a rock outcropping adjacent to the falls. On the last day plan on camping on the south end of Friday Bay, where this route leaves the lake. Although there are thirty campsites on the lake, only three are located in Friday Bay. Get one early.

Leave Crooked Lake by portaging 90 rods from Friday Bay to Papoose Creek, paddle the creek to Papoose Lake, continue into Chippewa Lake, and then paddle into Niki Lake. Next, portage 45 rods to Wagosh Lake. A 300-rod portage separates Wagosh Lake and Gun Lake. Gun Lake is an accommodating lake for overnight camping before starting the journey back to Mudro Lake. Gun Lake covers 358 acres, is 57 feet deep, and has walleye, northern pike, smallmouth bass, and panfish in its depths. Five campsites are spread around the lake.

From Gun Lake portage 45 rods to Fairy Lake and 15 rods to Boot Lake. Leave Boot Lake by a 35-rod portage to Fourtown Lake. An alternate route is available, which is possibly easier, but less interesting: Portage to Bullet Lake, then to Moosecamp Lake, and follow the Moosecamp River from the east end of this lake to Fourtown Lake. If time permits another night's layover, consider Fourtown Lake. It covers 1,305 acres and has a maximum depth of 25 feet. It can offer good fishing for walleye, northern pike, and smallmouth bass. There are thirteen campsites available, but it is also a very popular lake, and they might fill early.

Return to Mudro Lake and the take-out point by the unnamed stream at the south end of Fourtown Lake.

Access: Start at the intersection of County Road 88 and the Echo Trail (County Road 116) and drive west on the Echo Trail for about 8.5 miles. Watch for the intersection with Forest Road 457 immediately west of Fenske Lake. Turn right on FR 457 and follow to a turnaround on the left side of the road just before crossing the bridge at the Picket Lake outlet. Put in here, and park along the road, out of the traffic lane. A private parking lot is available across from the Picket Lake outlet bridge, at the Chain Saw Sisters bar. A fee is charged for parking and canoe access. Alternately, continue on the Echo Trail to Nels Lake Road and parking lot. Paddle through Nels Lake and Picket Lake to Mudro Lake. The portages on this section, though, are impassable at times.

Shuttle: None.

Camping: Fenske Lake Campground. A fee is charged.

Food, gas, lodging: Ely.

For more information: Kawishiwi Ranger District (see appendix).

13 ⌇ South Hegman Lake

Entry points: 77, 78

Character: This rugged route heads north through small lakes and the Beartrap River to Iron Lake on the international border. Then it turns east and follows the border to Crooked Lake, where it bends south and traverses small lakes back to the entry point. Pictographs and waterfalls are enjoyed, fishing opportunities abound, and wildlife is about.

Length: 44 miles.

Average run time: 6 to 9 days, with sightseeing and fishing.

Skill level: Beginner.

Hazards: Wind on Iron and Crooked Lakes.

Maps: USGS: Iron Lake, Angleworm Lake, Fourtown Lake, Friday Bay.

The paddling: Portage 78 rods from the South Hegman Lake parking lot to the lake. South Hegman Lake covers 298 acres, is 55 feet deep, and has walleye, northern pike, and smallmouth bass for fishing. There are two campsites available. Portage 5 rods to North Hegman Lake, and paddle to the north end. Some exceptional, ancient Indian pictographs are displayed on the west bank near the inlet to Trease Lake. According to records, many groups elect to stay right on the Hegman Lakes and Trease Lake with possibly a side trip to Little Bass Lake. There are several campsites, and the fishing can be very good.

For those adventurous and energetic paddlers who want to continue, paddle north through Trease Lake, and portage 480 rods to Angleworm Lake. Angleworm Lake is long and narrow, covers 148 acres, is 11 feet deep, and has good walleye and northern pike fishing. There are seven campsites available, but hikers on the Angleworm Hiking Trail have access to them, also. Get one early, if staying over. Leave Angleworm Lake by portaging 40 rods to Home Lake. This lake covers 85 acres, has some 24-foot-deep water, and gives shelter to walleye and northern pike. Two campsites are available.

Portage 240 rods from Home Lake to Gull Lake. Gull Lake covers 196 acres, is 13 feet deep, and offers northern pike and sunfish to the angler. There are three campsites available. Continue by portaging 35 rods to Mudhole Lake and then 55 rods to Thunder Lake. Thunder Lake and adjoining Beartrap Lake are separated only by a 5-rod portage. The two lakes combined cover 310 acres, have walleye and northern pike, and four campsites. Ahead lies a 200-rod portage to the Beartrap River and a serious day's paddling before Peterson Bay at Iron Lake is reached. Most groups will want to stay over at Thunder/Beartrap to be rested for the next day.

After reaching the Beartrap River paddle downstream to Sunday Lake, find the outlet of the Beartrap River on the west shoreline, and continue downriver to Iron Lake. A 20-rod portage and a 65-rod portage will be encountered along the river. Try to get the campsite on Peterson Bay so as to be centrally located. If time permits, plan on staying at least two days, three would be better. It will take at least this long to properly enjoy what this lake has to offer.

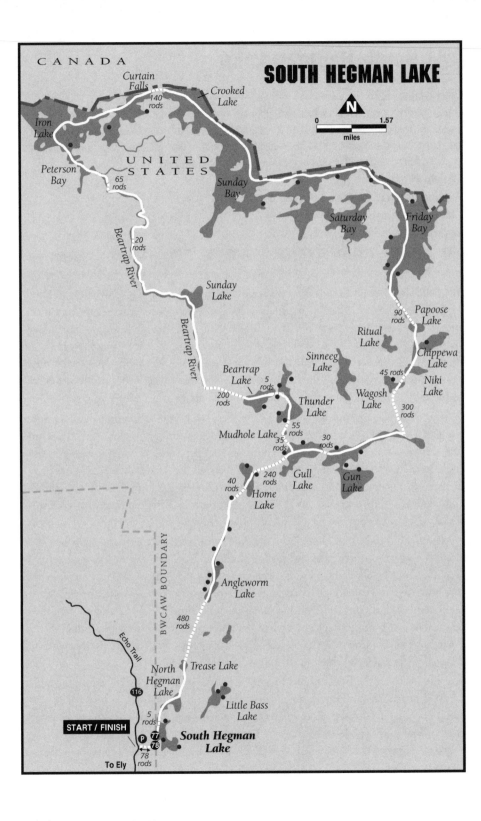

CANADA

SOUTH HEGMAN LAKE

Curtain
Falls
Crooked
Lake
140
rods

N

0   1.57
miles

Iron
Lake

UNITED
STATES

Peterson
Bay
65
rods

Sunday
Bay

Saturday
Bay

Friday
Bay

20
rods

Beartrap River

Sunday
Lake

Papoose
Lake
90
rods

Ritual
Lake

Chippewa
Lake

Beartrap River

Sinneeg
Lake

Niki
Lake

45 rods

Beartrap
Lake
5
rods

Wagosh
Lake

200
rods

Thunder
Lake

300
rods

Mudhole Lake
55
rods

35
rods

30
rods

Gun
Lake

40
rods

240
rods

Gull
Lake

Home
Lake

BWCAW BOUNDARY

Angleworm
Lake

480
rods

Echo Trail

116

North
Hegman
Lake

Trease Lake

Little Bass
Lake

5
rods

START / FINISH

P 77
78

South Hegman
Lake

To Ely
78
rods

Iron Lake is a boundary line lake that is about 3 miles long. It covers 2,300 acres, including about twenty-nine islands, is 60 feet deep, and has walleye, northern pike, and smallmouth bass holding along the rugged shorelines. There are nine campsites. Two picturesque waterfalls can be enjoyed. Rebecca Falls, which has a drop of 23 feet, is located in Canada, just north of Four-Mile Island. Before entering Canadian territory be sure to have permission or a border-crossing permit. See the introduction and chapter 10, Stuart River to Iron Lake Loop, for more information.

Leave Iron Lake by paddling east. A 140-rod portage separates Iron Lake from Crooked Lake. The portage reaches around the spectacular Curtain Falls waterfall. Here on the international border, the water drops 29 feet in a brawling display of falls and whitewater rapids. A beautiful lunch site is located on a rock outcropping adjacent to the falls.

Crooked Lake is a 10,904-acre lake with some 165-foot-deep water. It is about 16 miles long and spreads to 5 miles wide. Most every fish found in the BWCAW lives in its waters, and there are nine campsites in the area between Iron Lake and Friday Bay, where this route turns south. It will take most groups a day to travel from Peterson Bay at Iron Lake to Friday Bay. Study the map to avoid confusing Saturday Bay with Friday Bay. Bending south into Saturday Bay could result in a day's unnecessary paddling. Although there are thirty campsites on the lake, only three are located in Friday Bay. Get one as early as feasible. Crooked Lake offers excellent fishing for smallmouth bass, walleye, and northern pike; the sandy beaches invite sunbathers; and the many bays and rocky shorelines intrigue sightseers.

Leave Crooked Lake by portaging 90 rods from Friday Bay to Papoose Creek, paddle the creek to Papoose Lake, continue into Chippewa Lake, and then paddle into Niki Lake. Next portage 45 rods to Wagosh Lake. A 300-rod portage separates Wagosh Lake and Gun Lake. Gun Lake is an accommodating lake for overnight camping before starting the rugged journey back to the Hegman Lakes. Gun Lake covers 358 acres, is 57 feet deep, and has walleye, northern pike, smallmouth bass, and panfish in its depths. Five campsites are spread around the lake.

From Gun Lake portage 30 rods to Gull Lake, and from there on travel through familiar waters back to the put-in point.

Access: Start at the junction of County Road 88 and the Echo Trail (County Road 116), and drive 11 miles west on the Echo Trail to the South Hegman Lake parking lot. Portage 78 rods to South Hegman Lake.

Shuttle: None.

Camping: Fenske Lake. A fee is charged.

Food, gas, lodging: Ely.

For more information: Kawishiwi Ranger District (see appendix).

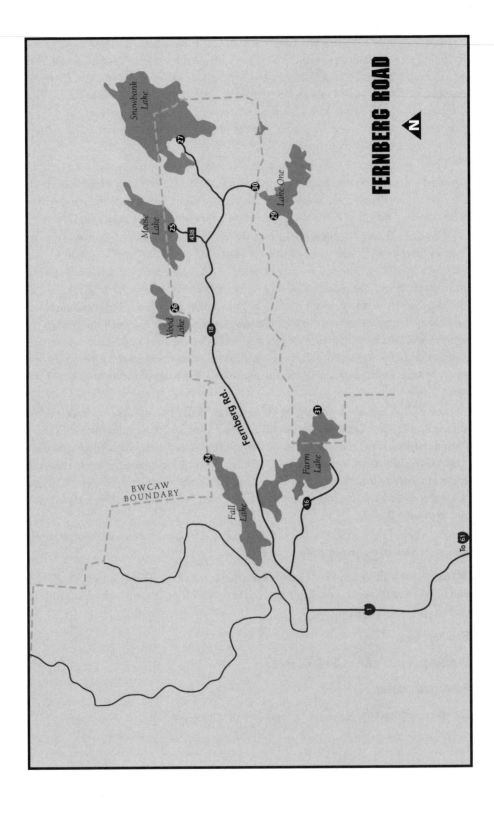

Fernberg Road Region

Fernberg Road extends east for 19 miles from the Kawishiwi Wilderness Station in Ely, to its terminus at the Lake One landing. The westernmost section of the road is connected to State Highway 169. It becomes Fernberg Road (County Road 18) when it crosses the Lake County line. The road is fairly straight and hard-surfaced. Moose Lake, the most popular entry point in the BWCAW, is located along this road. In fact, three of the six most popular entry points are located along this road.

The Kawishiwi Wilderness Center provides permits and up to date information for entry points along this road. Lodging, food, gas, showers, outfitters, and equipment are available in Ely.

14 Fall Lake to the Canadian Border and Return

Entry point: 24

Character: This is all lake paddling, on very large lakes at that. There are islands, scenic shorelines, and two waterfalls to explore and enjoy. The fishing can be quite good. The portages are not difficult, and you'll reach the Canadian border.

Length: 28 miles, average, much longer if the shorelines are followed.

Average run time: 3 to 4 days, or more.

Skill level: Beginner.

Hazards: Wind, waves, and motorboat wakes.

Maps: USGS: Basswood West and Farm Lake.

The paddling: This is an excellent trip for newcomers wanting to gain some BWCAW experience without removing themselves from outside help. Further, at any time during the outbound route, the trip can be aborted, and the paddlers can quickly return to the put-in point. A complete trip will reach the international border, which is a goal of many first timers.

The trip starts at the public landing at Fall Lake, possibly the most accessible entry point into the Boundary Waters. It is located only 3 miles from Ely, and the roads are hard surfaced. After leaving the landing paddle northwest. Skirt the southwest edge of Mile Island to find the Newton Falls Portage. This is an 80-rod portage alongside the connecting channel between Fall Lake and Newton Lake. The portage is quite easy and seems to be downhill.

After the Newton Falls Portage, follow Newton Lake about 2 miles northward to the Pipestone Falls Portage. Newton Lake is narrow with some fairly high shorelines; it is somewhat sheltered from the wind. There are several islands to explore, and the fishing can

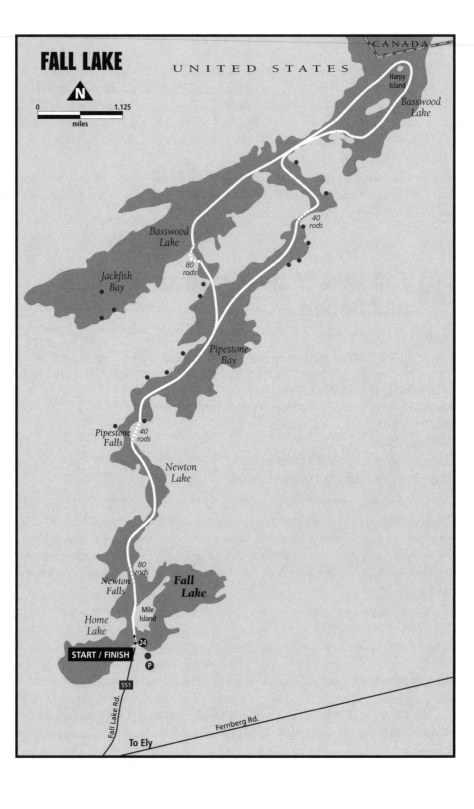

FALL LAKE

N

0 _____ 1.125
miles

CANADA

UNITED STATES

Harpy
Island

*Basswood
Lake*

40
rods

*Basswood
Lake*

80
rods

*Jackfish
Bay*

*Pipestone
Bay*

*Pipestone
Falls*   40
rods

*Newton
Lake*

80
rods

*Newton
Falls*   **Fall
Lake**

*Home
Lake*   Mile
Island

24

START / FINISH

P

551

Fall Lake Rd.

Fernberg Rd.

To Ely

be quite good for walleye and northern and smallmouth bass. There are two campsites on the northwest shoreline.

A 40-rod portage connects Newton Lake to Pipestone Bay. The portage is easy and is the last portage for the day. The bay is actually a part of Basswood Lake, although it seems to some paddlers like a lake in its own right. Pipestone Bay also offers good fishing and islands to explore. Most groups will be ready to call it a day and find a campground on the north end of Pipestone Bay. Fortunately, there are several, and at least one should be available.

The next day paddle westerly to enter Jackfish Bay, which is also a part of Basswood Lake. If time and weather permit, take a side trip to the south end of the bay and fish the reefs off the islands for walleyes. Finally, turn north and journey to the international border. Stay along the west shoreline where islands on the east side and the mainland on the west will reduce the velocity of the waves and boat wakes. Go north to the vicinity of Harpy Island, and find a campsite for the night; avoid camping on the Canadian side of the border without a permit. The fishing can be excellent around Basswood Falls and along the mainland shorelines and islands. Besides walleyes, bass, and northern pike, lake trout also inhabit Basswood. In spring they are found in shallow water. As the season progresses they move deeper and are harder to find.

Get an early start next morning to make it back to the Fall Lake put-in point. Go back south along the east shore of Jackfish Bay to see new territory. Watch for the small inlet that is the location of the portage back into Pipestone Bay. The portage is 40 rods and partially uphill. From there on follow familiar water to Pipestone Bay, portage into Newton Lake and from Newton Lake portage into Fall Lake and return to the put-in point.

Access: From Ely follow Fernberg Road 5 miles east. Turn left (north) on Fall Lake Road (Forest Road 551). Continue for about 1 mile to the public access and campground.

Shuttle: None.

Camping: Fall Lake campground. A fee is charged and reservations are recommended. Numerous campsites are along the canoe route.

Food, gas, lodging: Ely.

For more information: Kawishiwi Ranger District (see appendix).

Moose Lake to the Canadian Border and Return

Entry point: 25

Character: This route offers the paddler the opportunity to get to the international border rather quickly through some scenic lakes. A good part of the route follows the border. The portages aren't too strenuous, and the fishing can be quite good. Moose Lake is the most popular entry point in all of the BWCAW, and other people are apt to be nearby. Escape the crowds by portaging into some of the side trip lakes, such as Found Lake and Frog Lake.

Length: 32 miles.

Average run time: 4 days or more, depending on the time spent fishing. It has been done in 2 days.

Skill level: Beginner.

Hazards: Wind, waves, boat wakes, and collisions with motorized craft. Bears are unusually prevalent.

Maps: USGS: Ojibway Lake, Moose Lake.

The paddling: The canoe can be launched directly into Moose Lake. This is a busy landing and dozens of canoes might be in sight. Motors are allowed on Moose Lake and motorboats will likely be numerous. Moose Lake boat traffic is heavy because, in addition to being a short route to the border for canoeists, it offers the shortest route to Canadian customs at Prairie Portage and Quetico Provincial Park. It is also a popular route to Basswood Lake for motorized fishing boats. This route though offers beautiful lakes, good fishing, and a variety of trips and easy portages.

Moose Lake covers 1,030 acres and has a maximum depth of 60 feet. The length can be covered in a half day's paddling, if conditions are favorable. There are numerous buildings on the east shoreline outside the BWCAW boundary. From Moose Lake paddle north into Newfound Lake and then into Sucker Lake. This is about 8 miles total paddling and might be enough distance for the first day, if some fishing is done along the way.

There are no portages. Newfound Lake is about 40 feet deep and has about a 0.5-mile maximum width. Sucker Lake is narrow, also and has a maximum depth of 30 feet. There are several campsites at the north end of Sucker Lake, and if you get there early enough (usually before 4:00 P.M.) at least one should be available. If time and energy permit, there are opportunities for fishing for northern pike, walleye, and smallmouth bass in the nearby waters. Pitch camp and catch your dinner.

The next morning you will head into Birch Lake, either by a short, 5-rod portage from Sucker Lake or by paddling around the east shoreline of Sucker Lake and then heading east into Birch Lake. Taking the portage will save about one hour's paddling time. Either way, most groups will be able to paddle the length of Birch Lake in about a half day or less.

Go through Birch Lake, Carp Lake, Melon Lake, and into the Knife River, and, finally, Knife Lake. Under favorable conditions you can expect to reach Knife Lake in

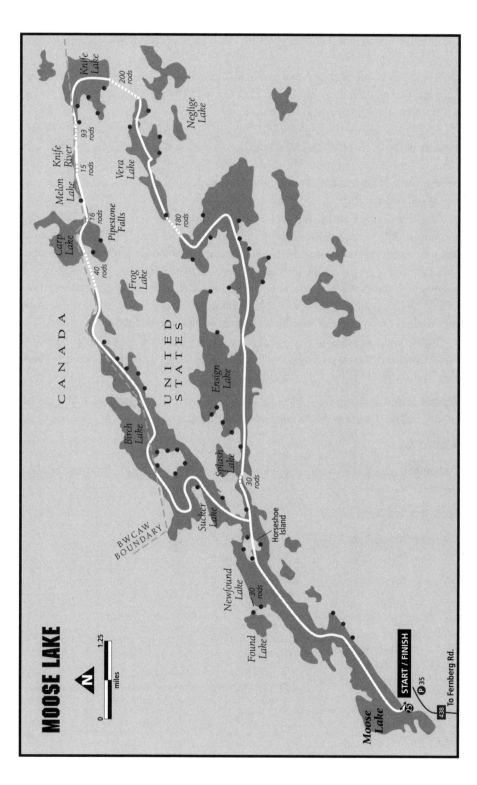

MOOSE LAKE

N

0 — 1,25 miles

CANADA

UNITED STATES

BWCAW BOUNDARY

Knife Lake

Neglige Lake

200 rods

93 rods

15 rods

Melon Lake

Knife River

Vera Lake

Carp Lake

16 rods

Pipestone Falls

40 rods

180 rods

Frog Lake

Ensign Lake

Birch Lake

Splash Lake

Sucker Lake

30 rods

Newfound Lake

Horseshoe Island

30 rods

Found Lake

Moose Lake

START / FINISH

P 35

25

438

To Fernberg Rd.

the afternoon, with plenty of time to set up camp for the evening. Walleye and northern pike fishing is quite good.

There is a 40-rod portage between Birch Lake and Carp Lake. Paddle through Carp Lake and portage 16 rods to tiny Melon Lake and then 15 rods to the Knife River. Portage 93 rods from the Knife River to Knife Lake.

Knife Lake was the home of the late Dorothy Molter. Molter was the last permanent resident allowed in the BWCAW. She lived there for about fifty years, all by herself in a log cabin of her own construction. She died in 1986. She was known as the "root beer lady" because she sold homemade root beer to passing paddlers. Two of her cabins were moved to Ely and reconstructed as a memorial.

The second night can be spent at Knife Lake; several campsites are available. The next morning paddle to the southwest corner to the portage to Vera Lake. This is the longest and toughest portage of the trip. It rises 80 feet and is 200 rods in length. Paddle through Vera Lake to the portage to Ensign Lake. It, also, is remarkable, being 180 rods long with a short climb and then a long descent to Ensign Lake. Realize that a productive brook trout fishery, Neglige Lake, lies just south of Vera Lake. If time permits, it is well worth working. Study the map to decide whether to portage or hike to it and shore fish.

Paddle to the west end of Ensign Lake, into Splash Lake, and then portage 30 rods to Newfound Lake. You are on familiar water now. Head south on Newfound Lake to Moose Lake and the put-in point.

Access: Follow Fernberg Road 16 miles northeast from Ely to Forest Road 438. Turn left (north) and go 3 miles to the Moose Lake public landing.

Shuttle: None.

Camping: Camp at Fall Lake Campground the night before the trip. Campsites are along the canoe route.

Food, gas, lodging: Ely.

For more information: Kawishiwi Ranger District (see appendix).

16 Wood Lake to the Canadian Border and Return

Entry point: 26

Character: This trip offers one of the most direct routes to the Canadian border. It crosses several small scenic lakes, loops through a part of gigantic Basswood Lake, and returns to the put-in point. It is an easy route for paddlers with some experience, but isn't too difficult for the novice, either. This region is usually not crowded. Moose, beaver, and bear have been sighted. The fishing is quite good.

Length: Approximately 24.5 miles.

Average run time: 3 days or more, with fishing and sightseeing.

Skill level: Beginner.

Hazards: Wind, waves, and storm-damaged trees (see introduction).

Maps: USGS quadrangles: Basswood East and Basswood West.

The paddling: This route starts with a 180-rod portage from Fernberg Road to Wood Lake. The path, except after a heavy rain, is firm, and it is used enough to be very visible. It has a level or falling gradient to Wood Lake. Canoes from nearby lodges are sometimes stored at the north end of the portage on Wood Lake. Otherwise, it is mostly a wilderness environment. This trip offers quiet and pleasant access to Basswood Lake.

Wood Lake is narrow, with an irregular shoreline. It covers 587 acres and has a maximum depth of 20 feet. Fishing can be quite good for walleye, northern pike, smallmouth bass, and panfish. The portage to Hula Lake is located at the extreme upper end of the second bay. Study the map closely to avoid wasted effort in finding this portage, which is 40 rods long. Hula Lake is shallow and can be choked with vegetation in late summer. The portage from Hula to Good Lake is 150 rods long.

Good Lake is made up of two segments, with a narrow channel connecting the two. The northernmost segment has a 65-rod portage along the west shore that extends northwest to Hoist Bay. Don't confuse this with the portage to Indiana Lake, which reaches easterly. Good Creek flows from Good Lake into Hoist Bay and offers the possibility of avoiding most of the portage if the water level is high enough to float a loaded canoe. It is worth checking out. A short, 2-rod portage is necessary at the mouth of the creek; and the creek may be clogged with vegetation in mid- to late summer. Good Lake is 50 feet deep, covers 183 acres, and holds walleyes, northern pike, and also lake trout in the early part of the season. Sand beach campsites are available.

Enter Hoist Bay, and paddle directly north about 3 miles to Washington Island and the Canadian border. If the winds are creating high waves or even if the weather looks threatening, stay close enough to shoreline to be safe. Campsites ring Washington Island and are found on Lincoln Island as well as most of the other nearby islands. This region can be a good place to spend the night. Fishing opportunities are excellent. Take care that you don't

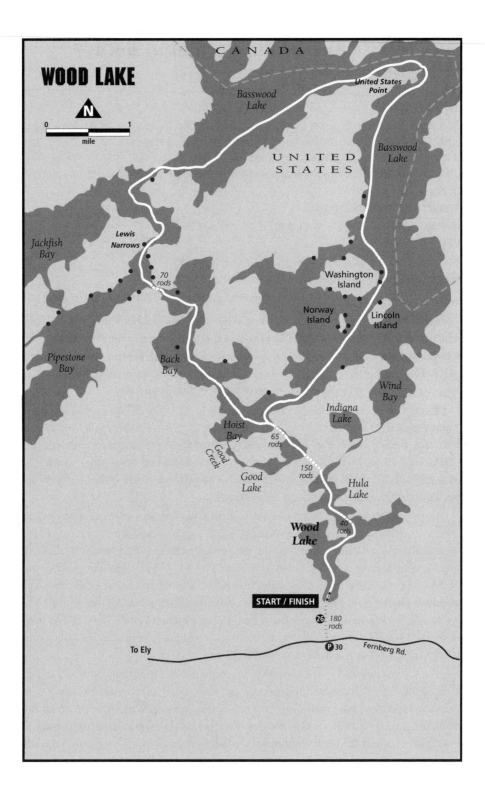

stray over the international border unless you have a border-crossing permit. Severe penalties have been meted out for this offense.

The next day paddle north along the shoreline of United States Point. Motors are not allowed north of Washington Island, and for hours you'll enjoy peace and quiet. Paddle around the point, and go south toward the head end of Jackfish Bay. At Jackfish Bay head east to Pipestone Bay, and go through the Lewis Narrows. Watch for the portage to Back Bay, which is located about 1 mile south of the narrows. This is a 70-rod portage.

There are several campsites in Back Bay and in Hoist Bay, which is connected by water to Back Bay. Camp in this region and resume paddling the next day in familiar territory as you head back through Hoist Bay to Good Lake, Hula Lake, Wood Lake, and the put-in point on Fernberg Road.

Access: Follow Fernberg Road 12 miles east from Ely. The entry point is on the north (left) side of Fernberg Road. There is parking for thirty vehicles.

Shuttle: None.

Camping: Fall Lake Campground. A fee is charged and reservations are recommended. Campsites are along the canoe route.

Food, gas, lodging: Ely.

For more information: Kawishiwi Ranger District (see appendix).

⊞ 17 Snowbank Lake Loop

Entry point: 27

Character: Snowbank Lake has resorts and motorboats. Once clear of Snowbank, though, a quality wilderness experience awaits on the smaller lakes that lie to the east. The portages are not overly rugged, and there is a great variety in the depths of the lakes and the appearance of the shorelines. Fishing for northern pike and walleyes is quite good, but a fantastic brook trout and splake lake can be enjoyed, also.

Length: About 20 miles.

Average run time: 3 days, with time spent fishing. This trip has been done in 1 day.

Skill level: Beginner.

Hazards: Motorboats and wind on the larger lakes.

Maps: USGS: Snowbank Lake, Ensign Lake East, Lake Insula.

The paddling: The canoe can be launched directly into Snowbank Lake. There are resorts and outfitters on the southern end of Snowbank, and during most of the year you will have to deal with wakes and powerboats. It might take about a half a day to paddle north to the Boot Lake Portage. If the wind is too strong to paddle north on the suggested route, simply reverse it and head east to the Parent Lake Portage.

There is a two-section portage into Boot Lake. The first is 50 rods, the second 30 rods, with a pond in between. Boot Lake takes less than an hour to cross, and then you will encounter the 220-rod portage to Ensign Lake. Ensign is about 4 miles long but is an excellent fishing lake and, in fact, a final destination for many anglers.

This trip only covers about 2 miles of Ensign Lake. Turn east at the put-in point and paddle around the peninsula to find the portage to Ashigan Lake. This is an excellent place to stop for the first day. Fishing is quite good for walleyes and northern pike, and there are several campsites on the southeastern section of the lake. Although this corner of the lake isn't as crowded as the western sections, it is wise to start looking for a campsite early in the day.

The next day can start with the 56-rod portage to Ashigan Lake and the 105-rod portage out of Ashigan to Gibson Lake. After this sweaty start, the rest of the day is all short portages. After negotiating Jitterbug Lake, where the water may be less than a foot deep, Ahsub Lake will be encountered. It is an excellent place to stop and fish. Try to get the campsite at the west end of the lake, near the portage to Disappointment Lake.

Schedule some serious fishing time at Ahsub, which covers 58 acres with a maximum depth of 78 feet. More than 22,000 brook trout have been stocked in this lake in the last few years. Brook trout over 18 inches long have been caught here. Large splake are present, also.

When you leave this location, only Disappointment and Parent Lakes separate you from Snowbank. Nevertheless, it will probably take most of the day to get back to the put-in point on Snowbank Lake. Snowbank Lake has excellent fishing and you might consider

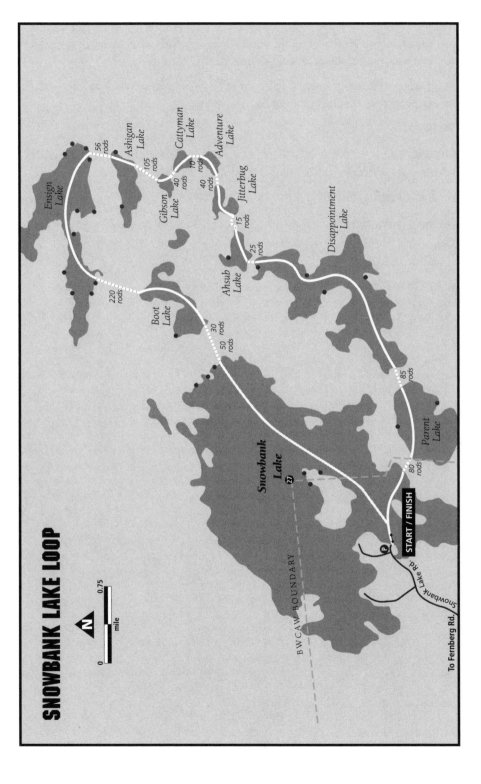

walleye or lake trout fishing, if time permits. A good strategy is to fish at night and get up in a bay where you are not apt to get run down by a motorboat. Have handy a good light to signal with, even if you don't want to leave it on all the time.

Access: Follow Fernberg Road 18 miles east of Ely to Snowbank Lake Road. Turn left and follow the road for 4 miles to the public boat landing.

Shuttle: None.

Camping: Camp at Fall Lake Campground the night before the trip. A fee is charged and reservations are recommended. Campsites are along the canoe route.

Food, gas, lodging: Ely, Winton.

For more information: Kawishiwi Ranger District, Superior National Forest (see appendix).

18 ﹏ North Kawishiwi River Loop

Entry point: 29

Character: Paddle across Ojibway Lake to find a unique eighteenth-century device that will allow the canoe to be rolled to Triangle Lake. The next portage will access the Kawishiwi River flowage. The rivers, and almost every mentioned lake, will offer good northern pike and walleye fishing. Scenic rapids and waterfalls abound. This route is usually not crowded.

Length: 20–24 miles.

Average run time: 3 days, with fishing and sightseeing.

Class: II–IV.

Skill level: Beginner.

Hazards: Rapids, bears, and insects.

Maps: USGS: Ojibway Lake, Gabbro Lake, Farm Lake.

The paddling: Put in at the public landing, outside the BWCAW boundary, at Ojibway Lake, and head south to Triangle Lake. The canoe can be transported to Triangle Lake on a rolling pin device and doesn't have to be carried. Motors are allowed in both lakes and when the fishing is good, boat traffic might be heavy. If time permits, at the start or end of the trip, lake trout and smallmouth bass fishing can be quite good in Ojibway Lake.

The portage into the entry point on the Kawishiwi River is 190 rods, one of the most lengthy portages on the trip. The Kawishiwi rivers have been called "flowages" and compared to long, narrow lakes, since they are mostly calm, extended pools, except where waterfalls and rapids signify a quick drop in elevation. Turn right (southwest) at the river and proceed down the main river to the fork. The river splits into the North Kawishiwi River and the South Kawishiwi River here. The South River continues southwest, but the North Kawishiwi River channel branches off to the northwest.

This trip initially follows the north river. About 3 miles downstream a long rapids can be portaged with a 210-rod carry. This portage is the main reason for running the river loop in this direction, because the portage is mostly downhill, falling almost 80 feet. The river and riverbank are scenic at this location, and there is a deep pool below the rapids for walleye fishing. Many paddlers linger here to enjoy its unique character.

After that portage there are only two short rapids to be lined. End the first day by leaving the river and portaging 144 rods into Clear Lake. Clear Lake is a picturesque 239-acre lake with an above average population of northern pike, along with walleyes and panfish. Reach this portage early to have a good chance of getting one of the five campsites available. Adjoining Eskwagama Lake has one legal campsite, but it requires a 100-rod portage from Clear Lake.

The second day, portage back into the South Kawishiwi River from either Clear Lake or Eskwagama Lake and proceed south to Gabbro Lake for fishing and sightseeing. An exploratory trip to Bald Eagle Lake is feasible, also. Early in the season the fishing can be excellent for northern pike and walleye on both of these large lakes. Alternately, you can

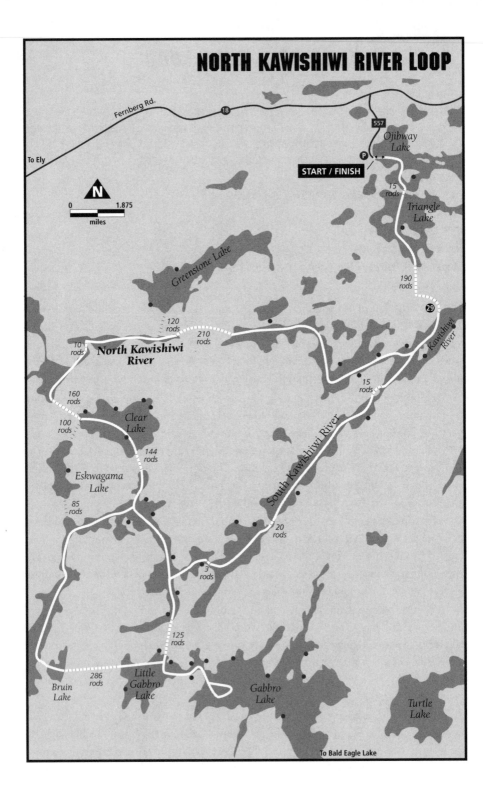

NORTH KAWISHIWI RIVER LOOP

Fernberg Rd.

18

557

Ojibway
Lake

To Ely

P

START / FINISH

15
rods

Triangle
Lake

N

0   1.875
miles

190
rods

29

Greenstone Lake

120
rods

210
rods

Kawishiwi River

10
rods

**North Kawishiwi
River**

15
rods

160
rods

100
rods

Clear
Lake

South Kawishiwi River

144
rods

Eskwagama
Lake

85
rods

20
rods

3
rods

125
rods

286
rods

Little
Gabbro
Lake

Gabbro
Lake

Bruin
Lake

Turtle
Lake

To Bald Eagle Lake

proceed down river to the Bruin Lake Portage, stay on Bruin Lake for the night, and negotiate the 286-rod portage into Little Gabbro Lake the next morning. Another alternative is to spend the second day fishing in the river maze south of Clear Lake. There are nine legal campsites in this good fishing area.

Next day head upriver to the point of entry and portage back to Triangle and Ojibway Lakes. Paddling upstream on this part of the river is not difficult, and the portages are short.

Access: From Ely follow Fernberg Road 14 miles east to Ojibway Lake Public Access Road (Forest Road 557). Turn right on FR 557 and follow the access road 0.5 mile to the public landing. There is one parking lot for day use and another for overnight parking.

Shuttle: None.

Camping: Fall Lake Campground. A fee is charged and reservations are recommended.

Food, gas, lodging: Ely.

For more information: Kawishiwi Ranger District (see appendix).

Lake One to Bald Eagle Lake

Entry point: 30
Character: This trip offers part lake and part river traveling. There is a good chance to see moose, shoot rapids, and fish for big northern pike. Bring plenty of film; the scenery is outstanding.
Length: About 24 miles.
Average run time: 3 to 4 days.
Class: Easy to intermediate.
Skill level: Beginner.
Hazards: Rapids, bears, and rough portages.
Maps: USGS: Snowbank, Ojibway, Gabbro Lake.

The paddling: Put in at the boat landing on Lake One. Turn a sharp right, head south, and try to stay along the west shoreline. This will lead to the Kawishiwi River channel.

The Kawishiwi River flows south for approximately 3 miles, then forks and becomes the South Kawishiwi River and the North Kawishiwi River. You will paddle southwesterly on the south river toward Little Gabbro Lake. There are some dangerous rapids between the put-in point and Little Gabbro Lake.

At the westerly bend of the river, directly north of Little "Gabby," an interesting choice can be made: Continue to follow the main channel to the portage to Bruin Lake, or portage directly into Little Gabbro. The Bruin Lake route adds 4 miles of paddling and over 200 rods of portaging. It offers a chance to fish the river on a productive, but under-utilized, stretch and an opportunity to occupy the solitary campsite on Bruin Lake. Bruin Lake is considered an average fishery for northern pike and perch.

Most paddlers will elect to forgo the Bruin Lake route and negotiate the arms and bays of the river to the 125-rod portage into Little Gabbro Lake. This will be a good place to camp after a fairly strenuous first day. Numerous campsites are available on Little Gabbro and adjoining Gabbro Lake. These two lakes have above average fishing for big northern pike and walleyes, and avid anglers could spend a day or even a week here. You are apt to have company as it is a popular fishing location, and also, entry point 33 is located at Little Gabbro.

On day two leave the Gabbros, and portage into Bald Eagle Lake. Bald Eagle Lake has an excellent population of black crappies and good northern pike fishing. Look for the portage to Turtle Lake on the north shoreline. Head north on the 185-rod portage to Turtle Lake. From here on you will see few other paddlers. Turtle Lake has above average fishing for northern pike. When it's time to move on, negotiate the portage to Clearwater Lake. Clearwater is a good place to camp the second day. This 641-acre lake has a maximum depth of 46 feet and can produce excellent northern pike fishing. It has four campsites, and if you get there early, at least one should be open.

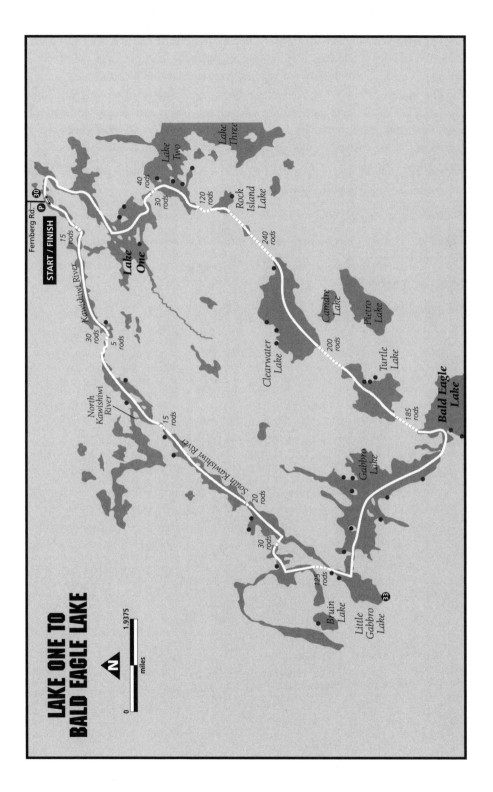

LAKE ONE TO
BALD EAGLE LAKE

N

miles
0   1.9375

Fernberg Rd. 1

START / FINISH

Kawishiwi River

15 rods

30 rods

5 rods

North Kawishiwi River

South Kawishiwi River

15 rods

20 rods

30 rods

125 rods

Bruin Lake

Little Gabbro Lake

Gabbro Lake

Bald Eagle Lake

185 rods

Turtle Lake

200 rods

Pietro Lake

Camdre Lake

Clearwater Lake

240 rods

Rock Island Lake

120 rods

30 rods

40 rods

Lake One

Lake Two

Lake Three

The third day will start with a 240-rod portage to Rock Island Lake. Rock Island Lake is small, and after you leave it only one portage separates you from Lake Two, which is joined to Lake One and the take-out point by two short lift-over portages.

The "numbered lakes," especially Lake One, are a maze of islands and directional changes. They can be quite confusing. Be sure and have a map and compass and study the map thoroughly. A friend of mine got confused on this complex and asked three different parties which way the landing was located. They pointed in three different directions.

Access: From Ely, follow Fernberg Road 19 miles east to its terminus at Lake One. A large parking lot lies adjacent to the boat landing.

Shuttle: None.

Camping: Fall Lake Campground. A fee is charged and reservations are recommended. Numerous campsites are along the canoe route.

Food, gas, lodging: Ely.

For more information: Kawishiwi Ranger District (see appendix).

⟨20⟩ Farm Lake Loop

Entry point: 31
Character: This trip has easy access, both lake and river paddling, scenic rapids and waterfalls, good fishing for brook trout and splake, and, mostly, easy portages.
Length: 22 miles.
Average run time: 3 to 4 days, with fishing.
Skill level: Beginner.
Hazards: Rapids.
Maps: USGS: Farm Lake, Ojibway Lake.

The paddling: This trip starts with an easy access into Farm Lake, which is 5 miles east of Ely. Farm Lake covers over 1,300 acres, and almost 2 miles of paddling are required to reach the mouth of the North Kawishiwi River. Farm Lake offers good fishing for walleyes, but motors are allowed and most paddlers hasten to reach the BWCAW boundary where only paddling is legal. Local outfitters will tow the canoe to the entry point for a fee.

The first day paddle up the North Kawishiwi River to the 210-rod portage around the long set of rapids, and consider taking a side trip to either Greenstone Lake or Conchu Lake for fishing and camping the first night. Greenstone Lake has one campsite and is reached by a 120-rod portage downstream from the rapids. It offers excellent walleye and northern pike fishing, covers 345 acres, and has a maximum depth of 72 feet. Conchu Lake, with one campsite, is only a 20-rod portage from the river channel but is located upstream from the long portage. Conchu Lake has brook trout and splake, covers 53 acres, and has a maximum depth of 67 feet.

Leave this area by continuing upstream to the fork of the North Kawishiwi River and the South Kawishiwi River. Several campsites are located at the junction of the rivers. Turn right (south) and follow the south channel downstream. Three short portages will be encountered, but the canoe can be lined through most of them. The only long portage will be the 70-rod carry from the river to Clear Lake. This is a good place to camp the second night.

Clear Lake is an above average northern pike lake with five campsites. Notice on the map that nearby Eskwagama Lake also has a campsite, and it offers good fishing. Next morning portage 144 rods north to the North Kawishiwi River and familiar water. Turn left (west) and return to Farm Lake and the take-out point.

If you decide to spend another night on the trip, consider portaging 120 rods to Pickerel Lake where two legal campsites are found. Pickerel Lake offers fishing for average sized northern pike. It is located on the north side of the river more than a mile downstream from the Clear Lake Portage.

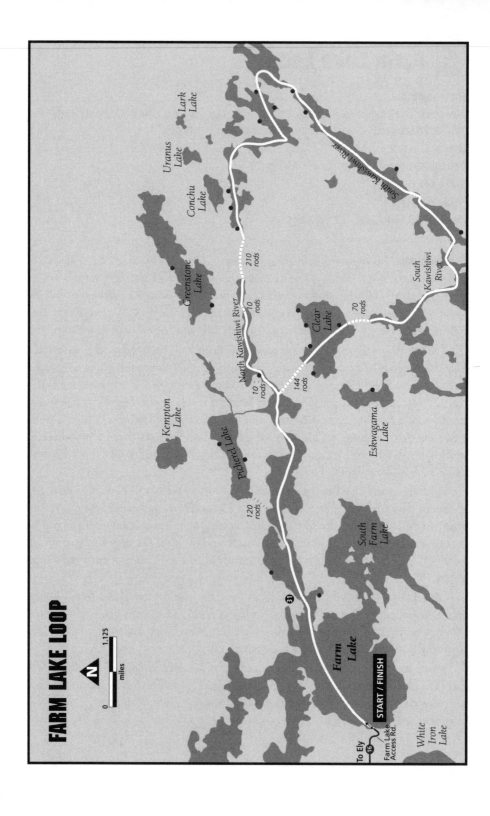

FARM LAKE LOOP

N

0 ————— 1.125
miles

To Ely

16

Farm Lake
Access Rd.

START / FINISH

White
Iron
Lake

Farm
Lake

31

South Farm
Lake

Eskwagama
Lake

120
rods

Pickerel Lake

Kempton
Lake

North Kawishiwi River

10
rods

10
rods

144
rods

Clear
Lake

70
rods

210
rods

Greenstone
Lake

Conchu
Lake

Uranus
Lake

Lark
Lake

South Kawishiwi River

South
Kawishiwi
River

Access: Follow Minnesota Highway 169 east from the International Wolf Center to St. Louis County Road 58. Turn right and follow CR 58 to County Road 16. Drive east on CR 16 for about 4 miles to Farm Lake Access Road. Follow the access road to the landing.

Shuttle: None.

Camping: Fall Lake Campground. A fee is charged and reservations are recommended. Many campsites are along the canoe route.

Food, gas, lodging: Ely.

For more information: Kawishiwi Ranger District (see appendix).

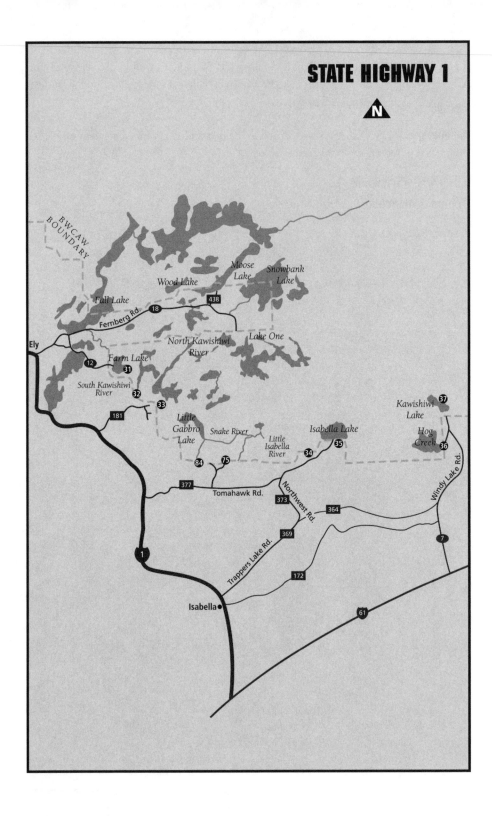

STATE HIGHWAY 1

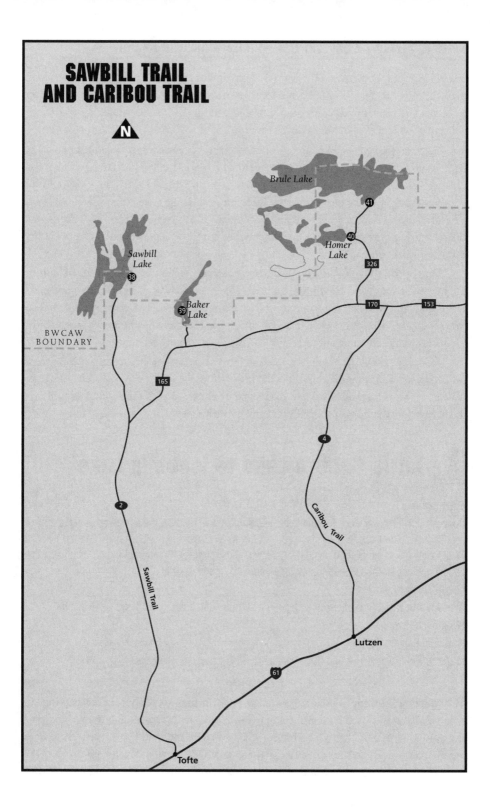

SAWBILL TRAIL
AND CARIBOU TRAIL

N

Brule Lake

41

40

Homer
Lake

326

Sawbill
Lake

38

170

153

Baker
Lake

39

BWCAW
BOUNDARY

165

4

2

Caribou Trail

Sawbill Trail

Lutzen

61

Tofte

State Highway 1 / Sawbill Trail and Caribou Trail Region

State Highway 1 leaves State Highway 61 approximately 5 miles north of Silver Bay along the Lake Superior shoreline. It reaches to Ely more than 70 miles northwest of Silver Bay. Highway 1 is a hardsurfaced road, but hilly and winding. It is also a wilderness road. Logging trucks are quite common. Drive with care.

There are no sizeable towns and most of the route is contained in Finland State Forest, Bear Island State Forest, or the Superior National Forest. The Sawbill Trail (County Road 2) leads directly from Tofte at State Highway 61 to Sawbill Lake. The Caribou Trail (County Road 4) winds north from the Lutsen area to Brule Lake, although Forest Road 170 and Forest Road 326 must also be negotiated to complete the trip. All entry points can be reached from either of the three mentioned routes by following the system of Superior National Forest roads.

None of the BWCAW entry points covered in this section is directly accessible from Highway 1. Most are reached from national forest trails that wind several miles northeast from the highway. Since the access routes are more complicated, paddlers tend to forego these routes in favor of the trips that lead directly to the Canadian border. Consequently, the access points are more apt to be available without advance registration.

The trips accessible from Highway 1 mostly have rivers as some part of their route. Except for Brule Lake and Alton/Sawbill Lakes the lakes tend to be small. The river valleys are populated with moose and other wildlife. Eagles soar overhead. Most of this region was not heavily damaged by the Independence Day storm. The trips are listed in numerical order.

Little Gabbro Lake to Isabella Lake

Entry point: 33
Character: This trip reaches two of the best fishing lakes in the BWCAW as well as one of the most scenic rivers. The Isabella River has good fishing for walleye and northern pike, and the Isabella River Valley offers excellent moose, deer, beaver, and bald eagle photographing opportunities. The paddling is not strenuous, and the portages aren't rugged.
Length: About 23 miles.
Average run time: 3 days or more, depending on the time spent fishing and sightseeing.
Skill level: Beginner.
Hazards: Rapids.
Maps: USGS: Boggberry Lake, Gabbro Lake, Quadga Lake, Isabella Lake.

The paddling: This trip starts as a 200-rod portage north of the Gabbro access parking lot. The portage trail is well used and easily followed. Put in at Little Gabbro Lake and proceed easterly through Little Gabbro Lake, Gabbro Lake, and Bald Eagle Lake. These lakes are interconnected, and no more portages are necessary the first day. Set up camp at the east end of Bald Eagle Lake near the mouth of the Isabella River. Gabbro Lake covers 1,174

Solitude on the water.

acres and is 50 feet deep, while Bald Eagle Lake covers 1,507 acres and is 36 feet deep. These lakes offer excellent walleye and northern pike fishing as well as smallmouth bass and crappie angling.

Leave Bald Eagle Lake by paddling up the Isabella River. The Isabella River is placid, and the current isn't hard to overcome, but it does have an abundance of bends. A long portage (190 rods) will be encountered shortly after passing the mouth of the Snake River. Take heart, though. Only shorter portages lie upstream. Continue up the Isabella River to Quadga Lake and set up camp. The mouth of the Little Isabella River is a landmark just downstream from the 70-rod Quadga Lake Portage.

Quadga Lake covers 248 acres and has a maximum depth of 35 feet. It has four camp-sites and above average fishing for northern pike and walleyes. The two campsites on the north shore are used by hikers on the Pow Wow Trail and are more apt to be occupied than the two on the east shore.

Alternately, campsites are available right on the Isabella River and at Rice Lake farther upstream. The river has fishing for northern pike and walleye. This region has a high pop-ulation of moose. Deer and beaver are regularly sighted. Keep the camera handy, and watch along the shoreline. Look upward to the branches of tall trees for bald eagles waiting for fish to appear in the river below.

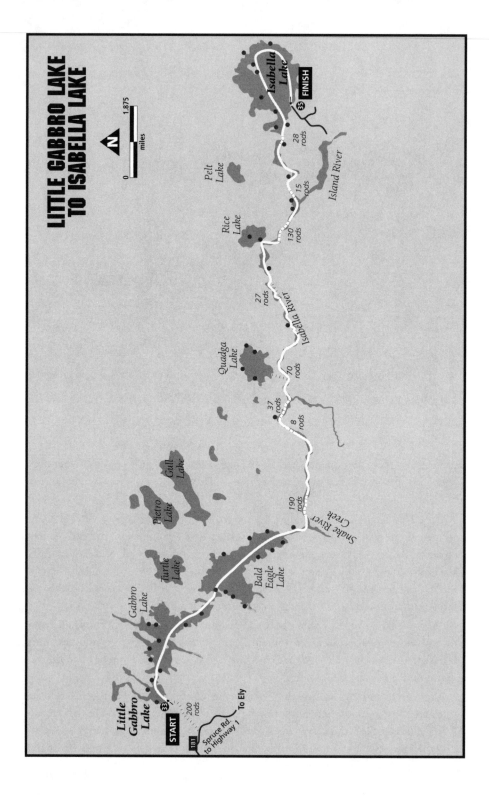

LITTLE GABBRO LAKE
TO ISABELLA LAKE

N

0   1.875
miles

Little
Gabbro
Lake

START

181

200
rods

Spruce Rd.
to Highway 1
To Ely

33

Gabbro
Lake

Turtle
Lake

Pietro
Lake

Gull
Lake

Bald
Eagle
Lake

Snake River
Creek

190
rods

8
rods

37
rods

70
rods

Quadga
Lake

Isabella River

27
rods

Rice
Lake

130
rods

Pelt
Lake

15
rods

Island River

28
rods

Isabella
Lake

FINISH

35

Six portages are encountered along the Isabella River the third day; the longest is 130 rods just upstream from Rice Lake. Most are only a fraction of that length. About 1 mile upstream from the long portage, the Island River joins with the Isabella, creating a fork. Take the left fork to Isabella Lake; the trip will end on Isabella Lake.

Variations of this trip can be taken from the Snake River or the Little Isabella River if the quota for the Little Gabbro Lake entry point is full. The Snake River offers the quickest way to get to Bald Eagle Lake and is in demand for fishing parties. It is necessary to portage 270 rods to put in at the Snake River, while the Little Isabella River portage is 20 rods. The Little Isabella River is a calm, meandering stream with heavily wooded shorelines. It meanders for 3 miles before reaching the Isabella River. It seldom is too low for good paddling. The trip will end on Isabella Lake (entry point 35).

Access: From Ely follow Minnesota Highway 1 11.5 miles east. Turn left on Spruce Road (Forest Road 181) and travel about 5.5 miles to the parking lot.

Shuttle: 32 miles one way. About 1.5 hours.

Camping: South Kawishiwi River Campground. A fee is charged. Numerous campsites are along the canoe route.

Food, gas, lodging: Ely.

For more information: Kawishiwi Ranger District (see appendix).

22 Isabella Lake to Perent Lake and Comfort Lake

Entry point: 35

Character: Base camp on Isabella Lake and take overnight trips up the Island River to Comfort Lake and up the Perent River to Perent Lake. This trip is very suitable for families or any party that wants an unhurried trip with both river and lake paddling. It also offers excellent opportunities for fishing and wildlife spotting. Both Isabella Lake and Perent Lake, as well as the rivers, have good walleye and northern pike fishing. The Perent River region has an abundant moose population.

Length: Approximately 7 miles one way to Perent Lake; approximately 9 miles one way to Comfort Lake.

Average run time: 5 to 7 days, or more.

Skill level: Beginner.

Hazards: Waves and high winds.

Maps: USGS: Isabella Lake, Perent Lake, Kawishiwi Lake.

The paddling: Start the trip at Forest Center on Isabella Lake. Forest Center was formerly the site of a large lumbering and logging operation. It was shut down in 1964, but artifacts and evidence of the town are still visible. Isabella Lake is accessed by a 35-rod carry in from the Forest Center parking lot.

Isabella Lake covers 1,516 acres and stretches about 2 miles east to west. It has a maximum depth of 19 feet. The water is murky, but the walleye and northern pike populations are above average and they bite well. Anglers cast crankbaits or troll crankbaits or spoons while they are paddling or wind drifting. Fishermen catch yellow perch with bait, small spinners, or flies.

Isabella is a large, relatively shallow lake, and brisk winds could create hazardous waves. Caution is recommended. Like canoeists always should, stay on land when the waves are too high. There are numerous islands and bays, however, that the paddler can use to diminish the effects of high wind if needed. No motors are allowed. There are a dozen campsites. If all the campsites are filled, consider starting one of the river trips recommended. Campsites are found along the rivers.

Start the Island River trip by locating the mouth of the Isabella River on the west shore of the lake. Follow the Isabella River downstream to the Island River confluence. Turn left, and paddle upstream on the Island River. Follow the Island River past the Forest Road 377 bridge, which, incidentally, is entry point 34, and continue upstream. The Island River has high scenic banks and little white water. Paddling upstream is not strenuous and coming back will be even easier. Continue upstream to Comfort Lake. Campsites are located along the river, and you can decide to stop for the night before you get to Comfort Lake, if desired. There are four short portages.

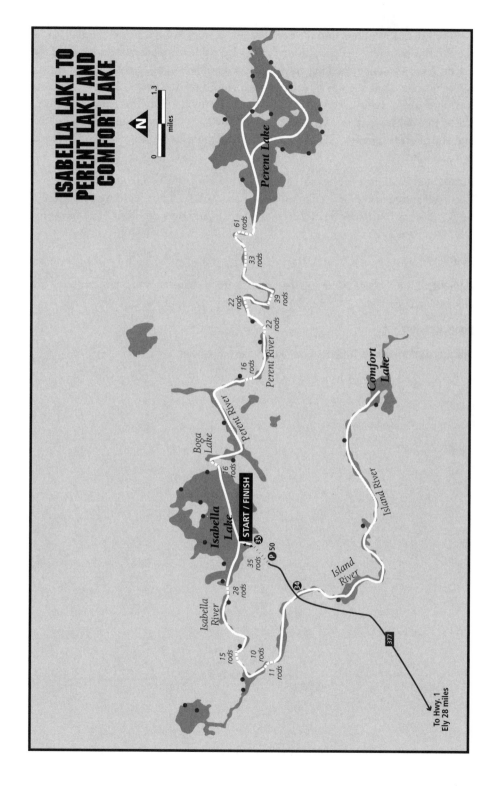

ISABELLA LAKE TO
PERENT LAKE AND
COMFORT LAKE

N

0   miles   1.3

Perent Lake

61
rods

33
rods

22
rods

39
rods

22
rods

Perent River

16
rods

Perent River

Boga
Lake

16
rods

START / FINISH

35

P 50

35
rods

28
rods

Isabella
Lake

Isabella River

15
rods

10
rods

11
rods

Comfort
Lake

Island River

Island
River

34

377

To Hwy. 1
Ely 28 miles

The Perent River flows into the east shoreline of Isabella Lake. Leave Isabella Lake at the mouth, and paddle upstream through Boga Lake, a hardly noticeable widening of the Perent River. Continue paddling easterly, for about 7 miles, to Perent Lake. There are twelve portages along the way. The longest is 61 rods from the river to Perent Lake. This is remote, scenic, game-filled territory and is very lightly traveled. The shoreline is steep, almost canyonlike, in spots. Perent Lake covers 1,800 acres, has a maximum depth of 28 feet, and fourteen campsites. It has a deeply indented shoreline and is not adversely affected by brisk winds.

Access: Drive Minnesota Highway 1 from Ely to Isabella. At Isabella turn left on Forest Road 369 and follow it for 7 miles to Forest Road 373. Continue northwest on FR 373 for 5.5 miles to Tomahawk Road (Forest Road 377). Turn right on FR 377 and follow for 5.5 miles to the landing.

Shuttle: None.

Camping: Little Isabella River Campground. A fee is charged. Numerous campsites are along the canoe route.

Food, gas, lodging: Ely.

For more information: Tofte Ranger District (see appendix).

Kawishiwi Lake Loop

Entry point: 37

Character: This trip offers a very unique opportunity to cross twenty-five lakes and four rivers in a week of paddling. Wild, remote territory is breached, fishing opportunities are endless. You'll cross the Lake/Cook county lines and the Laurentian Divide. Moose, beaver, and waterfowl are common and wolves are about. Abort the trip at Sawbill Lake and shuttle back to Kawishiwi Lake to save two days of paddling, if you're worn out.

Length: About 48 miles.

Average run time: 6 to 7 days, or longer. The trip has been done in 4 days.

Skill level: Beginner.

Hazards: Steep and rough portages; insects and wild animals are encountered.

Maps: USGS: Kawishiwi Lake, Lake Polly, Kelso Mountain, Beth Lake.

The paddling: The trip proceeds north from Kawishiwi Lake through six lakes to Malberg Lake, where it turns east and reaches through eight lakes to Mesaba Lake before heading south through six lakes. At Alton Lake you'll head west through five lakes back to Lake Polly before turning south and returning to Kawishiwi Lake.

Kawishiwi Lake covers 400 acres and has a maximum depth of 12 feet. Fishing success for walleye, pike, and northern pike is above average. On the first day you'll cross from Kawishiwi Lake into Square Lake, Kawasachong Lake, Townline Lake, Lake Polly, Koma Lake, and Malberg Lake, where you'll camp. The day includes six portages, the longest being 189 rods from Kawasachong to Townline Lake. They are evenly spaced, and even the longest is not overly difficult. This is a popular route as Malberg is a tremendous fishing lake for walleye and northern pike. Some experienced paddlers stop at Koma Lake since it is fairly common for the campsites at Malberg Lake to fill early in the day. Malberg Lake covers 404 acres and has a maximum depth of 37 feet. Walleyes are the most abundant fish in the lake and they average good size.

The second day leave Malberg Lake and head east. You're in for a fairly rough, but short, day. You will paddle through Frond Lake, Boze Lake, and the Louse River on the way to Trail Lake. Arrive early enough to get one of the two campsites available.

Trail Lake has good fishing for northern pike and this area is known for blueberries in season. On the way you will encounter nine portages, all are short except for a possible 190-rod carry from Boze Lake to the Louse River. This can be alternately paddled and portaged in high water. You will have to paddle upstream on the Louse River for about 2 miles. Beaver dams and boulder fields may slow progress.

The third day leave Trail Lake and paddle to Mesaba Lake. On the way you will encounter Tool Lake, Bug Lake, Dent Lake, and Chaser Lake before reaching Mesaba Lake. There are six portages. The longest is 130 rods from Dent Lake to Mesaba Lake, but two others are 125 rods in length. The portages are steep in spots and Bug Lake can be choked with vegetation and the portage to Chaser Lake muddy. Mesaba Lake covers 201

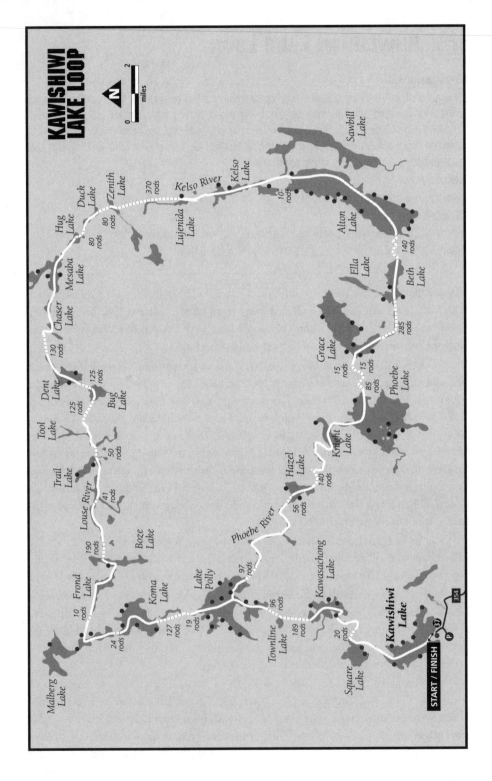

KAWISHIWI
LAKE LOOP

N

0 ___ 2
miles

Malberg
Lake

Frond
Lake

Trail
Lake

Tool
Lake

Dent
Lake

Louse River

Chaser
Lake

Mesaba
Lake

Hug
Lake

Duck
Lake

Zenith
Lake

Kelso River

Kelso
Lake

Sawbill
Lake

Lujenida
Lake

370
rods

80
rods

80
rods

80
rods

130
rods

125
rods

125
rods

Bug
Lake

50
rods

41
rods

10
rods

190
rods

Boze
Lake

Koma
Lake

127
rods

19
rods

24
rods

Lake
Polly

Townline
Lake

96
rods

189
rods

97
rods

Phoebe River

56
rods

Hazel
Lake

140
rods

Knight
Lake

Grace
Lake

15
rods

15
rods

85
rods

Phoebe
Lake

285
rods

Ella
Lake

Beth
Lake

140
rods

Alton
Lake

10
rods

Kawasachong
Lake

20
rods

Square
Lake

Kawishiwi
Lake

START / FINISH

P

37

354

acres and has a maximum depth of 65 feet. Some lake trout are known to inhabit the lake, but northern pike are the dominant gamefish. Mesaba Lake has three campsites and at least one should be open. Some parties stop for a day or two to rest up.

The fourth day you will leave Mesaba Lake and head south to Alton Lake. On the way pass through Hug Lake, Duck Lake, Zenith Lake, Lujenida Lake, and Kelso Lake. There are five portages; the two 80-rod portages are uphill, and there is a challenging carry of 370 rods between Zenith Lake and Lujenida Lake. Reportedly, when the water is high, the canoe can be lined or paddled down the Lujenida Lake inlet stream to save 170 rods of carrying. Trailside ponds also can be utilized to save some carrying, although most people prefer to walk the distance. You will pass over the Laurentian Divide on this portage. North of the divide water flows north to the Arctic Ocean; south of the divide it flows south to the Atlantic Ocean.

Alton Lake covers 1,093 acres and has a maximum depth of 72 feet. It is almost 3 miles long. Trophy anglers will want to do some serious fishing. The size of the walleyes and northern pike averages far above normal. Alton is also known as a good smallmouth bass fishery. There are more than a dozen campsites available. If your energy level is still up, paddle to the south end of the lake to camp. If fatigue has set in, portage a short distance into adjoining Sawbill Lake and shuttle approximately 25 miles back to Kawishiwi Lake.

If you elect to continue, head west to Hazel Lake the fifth day. On the way you will encounter Beth Lake, Grace Lake, Phoebe Lake, and Knight Lake. There are seven portages, the longest being a 285-rod carry from Beth Lake to Grace Lake. All of the portages seem to be downhill. You might consider stopping at Phoebe Lake or Grace Lake; they do have several campsites, but they also receive spillover paddlers from Alton and Sawbill Lakes, and the sites might be occupied. Knight and Hazel Lakes are beyond the popular regions. Watch for moose and beaver; fish for northern pike and walleyes.

Leave Hazel Lake early the sixth day, and head down the Phoebe River to Lake Polly and familiar territory. You will encounter four short portages to reach Lake Polly. You can probably reach Kawishiwi Lake the sixth day if you keep moving through three portages and two lakes.

An alternate, and much easier, trip from Kawishiwi Lake can be taken by heading north to Lake Polly. Then turn east and follow the Phoebe River through Hazel Lake and the other five lakes to Sawbill Lake. Shuttle back to Kawishiwi Lake.

Access: Drive from Ely to Isabella on Minnesota Highway 1. Turn left on Forest Road 172 and follow it east for 12 miles to County Road 7. Follow CR 7 north for 11 miles to Forest Road 354. Follow FR 354 north for 4 miles to Kawishiwi Lake.

There is an alternate route from the Sawbill Trail: Follow the Sawbill Trail (County Road 2) north from Tofte to County Road 3. Turn left (west) on 3 and follow to Forest Road 354. Turn right (north) on FR 354 and proceed to the lake.

Shuttle: None, unless you abort the trip at Alton Lake. Then, a 25-mile shuttle to Kawishiwi Lake is needed.

Camping: Kawishiwi Lake campground is adjacent to the Kawishiwi Lake access; no fee is charged. Five sites are available. There are numerous public campgrounds within driving distance; a fee is charged and reservations are recommended. There are approximately eighty-five campsites on the paddling route.

Food, gas, lodging: Ely, Tofte, Grand Marais.

For more information: Contact Kawishiwi Ranger District (see appendix).

24 Sawbill Lake Loop

Entry point: 38

Character: This trip takes you through some large, busy lakes to a series of smaller, seldom visited lakes and the wild and remote Frost River system. Moose gravitate to the Frost River region and a dozen adults have been sighted on a single trip. The scenery is spectacular. Lake trout, walleyes, or northern pike are found in most all of the lakes. This trip is for the physically fit or groups with discretionary time.

Length: 33 miles.

Average run time: 5 to 7 days.

Skill level: Beginner.

Hazards: Storm-damaged trees (see introduction).

Maps: USGS: Kelso Mountain, Cherokee Lake.

The paddling: Put in on 944-acre Sawbill Lake and paddle north toward the Ada Creek Portage. The lake is about 5 miles long, and it might take more than half a day to reach Ada Creek. Negotiate the two 80-rod portages on Ada Creek, pass through Skoop Lake, and continue north to the 189-rod portage to Cherokee Creek. Cherokee Creek leads to Cherokee Lake, which has about twenty campsites and offers a place to camp for the first night. Cherokee Lake covers over 1,000 acres and is 142 feet deep. It offers fishing for big northern pike and lake trout.

Next morning, portage 15 rods to Gordon Lake, paddle to the north end, and look on the west shore for the 140-rod portage to Unload Lake. Negotiate this and the short portage to Frost Lake. Frost Lake covers 313 acres, is 80 feet deep, and is well known for lake trout fishing. It also has northern pike and perch. There are campsites available for overnighting if the fish are biting and you're interested in staying over.

Leave Frost Lake by the 130-rod portage to the Frost River, and then head west through a succession of small lakes connected by the river. Campsites are scarce; you can decide to stop at Chase Lake, where a single campsite is found on adjoining Bologna Lake, or (recommended) push on another 4 miles to Afton Lake. Afton Lake covers 50 acres and has northern pike fishing and a single campsite. This is wild and remote territory—some groups stay awhile and savor it.

The next day is a rough one. Paddle through Fente Lake, and find the second longest portage of the trip, 340 rods from Fente Lake to Hub Lake. Then after paddling Hub Lake portage 105 rods to Mesaba Lake. Continue through Mesaba, portage 80 rods to Hug Lake, and then 90 rods to Zenith Lake. Most groups will want to stop here and rest up for a day or so before tackling the 370-rod portage to Lujenida Lake. In high-water periods this portage can be fragmented by utilizing the inlet stream to Lujenida Lake and some trailside ponds.

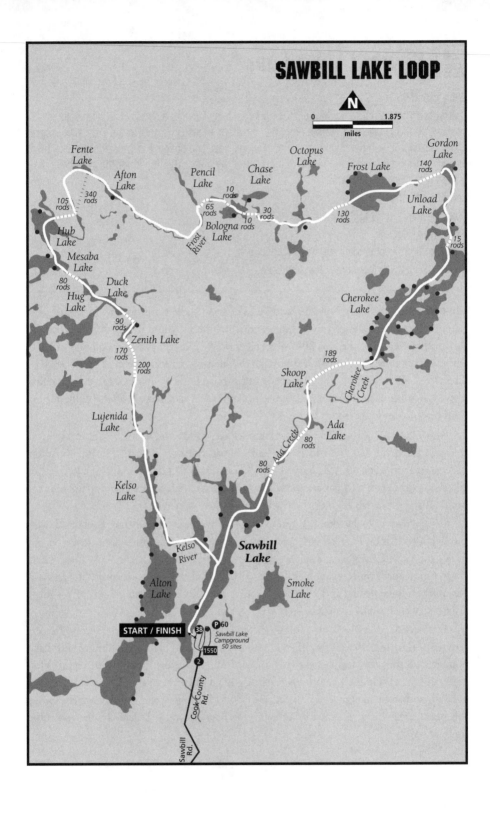

Take heart, though. That is the last noticeable portage of the trip. From here on you have the luxury of paddling down the Kelso River to Kelso Lake, going back into the Kelso River, and heading east back to Sawbill Lake and the take-out point.

Keep in mind this is only one of the possible trips from Sawbill Landing. A rewarding two or three day popular trip with good fishing and short portages goes through Sawbill Lake, turns east through Smoke Lake and Burnt Lake, turns north through Kelly Lake, Jack Lake, and Weird Lake to the Temperance River Flowage, and finally turns west to Cherokee Lake. From there it heads south again back to Sawbill Lake.

Access: Follow the Sawbill Road 22 miles from Tofte on the Lake Superior Shore. Sawbill Lake and campground are at the end of the trail.

Shuttle: None.

Camping: Camp right at the lake in the Sawbill Lake Campground. There are fifty sites; a fee is charged and reservations are recommended.

Food, gas, lodging: Grand Maria, Grand Portage, Tofte.

For more information: Tofte Ranger District (see appendix).

25 Baker Lake to Bower Trout Lake

Entry point: 39

Character: This is an easy but substantial trip, designed for a family or the angler who can't put in to Brule Lake because the quota is filled. Each sizeable lake on the route has good fishing, and Brule Lake alone could keep an angler busy for weeks. The trip from Brule Lake to the take-out point is rimmed with high, scenic hills. The South Brule River system of lakes has sparkling clear water and easy portages. Independence Day–storm affected area.

Length: About 24 miles.

Average run time: 3 days to a week or more, with fishing and "wind days."

Class: Vern River: I; Temperance River: I

Skill level: Beginner.

Hazards: High wind and waves on Brule Lake. Storm-stressed trees.

Maps: USGS: Kelly Lake, Cherokee Lake, Brule Lake, Eagle Mountain, Lima Mountain.

The paddling: Launch the canoe at shallow, weedy Baker Lake, and paddle to the northwest corner to find the 10-rod portage to Peterson Lake. Peterson Lake is also shallow, but it covers 104 acres and has walleye and northern pike fishing, as does adjoining Kelly Lake. Kelly Lake covers 188 acres, is long and narrow, and resembles a river flowing between steep bluffs. Paddle north on Kelly Lake for about 2 miles to the 65-rod portage to Jack Lake. Jack Lake covers 127 acres, is irregularly shaped, and extends north for about 1.5 miles to a 12-rod portage to Weird Lake. Weird Lake is much smaller—only 47 acres. It is very shallow, but also has a population of walleye and northern pike.

After conquering Weird Lake, portage 80 rods to the Temperance River. Paddle a short distance, then portage 240 rods to South Temperance Lake. South Temperance Lake is more square than long, has several islands, covers 258 acres, and has a maximum depth of 58 feet. There is evidence here of the 1995 South Temperance fire. Northern pike are about the only fish that inhabit this lake. Follow the east shoreline to the bay that extends east to Brule Lake. There are several campsites on South Temperance Lake and the west end of Brule Lake; either spot is a good place to camp for the first day. The fishing will probably be better on Brule Lake than South Temperance Lake.

Brule Lake covers over 4,500 acres and has more length than width, with some very deep water that harbors lake trout. There is a good population of walleye and an excellent population of fast growing and good sized northern pike. Smallmouth bass are also present in good numbers.

Brule Lake is about 8 miles long from east to west. Even without fishing and with favorable winds, it requires steady paddling to reach Brule Bay—which is adjacent to Vernon Lake—in one day. It would be a pity not to spend at least one day just exploring and fishing the shoreline of this watery world, however. No motors are allowed on Brule Lake even though it is one of the largest lakes in the BWCAW. It is dotted with sixty-seven islands and sits in the shadow of Eagle Mountain, the highest point in Minnesota. Many

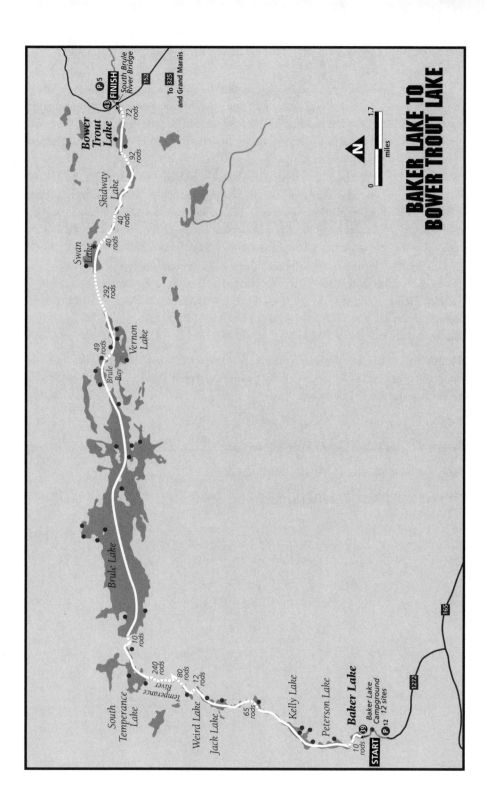

BAKER LAKE TO
BOWER TROUT LAKE

South Brule
River Bridge

FINISH
43

P 5

152

To 325
and Grand Marais

Bower
Trout
Lake

72
rods

92
rods

Skidway
Lake

40
rods

Swan
Lake

40
rods

292
rods

49
rods

Vernon
Lake

Brule
Bay

Brule Lake

10
rods

South
Temperance
Lake

240
rods

Temperance River

80
rods

12
rods

Weird Lake

Jack Lake

65
rods

Kelly Lake

Peterson Lake

Baker Lake

Baker Lake
Campground
12 sites

P 12

39

START
10
rods

N

0   miles   1.7

165

1272

people land the canoe and hike the bluffs to find a place high enough to overlook this very picturesque waterway.

There will surely be other paddlers about, but the lake is large enough to allow you to completely escape crowds. Keep aware at all times that brisk winds can whip up very high waves on this lake. Do what paddlers have always done to keep themselves safe: Wear your personal flotation device (PFD), and stay close enough to an island or shoreline to get out of harm's way if wind suddenly whips up.

The last day can be busy as you head for the take-out point. Leave Brule Lake at Brule Bay by portaging 49 rods to Vernon Lake, and paddling east to the long (292 rods) portage to Swan Lake. There are a series of portages passing Skidway Lake, Dugout Lake, and Marshall Lake. Finally only one 92-rod portage remains to reach Bower Trout Lake and the take-out point. In high water some of these portages can be avoided.

Commercial shuttle service will probably be available, but some groups have two vehicles or make other arrangements to take their vehicle to the take-out point so it will be waiting. Keep in mind that the route can be reversed to return to Baker Lake if arranging a shuttle is too wearisome. Further, you can take out at Brule Lake landing to shorten the shuttle or if an emergency develops.

Access: Follow the Sawbill Road (County Road 2) north from Tofte 17 miles to Forest Road 170. Turn right and follow FR 170 5 miles to Forest Road 1272. Continue to the parking lot and Baker Lake access.

Shuttle: 21 miles one way. About 1.5 hours.

Camping: Baker Lake Campground, no fee; Crescent Lake Campground, a fee is charged.

Food, gas, lodging: Grand Marais, Tofte, Schroeder.

For more information: Tofte Ranger Station (see appendix).

26 Homer Lake

Entry point: 40

Character: This trip has big lakes, small lakes, creeks, and rivers. Only two of the portages are longer than 160 rods. Spectacular hills and rocky cliffs surround clear water lakes, and the fishing for walleye, northern pike, and lake trout can be fulfilling. Wildlife is about. Solitude is easy to find. You cross the Laurentian Divide. You can even find a hot shower and groceries on the way back. When you finish this trip you will be a seasoned paddler, if you weren't before. Independence Day storm–affected area.

Length: 50 miles.

Average run time: 5 to 10 days.

Skill level: Beginner.

Hazards: Wind and waves on Brule and Cherokee Lakes and rough, boulder-strewn portages.

Maps: USGS: Brule Lake East, Cherokee Lake, Sawbill Camp.

The paddling: Put in directly at Homer Lake. Homer Lake covers 516 acres and motors are allowed on part of it. Paddle west from the boat landing to the 6-rod portage to Whack Lake. If plenty of time is available, instead of going to Whack Lake, consider heading south to the Vern River to reach Vern Lake by the longer but more scenic route. Most paddlers think it's worth the effort. Follow long, slender, 230-acre Vern Lake to the west end and portage 65 rods to Juno Lake. This is a steep and hilly portage. Juno Lake is comparative to Vern Lake in size, configuration, and fish populations of walleye, northern pike, and panfish. Leave Juno Lake by a 70-rod, easy portage to Jock Mock Bay of Brule Lake. Most groups consider this far enough for one day and find a campsite. There are several in the vicinity of Jock Mock Bay. Fishing can be quite good in Brule Lake for walleye, northern pike, and lake trout.

Next morning paddle around Jock Mock Point and head to the northwest corner of Brule Lake. Find the bay that leads to the portage to Cam Lake. This 100-rod portage is mostly uphill and strewn with rocks. Cam Lake is a 66-acre lake that has only mediocre fishing for northern pike, and most paddlers will press on to better lakes ahead. The next portage from Cam Lake to Gasket Lake is 45 rods and not difficult; however, the following 75-rod portage from Gasket Lake to Vesper Lake climbs over the Laurentian Divide and will take its toll. Take heart, though, there is only one more portage for day two to the recommended campsite at Town Lake. This 110-rod portage is not steep, but it is strewn with boulders and care must be taken to avoid an accident.

Town Lake covers 94 acres, has some 60-foot-deep water, and can produce excellent northern pike fishing. There are several campsites and, if the Town Lake sites are occupied, only a 10-rod portage separates Town Lake from Cherokee Lake and about twenty additional campsites. This is a good place to base camp and fish for a day or two, although you will probably have plenty of company.

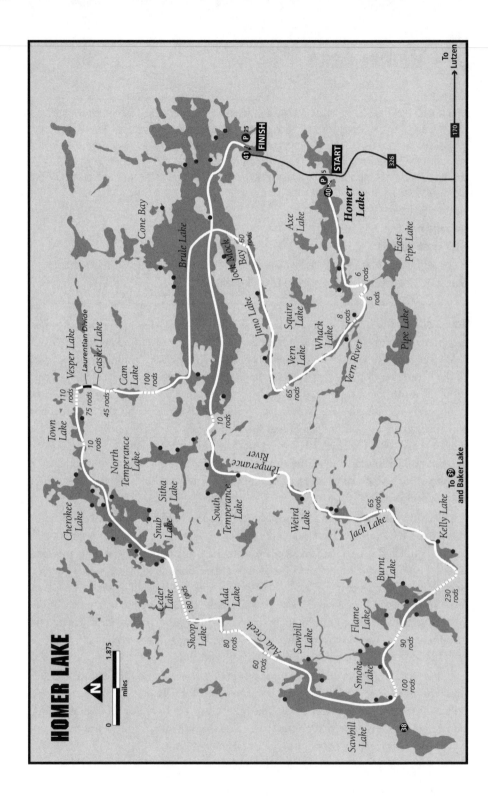

HOMER LAKE

N

0   1.875
miles

To Lutzen

170

326

START

40 P S

Homer Lake

41 P 25
FINISH

East Pipe Lake

Pipe Lake

Axe Lake

Squire Lake

6 rods

6 rods

Whack Lake

8 rods

Vern Lake

Vern River

65 rods

Juno Lake

Jock Mock Bay

60 rods

Cone Bay

Brule Lake

Vesper Lake

Laurentian Divide

Gasket Lake

Cam Lake

100 rods

110 rods

75 rods

45 rods

Town Lake

10 rods

10 rods

North Temperance Lake

Sitha Lake

South Temperance Lake

Temperance River

Cherokee Lake

Snub Lake

Ceder Lake

180 rods

Skoop Lake

Ada Lake

80 rods

60 rods

Ada Creek

Weird Lake

Jack Lake

Kelly Lake

65 rods

To 39 and Baker Lake

230 rods

Sawbill Lake

Flame Lake

Burnt Lake

Smoke Lake

90 rods

100 rods

Sawbill Lake

38

When ready, portage into Cherokee Lake, head to the south end, and find Cherokee Creek. Paddle the creek to Ceder Lake and portage 180 rods south to Skoop Lake. From there on it is only a series of easy portages and paddling to sprawling, busy Sawbill Lake. (For more information see chapter 24, Sawbill Lake Loop.) Find a campsite on Sawbill Lake. An outfitter at the south end of the lake has a grocery store, hot showers, and other amenities, if you need supplies.

When you leave Sawbill Lake, portage 100 rods east to Smoke Lake and then 90 rods to Burnt Lake. Smoke Lake and Burnt Lake are well worth considering for some serious fishing time. They have substantial populations of walleye and northern pike. Each has several campsites. When you leave portage a whopping 230 rods to Kelly Lake and head north.

Continue through Jack Lake, Weird Lake, the Temperance River, and South Temperance Lake. This is a fitting place to camp, or you can turn east and portage 10 rods back into the west end of Brule Lake, where more campsites are available. The take-out point is entry point 41, located at the southeast end of Brule Lake. This is only about 1.5 miles from the put-in point on Homer Lake, and you can walk back to your vehicle.

This is a long trip, but there are several ways of shortening it, even after you start. If, by the time you get to Cherokee Lake, you decide to shorten the trip, leave Cherokee Lake by the portage to Snub Lake, located in the southeast corner of Cherokee. Study the map. This route will lead through the Temperance Lakes back to Brule Lake and the take-out point. This is about one day's serious paddling. The trip can even end at Sawbill Lake (entry point 38), if desired. And even after you reach Kelly Lake, it is only a 10-rod portage south to Baker Lake and entry point 39. Commercial shuttle service to all of the mentioned take-out points is available at Sawbill Lake.

Access: Start 1 mile north of Lutzen on U.S. Highway 61, and follow the Caribou Trail west (County Road 4) 18 miles to Forest Road 170. Turn left and follow FR 170, 1.5 miles to Forest Road 326 (Brule Lake Road). Turn right and continue for 6 miles to the Homer Lake access.

Shuttle: 18 miles one way. 1 hour.

Camping: Crescent Lake Campground. A fee is charged and reservations are recommended. Numerous campsites are along the canoe route.

Food, gas, lodging: Grand Marais.

For more information: Tofte Ranger District (see appendix).

27 Brule Lake

Entry point: 41

Character: This trip heads north from gigantic Brule Lake through two chains of lakes and one river, before returning to the put-in point. A variety of lakes and one river are encountered. Tall, scenic bluffs border some of the lakes. Fishing for walleye, northern pike, and smallmouth bass can be productive. A moose might be sighted; beaver, mink, and otter inhabit the region as well. Waterfowl, eagles, and osprey are common here.

Length: About 32 miles.

Average run time: 4 to 8 days, with time spent fishing.

Skill level: Beginner.

Hazards: Wind and waves on Brule and Cherokee Lakes.

Maps: USGS: Brule Lake, Cherokee Lake, Gunflint Lake.

The paddling: Launch the canoe at the southeast corner of gigantic Brule Lake, paddle northwest to Cone Bay, and follow the Cone Lake island chain northward. There are short portages between South Cone Lake, Middle Cone Lake, and North Cone Lake. In highwater periods the canoe will not have to be taken out of the water. The Cone Lakes have northern pike, walleye, and smallmouth bass.

The portage from North Cone Lake to Davis Lake is 165 rods. Davis Lake is a good place to camp the first night. It has two campsites and northern pike fishing. When you leave Davis Lake, prepare for a strenuous day. First a whopping 305-rod portage to Kiskadinna Lake looms. This is a level portage, but it can be muddy in places. (The long portage from Davis Lake to Kiskadinna Lake can be avoided by a side trip. Turn east at North Cone Lake, portage 152 rods to Cliff Lake, then portage and paddle through Wanihigan Lake to Winchell Lake, turn north and portage 50 rods to Omega Lake, then turn west and portage 32 rods to Kiskadinna Lake. The portages are easier, but little time will be saved. It is 5 miles farther.) Then, after a short paddle west on Kiskadinna Lake, a steep 185-rod downhill portage to Muskeg Lake is encountered. Take heart, though. Only a 24-rod portage separates Muskeg Lake from Long Island Lake.

Camp at Long Island Lake, rest up, and enjoy the fishing. Long Island Lake covers almost 1,000 acres, has some 70-foot-deep water, and can provide excellent lake trout fishing. It is a popular spot, being an easy paddle from both Ham Lake or Sawbill Lake. It has more than a dozen campsites, but it is prudent to pick one early.

Leave Long Island Lake by finding the Long Island River at the west end of the lake. Paddle up the river to Gordon Lake, and portage 15 rods to Cherokee Lake. Cherokee Lake covers over 1,000 acres and has a 142-foot maximum depth. It is well known for big northern pike and lake trout fishing. Both campsites and campers are numerous.

Leave Cherokee by portaging 140 rods past Snub Lake to Sitka Lake. Leave Sitka by a 105-rod portage from the southeast shore that leads to North Temperance Lake. This portage passes over the Laurentian Divide and it climbs 89 feet. Next, portage 55 rods to

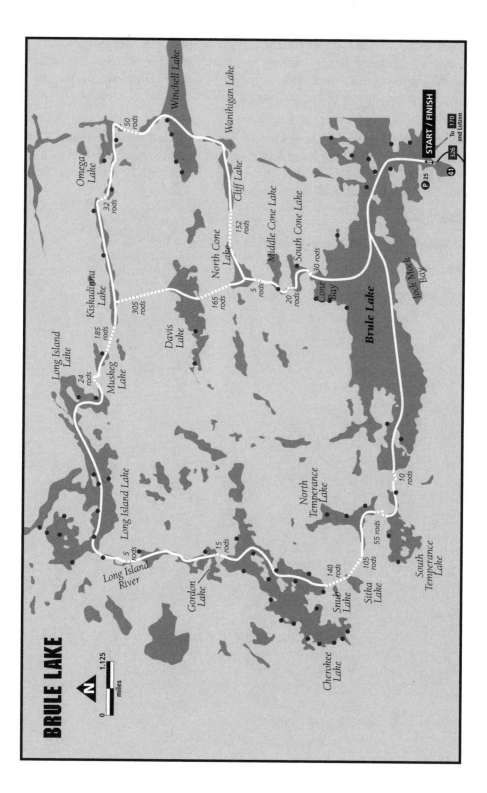

BRULE LAKE

N

0 — 1,125
miles

Winchell Lake

Wanihigan Lake

50 rods

Omega Lake

32 rods

Cliff Lake

152 rods

North Cone Lake

Kishadinna Lake

305 rods

165 rods

Davis Lake

Middle Cone Lake

South Cone Lake

30 rods

5 rods

20 rods

Long Island Lake

185 rods

24 rods

Muskeg Lake

Cone Bay

Brule Lake

Jock Mock Bay

Long Island Lake

Long Island River

5 rods

10 rods

North Temperance Lake

15 rods

Gordon Lake

55 rods

105 rods

Sitka Lake

140 rods

Snub Lake

South Temperance Lake

Cherokee Lake

START / FINISH

To 170 and Lutzen

326

41

P 25

South Temperance Lake. If time permits, consider stopping at the Temperance Lakes for fishing and sightseeing. Both can be very productive. Only a very short portage separates South Temperance Lake from the west end of Brule Lake. Depending on the wind, though, reaching the east end of the lake and the take-out point may require a full day's paddling.

Access: Start 1 mile north of Lutzen on U.S. Highway 61, and follow the Caribou Trail (County Road 4) 18 miles to Forest Road 170. Turn left and follow FR 170 1.5 miles to Forest Road 326 (Brule Lake Road). Turn right and continue north for 6 miles to the Brule Lake public landing on the left side of the road.

Shuttle: None.

Camping: Crescent Lake Campground. A fee is charged.

Food, gas, lodging: Grand Marais.

For more information: Tofte Ranger District (see appendix).

GUNFLINT TRAIL

N

55 Saganaga Lake

C A N A D A

54
Seagull Lake

60

12

Magnetic Lake

North Lake

57 Gunflint Lake

Loon Lake

South Lake **58**

Daniels Lake

50 Cross Bay Lake
52
Brant Lake **51**

Duncan Lake **60** **61** **62**

Clearwater Lake

64

Missing Link Lake

Portage Lake

65

East Bearskin Lake

Meeds Lake **48**

47 Lizz Lake

Morgan Lake

45

U N I T E D   S T A T E S

Ram Lake

44

Brule Lake

43

Bower Trout Lake

Gunflint Trail

12

BWCAW BOUNDARY

61

Gunflint Trail

The Gunflint Trail (County Highway 12) starts at the town of Grand Marais on the shore of Lake Superior. It heads northwest from State Highway 61 to finally end at Gull Lake, 57 miles northwest of Grand Marais. The road is all hard-surfaced, and usually kept in top condition. It extends through some of the most remote and scenic territory in the BWCAW. Fallen trees from the July 4, 1999 storm can be seen on both sides from mid-trail to the end.

Although the trail reaches deep into the BWCAW, a corridor on each side of the highway is not part of the BWCAW. Private resorts and outfitters are located in this corridor, all along the trail. There are also both public and private campgrounds.

The Gunflint Ranger Station located in Grand Marais can issue permits and provide information on the seventeen entry points covered in this section. The Gunflint Trail entry points lakes commonly are deeper and with fewer islands than those located farther west. Many have high rocky shorelines. Two trips in the Daniels and Duncan Lakes area are planned for early fall when reservations are no longer needed. The trips are listed in numerical order by entry point.

Lodging, hot showers, groceries, cold drinks, and some equipment are available in Grand Marais.

28 Bower Trout Lake

Entry point: 43

Character: This trip starts in one of the most ruggedly scenic areas of the BWCAW, and picturesque hills are usually close at hand. Excellent fishing for walleye, northern pike, and lake trout is available. Brook and rainbow trout inhabit some lakes, also. The portages are mostly short, but two are long, steep, and rough. You will talk about this trip for years. Independence Day storm–affected area.

Length: About 32 miles.

Average run time: 4 to 6 days, with fishing and sightseeing.

Skill level: Beginner.

Hazards: Rough portages; high winds on Brule and Winchell Lakes.

Maps: USGS: Lima Mountain, South Lake, Eagle Mountain, Brule Lake, Gunflint Lake.

The paddling: The canoe can be launched right from the South Brule River bridge. Paddle west (upstream) to a 72-rod portage into Bower Trout Lake. There is an alternate way to reach Bower Trout Lake: From the South Brule River Bridge proceed north on Forest Road 152 for 0.25 mile to a two-track road leading to the left. Follow this road 0.45 mile past a gravel pit to a small parking lot. A 65-rod portage continues along the road to Bower Trout Lake.

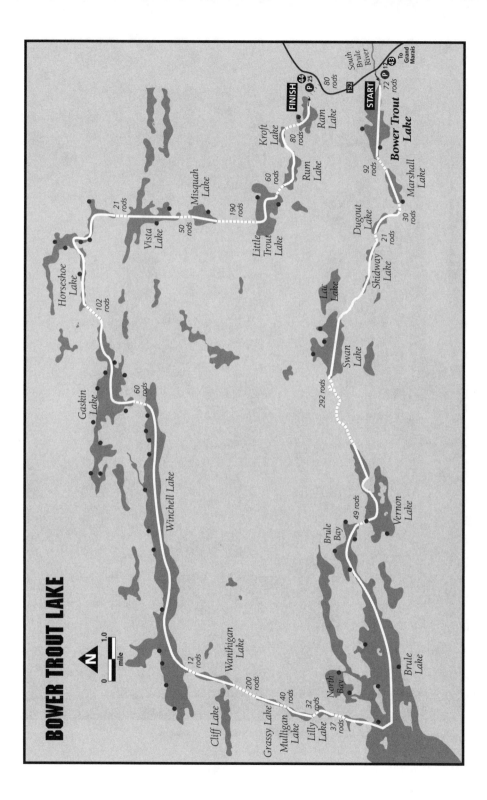

BOWER TROUT LAKE

N
0 mile 1.0

To
Grand
Marais

South
Brule
River

43

FINISH
44
P 25
80
rods

P 12
START
72
rods

152

Ram
Lake

Kroft
Lake
80
rods

Bower Trout
Lake

Rum
Lake
60
rods

Marshall
Lake

92
rods

Misquah
Lake
21
rods

Vista
Lake

50
rods

190
rods

Little
Trout
Lake

Dugout
Lake
30
rods

Horseshoe
Lake

Shidway
Lake
21
rods

102
rods

Lax
Lake

Gaskin
Lake
60
rods

Swan
Lake

292 rods

Winchell Lake

Vernon
Lake

49 rods

Brule
Bay

Cliff Lake

12
rods

Wanihigan
Lake

200
rods

Grassy Lake
40
rods

Mulligan
Lake

Lilly
Lake
32
rods

North
Bay

37
rods

Brule
Lake

Campsite near Gunflint Trail. Photo: Courtesy Minnesota Office of Tourism

Note that some maps list Bower Trout Lake as Lower Trout Lake. Covering 136 acres and only 6 feet deep, Bower Trout Lake can produce excellent northern pike, walleye, and sunfish catches. One group decided to troll a shadrap fishing plug while they were paddling to the Marshall Lake Portage. They finally had to stop fishing because they were spending too much time taking fish off the line!

The portage from Bower Trout Lake to Marshall Lake is 92 rods but fairly easy. Marshall Lake covers 62 acres, has some 16-foot-deep water, and, like the rest of the lakes in this chain, holds northern pike, walleye, and panfish. The 30-rod portage from Marshall Lake to Dugout Lake is almost level. It and Skidway Lake are really just wide stretches of the South Brule River, and even though maps show a portage between them, it doesn't exist. However, the stretch of river between Skidway Lake and Swan Lake almost disappears in two locations. This makes two 40-rod portages necessary. Both are easy.

Swan Lake is one of the most scenic of the BWCAW lakes. It has crystal clear water and spectacular hills ring the horizon. It covers 219 acres and has a maximum depth of 108 feet. Walleye and northern pike live here. Swan Lake has three campsites, including one on the north shore located at the site of an old logging camp. After almost a mile of portaging, many groups will be ready to stop here the first night. This beautiful lake can be trusted to rejuvenate tired bodies and provide restful sleep for the next day's journey.

The second day starts with a 292-rod portage to Vernon Lake. This portage is long, but fairly level, with a smooth path. Remnants of an old logging camp can be seen at the start. Vernon Lake is more than a mile long and covers almost 300 acres. It is very deep and has northern pike, walleye, and smallmouth bass in its clear waters. Only a 49-rod portage separates this lake from Brule Lake, but it is steep. Brule Lake is more than 80 feet higher than Vernon Lake.

After putting in at the Brule Bay section of Brule Lake, paddle west, along the north shore, for about 3 miles. Pass two large islands and the entrance to North Bay, and find the narrow, unnamed bay that reaches north to the portage to Lilly Lake. After this bay is located, 7 miles and more than a mile of portaging lie behind you for the day. Consider camping on one of the campsites nearby. Serious anglers will want to be rested and ready to fish Mulligan Lake when they get there. It is well populated with brook trout, and some are 18 inches long.

The third morning portage 37 rods to Lilly Lake and then 32 rods, mostly uphill, to Mulligan Lake. When situated in Mulligan Lake, unpack the fishing tackle and enjoy a few hours finessing the colorful brook trout. They should bite on spinners, worms, or flies. When ready, portage 40 rods to Grassy Lake. Grassy Lake is shallow and might hardly float the loaded canoe. The next portage to Wanihigan Lake is 200 rods but almost level and can be considered easy. Wanihigan Lake leads directly to Winchell Lake, which is surely one of the crown jewels of the region.

About 5 miles long and less than 0.25 mile wide, it resembles a strikingly scenic river. The south shore butts against high rock cliffs, and nearby hills tower above the water. Winchell Lake is 160 feet deep in spots and harbors lake trout and northern pike. It has about a dozen campsites and provides an excellent location to stop, rest, and fish for at least a day. Winchell is a popular lake, and other campers will probably be about. Find your campsite early. Campers that can't locate a site can probably continue to Gaskin Lake, where eight campsites are provided.

The fourth day leave Winchell Lake from the northeast shore by portaging 60 rods to Gaskin Lake. This portage is easy, as is the 102-rod portage to Horseshoe Lake. Only a 21-rod portage separates Horseshoe and Vista Lakes. Both lakes have midrange depths and are configured as a series of long bays. Therefore, they are not affected too much by wind and are accommodating lakes to canoe fish. The Minnesota Department of Natural Resources (DNR) stocks walleye in these lakes, and eating-size fish are abundant. Campsites are plentiful, but the surroundings not as scenic as the previous lakes.

If you stop here, however, consider that a 190-rod, difficult portage lies ahead, between Misquah Lake and Little Trout Lake. Negotiating this portage on the fourth day, instead of the last, will divide the portages more evenly between the last two days.

A 50-rod portage to Misquah Lake lies ahead, then the dreaded 190-rod portage to Little Trout Lake. This portage is rocky but starts out fairly level. In the last quarter of the trip, however, it abruptly climbs two hills to Little Trout Lake. Little Trout Lake is known for good lake trout angling and has two campsites, if an overnight stop is favored. All the portages from Little Trout Lake to Forest Road 152 (the take out) are downhill. Still, with three lakes to cross and 275 rods of portaging yet to do, most groups will be glad to see the road. Ram Lake has trout, but Rum and Kroft Lakes are murky, not potable, and considered fishless.

Access: From U.S. Highway 61 in Grand Marais, follow the Gunflint Trail north for 17 miles to Forest Road 325. Turn left and follow FR 325 for 6 miles to Forest Road 152. Turn left and follow FR 152 0.5 mile to the Brule River bridge. Put in and paddle west to the portage to Bower Trout Lake.

Shuttle: Walk approximately 0.75 mile back to your vehicle.

Camping: East Bearskin Lake. A fee is charged. Numerous campsites are along the canoe route.

Food, gas, lodging: Grand Marais.

For more information: Gunflint Ranger District (see appendix).

꩜ 29 Ram Lake

Entry point: 44

Character: This is primarily a fishing trip. Lake trout, rainbow trout, and brook trout lakes are available, as well as walleye and excellent northern pike water. It is also useful for acquiring paddling and portaging experience in the BWCAW and connects to longer canoe routes, if the sought-after entry points are full.

Length: 8.5 miles.

Average run time: 3 days, with fishing.

Skill level: Beginner.

Hazards: Storm-damaged trees (see introduction).

Map: USGS: Lima Mountain.

The paddling: This trip starts with a steep, uphill, 80-rod portage from the road to Ram Lake. Ram Lake covers 67 acres, is 40 feet deep in spots, and has very clear water. It is a designated trout lake that is stocked and managed by the state. According to a recent survey, lake trout were most numerous, but some large rainbows are also present. Anglers should work this lake thoroughly. It is worth the effort. There are two campsites available if the fishing is too good to leave the first day.

Portage 80 rods to Kroft Lake, 55 rods to Rum Lake and 60 rods to Little Trout Lake. Kroft Lake and Rum Lake have murky water and are probably fishless. Little Trout Lake, though, is a hot spot for lake trout. Lake trout are known to be abundant and good-sized. It covers 123 acres and is 56 feet deep in some spots. Three campsites are available on this lake. It is a good first day camping location.

Leave Little Trout Lake by a rough 190-rod portage from the north shore to Misquah Lake. Misquah has one campsite, covers 60 acres, is 60 feet deep, and holds lake trout and brook trout. Vista Lake is reached by a 50-rod portage from the north shore of Misquah Lake. It covers 222 acres, is 47 feet deep, and has a fair walleye and northern pike population. Vista Lake has three campsites. It is a good second day camping location.

The third day paddle east to find and negotiate the 35-rod portage to Jake Lake. Cross this lake, and portage 59 rods to 82-acre Morgan Lake. It has an abundant northern pike population and some brook trout. Lux and Carl Lakes, connected to Morgan Lake by short portages, offer excellent northern pike fishing. Take out from the east end of Morgan Lake and portage east to Forest Road 152.

Access: Start at Minnesota Highway 61 at Grand Marais, and follow the Gunflint Trail (County Road 12) north for 17 miles to Forest Road 325. Turn left and follow FR 325 6 miles to Forest Road 152. Turn right and follow for 0.5 mile to the portage sign for Ram Lake.

RAM LAKE

N

0   0.5
           mile

152

152

P

320 rods

FINISH 45

5 rods

Morgan Lake

Carl Lake

59 rods

5 rods

20 rods

Jake
Lake

Lux Lake

35 rods

152

Sled
Lake

Fiddle
Lake

**Ram
Lake**

80
rods

P 6
44

80
rods

START

Kroft
Lake

55
rods

To Grand Marais

Rum
Lake

Vista
Lake

50 rods

Misquah
Lake

190
rods

60
rods

Little Trout
Lake

Slough
Lake

Shuttle: 5 miles one way. About 20 minutes.

Camping: East Bearskin Lake. A fee is charged. Several campsites are along the canoe route.

Food, gas, lodging: Grand Marais, Ely.

For more information: Gunflint Ranger Station (see appendix).

30 Morgan Lake

Entry point: 45

Character: This route begins with a long portage to some isolated lakes and ends at a boat landing on a busy lake. It connects to several longer routes that lead to the remote interior of the BWCAW and can be used as an alternate entry point in case your first choice is full. Fishing can be very good for trout, walleye, and northern pike. Moose are about. Independence Day storm–affected area.

Length: 13 miles.

Average run time: 2 to 3 days, with fishing.

Skill level: Beginner.

Hazards: High wind and motorboats on Poplar Lake.

Maps: USGS: Lima Mountain, South Lake, Hungry Jack Lake.

The paddling: This trip begins with a 340-rod portage from Forest Road 351 to Morgan Lake. The portage path is fairly easy except for a narrow strip of boggy trail at the beginning. Good fishing is soon encountered. Morgan Lake has an abundant northern pike population and some brook trout. Lux, Carl, and Jake Lakes are connected to Morgan Lake by short portages. They have excellent northern pike fishing. The first day of the trip could be spent on these four lakes. Probably, few other anglers will be encountered. Two campsites are available.

Vista Lake is an easy 35-rod portage west of Jake Lake, and it, too, has a good northern pike and walleye population, as does adjoining Horseshoe Lake. There should be plenty of time for fishing on the trip north through Horseshoe Lake and into Caribou Lake. Caribou Lake has many campsites and is a good place to camp the second night. It covers 235 acres, is 20 feet deep, and has good walleye and northern pike fishing.

The third day portage to Swamp Lake. Swamp Lake covers 181 acres, is 10 feet deep, and historically has had an abundant walleye population. Enjoy fishing this lake, then portage to Poplar Lake. Paddle to the west end and the take-out point. Poplar Lake is outside the boundary waters; motors are allowed, resorts and cabins are numerous, and it is very busy in most seasons. Entry point 46 is at the east end of Poplar Lake. It is about 3 miles long and apt to be windswept. It is heavily stocked with walleyes and trout but also heavily fished. Unless staying at a resort on Poplar Lake, most canoeists use it for an entry and exit lake only. Take out at the excellent ramp and parking lot on the west end, and shuttle back to Morgan Lake. Commercial shuttle service is available from Poplar Lake.

Access: From Minnesota Highway 61 at Grand Marais, follow the Gunflint Trail 21 miles northwest to Forest Road 152. Turn left and follow to Forest Road 315. Turn right and follow for about 2 miles to the Morgan Lake Portage.

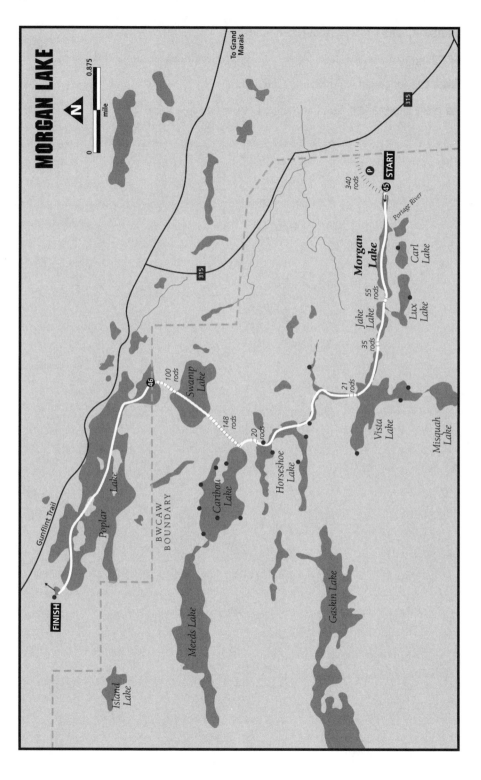

MORGAN LAKE

N

0   0.875
mile

To Grand
Marais

315

340
rods

START
45

P

Portage River

Morgan
Lake

Carl
Lake

55
rods

Lux
Lake

Jake
Lake

35
rods

315

21
rods

Vista
Lake

Misquah
Lake

46

100
rods

Swamp
Lake

148
rods

20
rods

Horseshoe
Lake

Caribou
Lake

BWCAW
BOUNDARY

Gunflint Trail

Poplar
Lake

FINISH

Meeds Lake

Island
Lake

Gaskin Lake

Shuttle: 8 miles one way. About 30 minutes.

Camping: East Bearskin Lake. A fee is charged, reservations recommended.

Food, gas, lodging: Grand Marais, Grand Portage.

For more information: Gunflint Ranger District (see appendix).

③¹ Meeds Lake

Entry point: 48

Character: This trip crosses eleven lakes. Only three of these are large lakes, where wind could be a problem. Most portages are short; all are easy. Fishing opportunities for northern pike, walleye, and trout abound. Independence Day storm–affected area.

Length: 16 miles.

Average run time: 3 to 5 days, with fishing and sightseeing.

Skill level: Beginner.

Hazards: Wind and motorboats on Poplar Lake and wind on Meeds Lake. Storm-stressed trees.

Maps: USGS: South Lake and Hungry Jack.

The paddling: Launch the canoe at the west end of busy, noisy Poplar Lake, and paddle about 2 miles to the Meeds Lake Portage. This 220-rod portage is usually damp and always rough and hilly, but it is a quick way to escape the crowds. Meeds Lake covers about 400 acres, is 41 feet deep, and is well known as a good walleye fishing lake. Find the 270-rod portage to Swallow Lake at the southwest end of Meeds Lake. This portage is easy, as is the 98-rod portage from Swallow Lake to Pillsbery Lake. Swallow and Pillsbery are small lakes that are not considered good for fishing. Pillsbery has one campsite; Swallow has none. After the 58-rod portage to Henson Lake, most groups will be ready to stop. Henson covers 146 acres, has a northern pike population, five campsites, and is an agreeable place to layover.

The next morning portage 88 rods to Gaskin Lake. Gaskin is a large lake with numerous campsites and offers good fishing, as do the rest of the lakes scheduled for day two: Jump Lake, Allen Lake, and Horseshoe Lake. Horseshoe Lake is a pleasant and convenient location for camping the second night. It has excellent walleye and perch populations and seven campsites.

The third morning starts with a 20-rod portage to Caribou Lake. Caribou has good fishing and numerous campsites. After leaving Caribou portage to Lizz Lake and then on to Poplar Lake. No more campsites are available until the take-out point at the west end of Poplar Lake. However, this is only about a 6-mile run and shouldn't be worrisome unless a strong wind is blowing across Poplar Lake.

This route can be reversed if (rarely) a reservation is available for entry point 47, Lizz Lake. The Lizz Lake entry is much more popular than the Meeds Lake entry because the portages are easier to manipulate. Consequently, this entry point might be all booked up.

Access: From Minnesota Highway 61 in Grand Marais, follow the Gunflint Trail (CR 12) 31 miles north to Poplar Lake. Access is on the western tip of the lake.

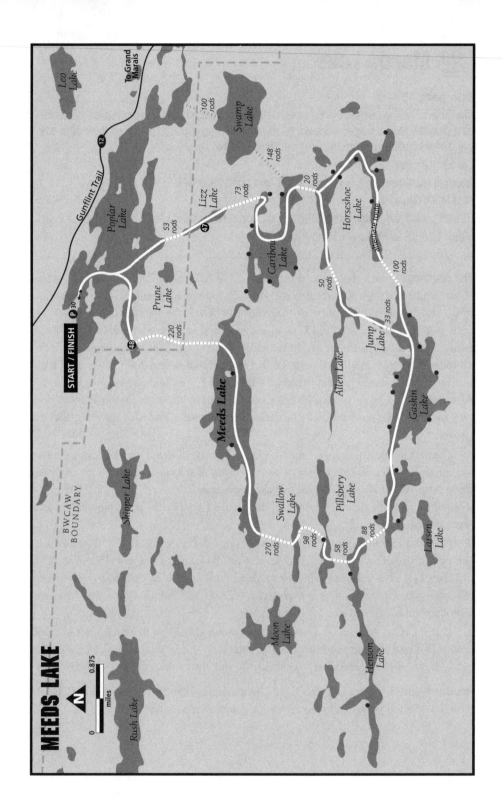

Shuttle: None.

Camping: Flour Lake Campground and Iron Lake Campground. A fee is charged. Numerous campsites are available along the route.

Food, gas, lodging: Grand Marais, Ely, Grand Portage.

For more information: Gunflint Ranger District (see appendix).

32 Skipper–Portage Lakes

Entry point: 49

Character: This route reaches south from the Iron Lake Campground to a series of lakes that extend west to Long Island Lake. Then it returns on the same lakes. It is a seldom-used route, best suited for energetic paddlers. It should yield excellent northern pike fishing. It is, also, an exceptional route for moose hunting with a camera. The first day portages are easy, but the second day is rugged. It connects to dozens of other routes at Long Island Lake, and the entry quotas are seldom filled. Independence Day storm–affected area.

Length: 27 miles.

Average run time: 4 to 6 days, with fishing and sightseeing.

Skill level: Beginner.

Hazards: None.

Maps: USGS: South Lake, Gunflint Lake, Long Island Lake.

The paddling: Launch the canoe at Iron Lake, which is outside the BWCAW boundaries, portage to Portage Lake and from Portage Lake portage 220 rods to One Island Lake. This small (28 acres) lake has fishing for northern pike and perch and is only a 60-rod portage from Rush Lake. Rush Lake covers 316 acres and connects by water to long, slim, 248-acre Banadad Lake. There is a short portage between the two. Both lakes have fishing for northern pike; Rush Lake has the highest population. It is almost mandatory that the first night of the trip be spent on one of these lakes. They have eight campsites. There are no more campsites until Long Island Lake. About 8 miles and 574 rods of portaging lie between Rush and Long Island Lakes.

The second day will require more portage time than paddling. Leave Banadad Lake and portage 94 rods to Sebeka Lake, then 180 rods to Ross Lake, followed by a 200-rod portage to Cave Lake. Going west the portages are mostly downhill, but the trail can be wet, marshy, and rough. By the time the 105-rod portage to Long Island Lake is negotiated, most paddlers will be ready to camp for the day. Grab the first campsite you see if it is midsummer. Long Island gets destination traffic from Sawbill Lake and stopover visitors from several popular routes and is therefore quite busy.

Long Island Lake is a picturesque, watery world. It covers almost 900 acres in a series of bays, points, and inlets. It is almost 70 feet deep and harbors big lake trout and northern pike. This lake has more than a dozen campsites. When it is time to head back, just retrace the route back to Iron Lake. The first day will be tough, as the portages are uphill. Also, remember that there are no other designated campsites after leaving Rush Lake until Iron Lake Campground. Plan accordingly.

If there is some means of shuttling, a shorter and easier alternate route from Long Island Lake is at hand. Just head north from the big lake, through Karl Lake, Lower George Lake, Rib Lake, and Cross Bay Lake to entry point 50 (see Gunflint Trail map). It is

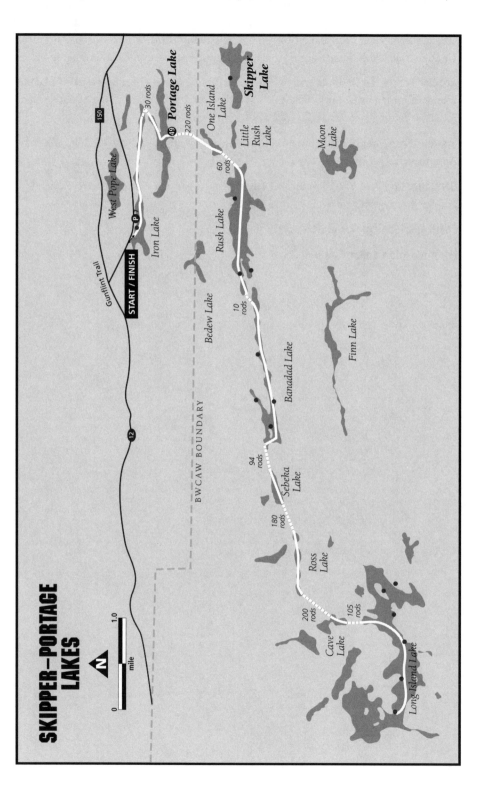

SKIPPER–PORTAGE LAKES

N

0   mile   1.0

Gunflint Trail

150

12

West Pope Lake

Iron Lake

P 7

START / FINISH

30 rods

40 **Portage Lake**

220 rods

One Island Lake

Little Rush Lake

Skipper Lake

Moon Lake

60 rods

Rush Lake

BWCAW BOUNDARY

Bedew Lake

10 rods

Banadad Lake

Finn Lake

94 rods

Sebeka Lake

180 rods

Ross Lake

200 rods

105 rods

Cave Lake

Long Island Lake

accessed from Ham Lake and a short stretch of County Road 47 leading south from the Gunflint Trail. From Ham Lake boat landing shuttle back to Iron Lake Campground.

Access: Follow the Gunflint Trail northwest for 38 miles from U.S. Highway 61 in Grand Marais. Turn left at County Road 92, and follow for 1 mile to Iron Lake Campground. The boat landing is located 0.25 mile south on Forest Road 150.

Shuttle: None, unless the alternate route is used. It is approximately 12 miles one way. Approximately 45 minutes.

Camping: Iron Lake Campground. A fee is charged and reservations are recommended. Numerous campsites are along the canoe route.

Food, gas, lodging: Grand Marais, Ely, Grand Portage.

For more information: Gunflint Ranger District (see appendix).

33 | Missing Link Lake to Little Saganaga Lake

Entry point: 51

Character: This is a lengthy trip that reaches through big lakes with scenic islands and small lakes with rocky outcroppings. The surroundings are hilly and picturesque. There is only one long portage. Trout fishing opportunities abound, and moose are frequently seen. Log bridges and an antiquated log cabin can be seen, too.

Length: 22 miles.

Average run time: 3 to 5 days or more, with fishing and sightseeing.

Skill level: Beginner.

Hazards: Wind on the large lakes, rough portages, and blowdowns.

Maps: USGS: Gillis Lake, Ogishkemuncie Lake, Long Island Lake.

The paddling: Launch the canoe outside the BWCAW at Round Lake, and paddle to the south end. Portage 140 rods on a steep uphill trail to Missing Link Lake. Here a decision must be made. Either take one of the three campsites on Missing Link Lake and spend the day fishing for the brook trout and rainbow trout in this lake and adjoining Mavis Lake, or portage 366 rods to Tuscarora Lake. Paddlers making this journey for the second time or those getting a late start usually stop at Missing Link Lake and enjoy the fishing for at least one day.

The Tuscarora Lake Portage is rocky, narrow, and steep in spots, and most paddlers that elected to continue through Missing Link Lake will want to stop and rest at Tuscarora Lake. Fortunately, it has an abundance of campsites. This lake covers over 800 acres and is 130 feet deep. It offers good fishing for lake trout and northern pike. The shoreline and even some overlooking campsites have scenic exposed rock outcroppings.

Compared to the first day, the second day is easy. It starts with a 68-rod portage to Owl Lake, followed by a 56-rod portage to Crooked Lake. This lake covers 320 acres, is 75 feet deep, and can be an excellent lake trout fishery. Anglers will want to spend some time on this lake. Turn south here and portage to Tarry Lake and through it to Mora Lake. This is a reasonable location for the third night campsite. It covers 247 acres, has several campsites, and offers fair fishing for northern pike.

Leave Mora by the 45-rod portage to huge, sprawling Little Saganaga Lake. It has an abundance of islands, deep bays, and points. It covers almost 2,000 acres, stretches about 3 miles from north to south, and is 150 feet deep in spots. Fish species include lake trout and northern pike. At least one day should be spent exploring and fishing this water world. Even though about twenty-five campsites are found here, get your campsite early. It is a very popular lake.

Leave Little Saganaga by the 90-rod, rather steep, portage to Virgin Lake, which has no fish, then negotiate the 20-rod portage to Powell Lake, which covers 40 acres, is 75 feet deep, and has lake trout. From Powell Lake portage 33 rods to French Lake. It covers 128 acres, is 135 feet deep, and also has lake trout. From this lake a choice of routes to Gillis

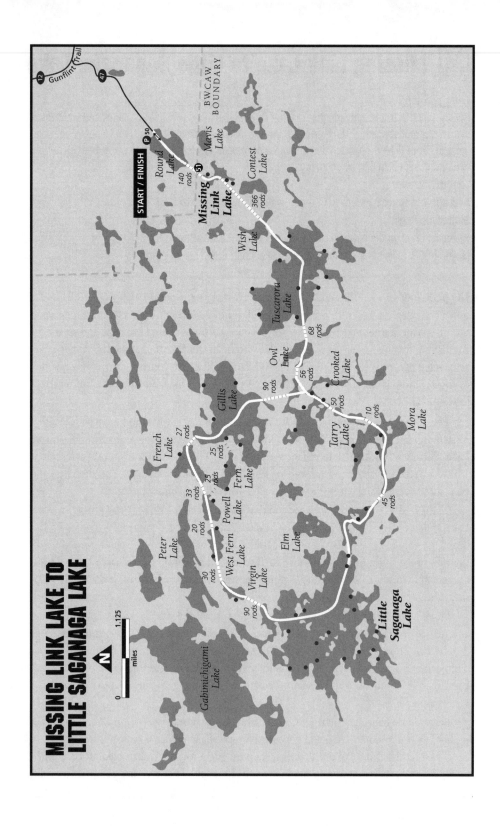

MISSING LINK LAKE TO LITTLE SAGANAGA LAKE

N

0   1,125

miles

Gunflint Trail

12

47

P 50

START / FINISH

Round
Lake

140
rods

51

Mavis
Lake

BWCAW
BOUNDARY

**Missing
Link
Lake**

Contest
Lake

366
rods

Wish
Lake

Tuscarora
Lake

68
rods

Owl
Lake

Crooked
Lake

56
rods

90
rods

Gillis
Lake

27
rods

French
Lake

25
rods

50
rods

10
rods

Mora
Lake

Tarry
Lake

25
rods

Fern
Lake

33
rods

Powell
Lake

Peter
Lake

20
rods

Elm
Lake

West Fern
Lake

30
rods

Virgin
Lake

45
rods

90
rods

Gabimichigami
Lake

**Little
Saganaga
Lake**

Canoeing Tuscarora Lake. Photo: Courtesy Minnesota Office of Tourism

Lake is at hand: Portage to Fern and then portage from Fern to Gillis, or portage directly to Gillis Lake. Fern Lake has fishing for lake trout and northern pike but only one campsite.

Gillis Lake covers 703 acres, is 180 feet deep, and has good fishing for lake trout and northern pike. It has a half dozen campsites and is an excellent location for staying overnight, if an unoccupied campsite is available.

Leave Gillis Lake from the south end on a 90-rod portage to Crooked Lake. From there head back northeast to Round Lake and the take-out point on the route used previously.

Access: From U.S. Highway 61 at Grand Marais, follow the Gunflint Trail 49 miles north to County Road 47. Turn left on CR 47 and follow it for 0.75 mile to Forest Road 1495. Turn right on FR 1495 and follow it for 0.75 mile to the parking lot.

Shuttle: None.

Camping: Trail's End Campground. A fee is charged and reservations are recommended.

Food, gas, lodging: Grand Marais.

For more information: Gunflint Ranger District (see appendix).

34 Brant Lake to Kekekabic Lake

Entry point: 52

Character: This trip goes west through several small lakes and accesses three large, popular, base camp lakes. It connects to routes from other entry points. The fishing opportunities for lake trout are plentiful, and brook trout are available. The large lakes are studded with scenic islands and Gabimichigami Lake has 400 foothills rising from its shorelines. Moose, beaver, mink, and otter are frequently seen. Some of the portages are rugged but not exceptionally long. The return trip retraces the route, with alternate routes mentioned. Independence Day storm–affected area.

Length: Approximately 30 miles.

Average run time: 4 to 6 days, with fishing and sightseeing.

Skill level: Beginner.

Hazards: Rough portages, wind on large lakes, storm-damaged trees (see introduction).

Maps: USGS: Ogishkemuncie Lake, Gillis Lake, Long Island Lake.

The paddling: Launch the canoe at Round Lake and paddle to the southwest corner of the lake to find and negotiate the 85-rod portage to West Round Lake. Cross this lake, and portage 50 rods to Edith Lake and then 36 rods to Brant Lake. Brant Lake covers 121 acres and is 80 feet deep. Northern pike and perch live in its depths. There are three campsites on Brant Lake. They are the last ones available until Peter Lake, except for two at adjacent French Lake. Peter Lake is about an average day's paddling and portaging from Round Lake.

From Brant Lake portage 100 rods over a hill to tiny Gotter Lake and then 10 rods to Flying Lake. Continue by a 90-rod carry to Fay Lake. Fay Lake covers 77 acres and has trout living in its depths. There is an alternate route for brook trout fishing: Portage to Bingshick, then to Glee Lake, and finally to Fay Lake. Bingshick Lake covers 44 acres, is 37 feet deep, and has been heavily stocked with brook trout for several years. Of course hikers fish it also. Leave Fay Lake by a 45-rod portage from the northwest corner to War Club Lake. Between Fay Lake and Seahorse Lake cross the well-known Kekekabic Hiking Trail, twice.

From War Club Lake portage 15 rods to Seahorse Lake, then turn south and find the 25-rod portage to French Lake. French Lake covers 128 acres and is 135 feet deep in one place. It is considered to be good lake trout fishing. When it is time to leave French Lake, the longest and last portage of the day looms ahead: the 132-rod carry from French Lake to Peter Lake. This portage crosses a 100 foot rise in elevation.

Peter Lake covers almost 300 acres and is 120 feet deep. It has lake trout angling. There are three campsites on this lake, and it is an excellent location for the first night's camping. Most paddlers will be satisfied to stop here to rest and fish.

Next morning leave this lake by portaging from the northwest corner 39 rods to Gabimichigami Lake. "Gabi" is expansive, at 1,236 acres of water, and exceptionally deep, at 209 feet. In its clear water live trout, northern pike, and perch, and the fishing can be

BRANT LAKE TO KEKEKABIC LAKE

N

0   2.75
miles

Kekekabic Lake

15 rods

Kek Lake

Kekekabic Ponds

15 rods

Eddy Lake

15 rods

15 rods

Jenny Lake

Annie Lake

Ogishkemuncie Lake

60 rods

115 rods

15 rods

Mueller Lake

39 rods

Agamok Lake

Gabimichigami Lake

Little Saganaga Lake

Howard Lake

Seahorse Lake

War Club Lake

Peter Lake

132

25 rods

15 rods

45 rods

Glee Lake

90 rods

Fay Lake

French Lake

West Fern Lake

Virgin Lake

BWCAW BOUNDARY

Bingshick Lake

Gotter Lake

100 rods

Flying Lake

Brant Lake

36 rods

50 rods

85 rods

Edith Lake

32

West Round Lake

P 50

Round Lake

START / FINISH

47

1495

To Grand Marais

fantastic for serious and knowledgeable anglers. There are eight campsites on this water wonderland. High scenic hills line its western shoreline, and the view is breathtaking from some of the campsites. Because of its scenic appeal and location, it is a popular lake also, and if staying over is planned, find a campsite by 1:00 or 2:00 P.M.

There are short portages from Gabi to Agamok Lake but also a 115-rod Agamok Lake to Mueller Lake carry and a 60-rod steep and rugged portage from Mueller Lake to Ogishkemuncie Lake. "Muncie" Lake has about a dozen campsites and is a very beautiful, island-studded, and popular lake often filled to capacity. Get your site early. Between Agamok Lake and Mueller Lake, watch for a wooden bridge on the Kekekabic Hiking Trail. It crosses over a thrilling waterfall.

Leave Ogishkemuncie Lake by a short portage to Annie Lake, followed by equally short portages to Jenny Lake and Eddy Lake. Then a pair of short portages through Kekekabic Ponds and a short carry will deliver you to Kekekabic Lake. Kekekabic Lake is remarkable, even by BWCAW standards. It covers 1,905 acres and is 195 feet deep. Lake trout live in the depths. It has fourteen campsites, but if you intend to stay over, get one early.

Reverse the route to return to Round Lake. If returning over the exact same route seems unexciting, study the map. There are several slightly different routes back to Round Lake. Realize, however, that most people will not even recognize most of the surroundings, even if they return over the same route. There are just too many shorelines, islands, and bluffs to recall.

Access: Start on U.S. Highway 61 at Grand Marais, and follow the Gunflint Trail 49 miles north to County Road 47. Turn left and follow this road for 0.75 mile to Forest Road 1495. Turn right and follow for 0.75 mile to the parking lot. Paddle west from Round Lake through West Round Lake and Edith Lake to Brant Lake.

Shuttle: None.

Camping: Trail's End Campground. A fee is charged and reservations are recommended. Numerous campsites are along the canoe route.

Food, gas, lodging: Grand Marais.

For more information: Gunflint Ranger District (see appendix).

35 Seagull Lake to the South Arm of Knife Lake

Entry point: 54

Character: The trip starts and ends at busy Seagull Lake where motors are allowed and people abound. Most of the journey is outside the legal limits for motors, though. Some very scenic lakes are enjoyed; and part of the trip follows the international border. There are no rugged portages. Enjoy a spectacular waterfall, find the homesite of a gold prospector named Benny Ambrose, and negotiate the Monument Portage. There is fishing for brook trout, lake trout, northern pike, walleye, and bass. Independence Day storm–affected area.

Length: 50 miles.

Average run time: 6 to 8 days, with fishing and sightseeing.

Skill level: Beginner.

Hazards: Wind on the large lakes and wind-damaged trees (see introduction).

Maps: USGS: Basswood Lake, Saganaga Lake.

The paddling: Launch the canoe at the public access point on Seagull Lake and head southwest. If you get an early start, motorboats will be less of a factor. It is about 6 miles across Seagull Lake to the 20-rod portage to Rog Lake. Rog Lake covers 55 acres, is 40 feet deep, has a campsite, and offers fishing for brook trout. If time permits, try catching enough for a delicious meal. Then find and negotiate the 65-rod portage to Alpine Lake. This can be the stop-over point for the first day's paddling.

Alpine Lake covers 839 acres, is 65 feet deep, and has over twenty campsites. It is configured in a series of loops and arms, with large islands taking up part of the lake basin. This offers privacy to almost every campsite and reduces the effect of wind. Alpine Lake has walleye, smallmouth bass, and abundant whitefish.

Leave Alpine Lake by a 45-rod portage to Jasper Lake. Jasper Lake covers 239 acres and is 125 feet deep in one place. It has seven campsites and is a good second choice for the first day's camping, if all the sites are taken on Alpine Lake. This lake has fishing for walleye and lake trout. Kingfisher Lake is a short 25-rod portage from Jasper Lake, and it, too, offers fishing for lake trout and walleye. From Kingfisher Lake portage 38 rods to Ogishkemuncie. This is a good place to spend the second night. See chapter 34, Brant Lake to Kekekabic Lake for more information on this lake, as well as for Annie and Jenny Lakes.

The third morning portage out of Ogishkemuncie Lake to Annie, Jenny, and Eddy Lakes. Consider the northern pike fishing opportunities offered by 134-acre Eddy Lake. A DNR fish survey brought up a good population of big fish. From Eddy Lake it is only a short 25-rod portage to the South Arm of Knife Lake. Take time to admire the waterfall on the creek connecting Eddy and Knife Lakes. It is best viewed from the east side of the creek. Knife Lake is practically an inland sea at 5,536 acres. It has a maximum depth of 135 feet and a good population of lake trout, northern pike, walleye, and smallmouth bass.

SEAGULL LAKE TO THE
SOUTH ARM OF KNIFE LAKE

N

0   1.66
miles

C A N A D A

U N I T E D
S T A T E S

American
Point

Saganaga
Lake

Munker
Island

Gold
Island

Saganaga
Corridor

Seagull River

Trail's End
Campground

Gunflint Trail

START / FINISH

54

P

12

Seagull
Lake

BWCAW
BOUNDARY

Seagull
Lake

Rog
Lake

20
rods

65
rods

45
rods

Alpine
Lake

25
rods

Kingfisher
Lake

Jasper
Lake

38
rods

Ogishkemuncie
Lake

10
rods

Swamp
Lake

80
rods

Otter Track
Lake

Ester Lake

Hanson Lake

40
rods

50
rods

Eddy
Lake

Jenny
Lake

15 rods

15
rods

Annie Lake

South Arm of
Knife Lake

25 rods

Turn northeast on the South Arm and paddle to the very short portage to Hanson Lake. Hanson Lake covers 300 acres and has lake trout and northern pike in its clear water. Continue to head northeast by another short portage to Ester Lake and then to Otter Track Lake on the international border. Otter Track Lake is long and narrow and bordered with high, rocky bluffs. This is the lake that Benny Ambrose lived on for sixty years as he hunted for gold in the area. He died in 1982 at the age of eighty-four; a plaque commemorating his life has been cemented into the base of a cliff here. Paddle east on Otter Track Lake and find the 80-rod Monument Portage to Swamp Lake. Along this portage is a large, steel marker marking the international boundary, which gives the portage its name.

Swamp Lake covers 208 acres, is 25 feet deep, and has walleye, northern pike, and perch in its depths. Most paddlers will want to move through Swamp Lake to the short portage to Saganaga Lake and find a campsite. Campsites are plentiful on the stretch between Swamp Lake and American Point. Motorboats are not allowed west of American Point.

Saganaga Lake covers 17,593 acres, is 280 feet deep in places, and has a good population of walleye. It is known for yielding big lake trout and has abundant northern pike. It is a very good fishing lake, but motorboats are allowed and the lake is apt to be humming with activity in most seasons.

There are no portages on this last day, but at least eight miles of water lie ahead before the take-out point on Seagull Lake is reached. If it is windy, stay close to the shoreline of American Point, and pass south of Gold Island to maintain a safe heading. Continue east to the Saganaga Corridor and the Seagull River. Paddle down the river to Seagull Lake and the take-out point.

Access: Start on U.S. Highway 61 at Grand Marais and follow the Gunflint Trail 54 miles north to Seagull Lake Access Road. Turn left and follow for 0.25 mile to the parking lot.

Shuttle: None.

Camping: Camp at Trail's End Campground. A fee is charged and reservations are recommended. Numerous campsites are along the canoe route.

Food, gas, lodging: Grand Marais, Grand Portage.

For more information: Gunflint Ranger District (see appendix).

Entry point: 55

Character: This is an introductory trip to the BWCAW. It is a good fishing trip but very appropriate for nonanglers, also. There are only three short portages. Scenic, island dotted lakes are crossed, including the notable Red Rock Lake. Almost every fish available in the BWCAW can be caught, including brook trout. Motorboats are allowed, and people will probably be seen or heard in most areas. Fire scars from the Roy Lake fire and the Romance Lake fire are visible, as well as damage from the July 4, 1999, windstorm.

Length: 24 miles.

Average run time: 3 to 6 days, with fishing and sightseeing.

Skill level: Beginner.

Hazards: High wind on the large lakes, storm-damaged trees (see introduction), motorboat wakes.

Map: USGS: Saganaga Lake.

The paddling: Launch the canoe directly into Seagull Lake at the Trail's End Campground boat landing, and head north up the Seagull River. Usually this river has only minimal flow, and upstream from Seagull Falls paddling against the current isn't difficult. Seagull Lake has walleye and smallmouth bass. Experienced anglers often put out a trolling lure while moving up the river. Continue to move north up the river to the Saganaga Corridor and finally emerge into gigantic Saganaga Lake. Realize, also, that Seagull Lake and the Seagull River can be bypassed by using the boat landing on the Saganaga Corridor.

After reaching Saganaga Lake several options are available. A favorite route is to continue north to the international border, bypassing enormous Munker Island on its west side. At the border turn west and follow it to American Point. Find a campsite here early in the afternoon for the first night. Motors are not allowed west of the point, so the campsites are often peaceful. Spend any leisure time fishing. Work the edges of the islands for walleyes, northerns, and bass, and troll the deepest water for lake trout. Wind can be an important factor on this part of Saganaga Lake. Stay safe by not venturing too far from a mainland or island shoreline, even if it means extra paddling. Saganaga Lake covers 17,593 acres, is 280 feet deep in places, and has a good population of walleye. It is known for yielding big lake trout and has abundant northern pike and smallmouth bass. It is a very good fishing lake, but motorboats are allowed and the lake is apt to be humming with activity in most seasons. Do as much traveling early in the morning as possible on big lakes. Usually the wind speed is lowest at that time.

The second morning follow the east shore of American Point into the Red Rock Bay portion of Saganaga Lake. Exploring and fishing both can be quite rewarding. Take time to enjoy both. Eventually, work south and negotiate the 10-rod portage to Red Rock Lake. This is an attractive, island-studded lake with bluffs bordering the shorelines. Red Rock lake covers 353 acres, has a maximum depth of 64 feet, and offers excellent northern pike

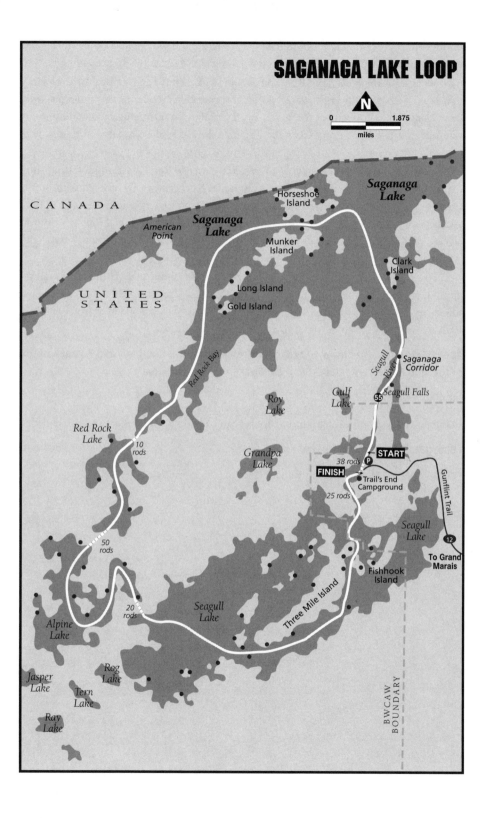

fishing, but lake trout, walleye, and smallmouth bass are also present in good numbers. The campsites are located far apart, and this is a good place to camp for the second night.

The next morning portage 50 rods to Alpine Lake. Alpine Lake covers 839 acres, is 65 feet deep, and has over twenty campsites. It is configured in a series of loops and arms, with large islands taking up part of the lake basin. This lake also offers privacy to almost every campsite and usually is not windswept. Alpine Lake has walleye, smallmouth bass, and abundant whitefish.

Next morning avid anglers will want to portage over to Rog Lake for brook trout fishing. Rog Lake covers 55 acres, is 40 feet deep, and has been heavily stocked with brook trout for many years. If time permits, try catching enough for a delicious meal. Then find and negotiate the 20-rod portage to Seagull Lake. Seagull Lake covers 4,032 acres and is several miles long. It has a good population of lake trout, walleye, smallmouth bass, and northern pike. In spite of heavy fishing, it maintains abundant fish numbers.

Cross Seagull Lake and find the take-out point on the south side of Trail's End Campground, about 0.25 mile from the put-in site. Walk back to your vehicle. Consider that this entire route can be reversed when a strong northwest wind is blowing by heading south from the Trail's End Campground to access Seagull Lake first.

Access: From U.S. Highway 61 at Grand Marais, follow the Gunflint Trail 56 miles north to the Trail's End Campground and the end of the Gunflint Trail.

Shuttle: None.

Camping: Trail's End Campground. A fee is charged and reservations are recommended.

Food, gas, lodging: Grand Marais.

For more information: Gunflint Ranger District (see appendix).

Magnetic Lake to Saganaga Lake

Entry point: 57

Character: This trip follows the Voyageurs route along the international border from Magnetic Lake north to Saganaga Lake. It offers peaceful lakes, placid stretches of rivers, roaring waterfalls, and white-water rapids. Both the Pine River and the uniquely picturesque Granite River are followed downstream. This trip is a short, but favorite, route for many who enjoy shooting rapids or retracing ancient routes. The fishing is good along the entire trip. Independence Day storm–affected area.

Length: 26 miles.

Average run time: 3 to 5 days, with fishing and sightseeing.

Class: II–III.

Skill level: Beginner, if all the portages are used.

Hazards: Rapids, waterfalls, wind on Saganaga Lake, storm-damaged trees (see introduction).

Maps: USGS: Conners Island, Munker Island, Long Island Lake.

The paddling: Launch the canoe outside the BWCAW boundary at the public landing on the south shore of Gunflint Lake and paddle about 1.5 miles northwest to the 12-rod portage to Magnetic Lake. Magnetic Lake is named after Magnetic Rock, a deposit of iron about 1 mile west of the lake. It can affect compass needle headings. Magnetic Lake covers 31 acres and has some 90-foot-deep water. Lake trout fishing can be good in deep water and walleyes are found in mid-depths.

Leave Magnetic Lake by portaging 15 rods to the Pine River. Follow the Pine River downstream to Little Rock Falls, a 15-foot drop in the river. This is a scenic area used extensively as a lunch break. At the next carry, Blueberry Portage, the river separates into three arms. It requires a 30-rod portage. Not far downstream the river bends sharply to the east, only to return again and flow into Clove Lake. This convolution and the channel of a drainage creek from Clove Lake isolate a block of land known as Pine Island. Most paddlers portage across Pine Island to Clove Lake. This 110-rod portage eliminates a stretch of river with some difficult rapids. White-water enthusiasts may want to continue following the Pine River until it flows into Clove Lake.

Clove Lake covers 172 acres, is 25 feet deep, and has walleye, northern pike, and smallmouth bass within its basin. It has several campsites, if it is time to stop for the day. If all the campsites on Clove Lake are full, Larch Lake, a 25-rod portage to the west, has campsites, also. Leave Clove Lake by heading north on the Granite River. It requires a 48-rod portage. The next, Swamp Portage, requires a 72-rod carry. Leave the main channel and carry across land to a bay in the river, therefore bypassing an oxbow turn of the river. This portage can be eliminated by staying on the main channel of the river and running the rapids. Paddlers with intermediate skills can successfully negotiate all of these rapids, except for the center rapids. It requires a 25-rod carry. Experts can run them all in normal water flow. Keep in mind, however, that removing a disabled canoe from this area can be a difficult, expensive undertaking.

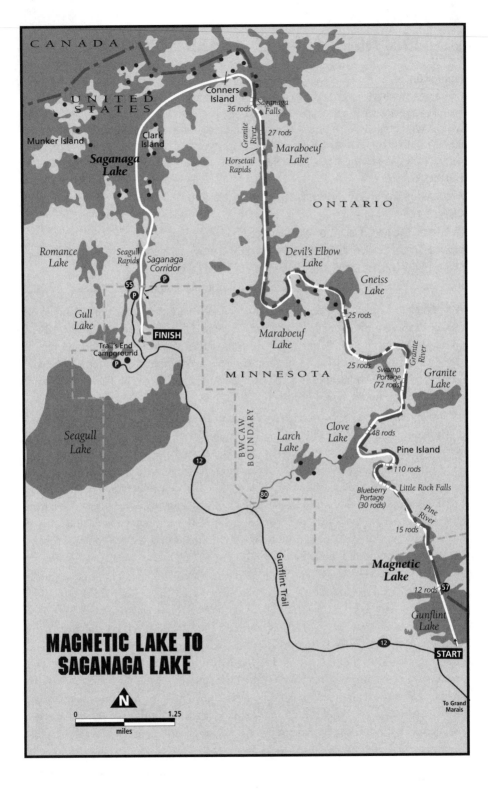

CANADA

UNITED STATES

Munker Island

Saganaga Lake

Clark Island

Conners Island

36 rods

Saganaga Falls

27 rods

Granite River

Horsetail Rapids

Maraboeuf Lake

ONTARIO

Romance Lake

Seagull Rapids

Saganaga Corridor

55

P

P

Gull Lake

FINISH

Trail's End Campground

P

Seagull Lake

Devil's Elbow Lake

Gneiss Lake

25 rods

Maraboeuf Lake

25 rods

Swamp Portage (72 rods)

Granite River

Granite Lake

MINNESOTA

BWCAW BOUNDARY

Larch Lake

Clove Lake

48 rods

Pine Island

110 rods

Blueberry Portage (30 rods)

Little Rock Falls

12

80

Gunflint Trail

Pine River

15 rods

Magnetic Lake

12 rods

57

Gunflint Lake

12

START

To Grand Marais

MAGNETIC LAKE TO SAGANAGA LAKE

N

0   1.25

miles

Continue downriver to the 25-rod portage to Gneiss Lake. Paddle into Devil's Elbow Lake, and then run a set of easy rapids to Maraboeuf Lake. Maraboeuf Lake is long and narrow, covers 900 acres, is 55 feet deep, and has fishing for walleye, northern pike, and smallmouth bass. It has several campsites and is a good place to stay over for sightseeing and fishing or searching for artifacts.

The portage out of Maraboeuf to the Granite River is around Horsetail Rapids. These twenty-seven rapids should not be run by anyone but an expert. The pool below the rapids is littered with artifacts from ancient and modern day voyageurs who thought otherwise. The next icon is Saganaga Falls, a roaring 5-foot cascade of white water. No one should attempt to run this maelstrom, although it is a pleasant place to rest and eat lunch.

Portage 36 rods around the falls and continue north into Saganaga Lake. Head south at the big lake, and find a take-out point on the Saganaga Corridor or at Trail's End Campground. Hopefully a vehicle will be waiting for you or you were transported to Gunflint Lake at the start of the trip. Outfitters in this area can arrange for transportation for a fee.

Access: Follow the Gunflint Trail 46 miles north of U.S. Highway 61 at Grand Marais to County Road 50. Turn right and follow for 0.5 mile to the public landing on Gunflint Lake. Magnetic Lake is accessed by paddling north across Gunflint Lake.

Shuttle: 13 miles one way. About 45 minutes round-trip.

Camping: Iron Lake Campground or Trail's End Campground. A fee is charged and reservations are recommended.

Food, gas, lodging: Grand Marais.

For more information: Gunflint Ranger District (see appendix).

South Lake to Hungry Jack Lake

Entry point: 58

Character: This is a very unusual and scenic trip that follows the border along part of the Voyageurs highway. On the north shore of Gunflint and North Lakes the remains of a historical town and a railroad can be found. A railcar can be used to haul the loaded canoe at one portage. The famous "Height of Land" Portage is negotiated and a wooden "stairstep" forms part of another portage. The world-renowned Rose Lake scenery can be photographed, and fishing opportunities abound.

From the public boat access it can be about a day's paddling to the east end of Gunflint Lake, especially if unfavorable winds diminish your progress. Get an early start. All five of the campsites are located at the east end. Independence Day storm–affected area.

Length: 23 miles.

Average run time: 3 to 5 days, with fishing and sightseeing.

Skill level: Beginner.

Hazards: Wind on the large lakes, motorboats, storm-stressed trees (see introduction).

Maps: USGS: Gunflint Lake, Long Island Lake, South Lake, Hungry Jack Lake.

The paddling: Launch the canoe at the public landing on the south shore of awesome Gunflint Lake, and paddle eastward along the Canadian border toward Little Gunflint Lake. Just traveling, fishing, and sightseeing the length of this lake can take up the first day or two. Gunflint Lake has tremendous fishing for lake trout, walleye, and northern pike. Ruins of bread baking ovens can be found on the north shore of this lake, where the town of La Blain once stood. There are five campsites on the east end of the lake, none in the midsection.

Leave Gunflint Lake by paddling to Little Gunflint Lake, and go through it to the 20-rod portage to Little North Lake. Private interests maintain a set of rails and a railroad car here for the public to use for portaging heavy boats or loaded canoes from one lake to the other. It should be used with care. Follow narrow Little North Lake to North Lake. North Lake covers 2,685 acres, but most of it lies in Canada. It offers fishing for walleye, northern pike, lake trout, and smallmouth bass. There are several campsites, if the fishing is too good to abandon quickly. On the Canadian shore the remains of an abandoned railroad and a railroad town can be found. An entry permit is required for entering Canadian waters.

The famous Height of Land Portage lies between North Lake and South Lake. This was the initiation point for rookies in the Voyageur ranks. It is commemorated with a sign. This portage also crosses the Laurentian Divide: Waters east of the divide flow easterly to Lake Superior, waters west of the divide flow north to Hudson Bay. This was significant to the early westbound Voyageurs because it meant they would be paddling with the current after they crossed it. Before that, coming up from Lake Superior, they were paddling upstream.

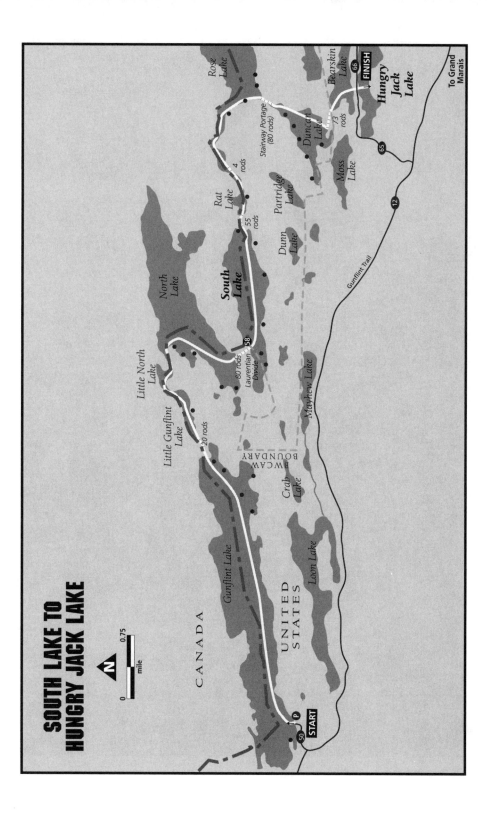

SOUTH LAKE TO
HUNGRY JACK LAKE

N

0   0.75
mile

CANADA

UNITED
STATES

Gunflint Lake

START
50
P

Little Gunflint
Lake

20 rods

Little North
Lake

North
Lake

Little North
Lake

58
80 rods
Laurentian Divide

South
Lake

55
rods

Rat
Lake

4
rods

Rose
Lake

Stairway Portage
(80 rods)

Dunn
Lake

Partridge
Lake

Duncan
Lake

73
rods

Bearskin
Lake

FINISH
66

Hungry
Jack
Lake

Moss
Lake

65

12

Gunflint Trail

To Grand
Marais

B.W.C.A.W.
BOUNDARY

Crab
Lake

Loon
Lake

Mayhew Lake

Stairway portage.

South Lake, the point of entry to the BWCAW, is an impressive wilderness border lake. It covers 1,143 acres—a substantial part of it lying in Canada—but it offers good fishing for lake trout, northern pike, and smallmouth bass. Motorboats are not allowed on this lake. There are several campsites, and it is good place to spend the second night.

Portage 55 rods to Rat Lake after leaving South Lake. Rat Lake is small and shallow, but it does have a smallmouth bass population. Leave Rat Lake by a very short portage to Rose Lake. Rose Lake is bordered by high, picturesque bluffs and has been described as the most heavily photographed lake in the BWCAW. It covers 1,404 acres, is 90 feet deep in spots, and has lake trout, walleye, and smallmouth bass for the catching. It also has several campsites for long layovers or overnighting.

Leave Rose Lake by an 80-rod portage to Duncan Lake. The first part of this portage is so steep that a wooden stairway has been built into the side of the hill. It is called Stairway Portage. At the top of the stairs, a scenic overlook offers a chance to photograph a stunning scene of the steep west shore of Rose Lake. A waterfall and a Border Lake Hiking Trail bridge can be seen from here, also. Some paddlers take time out to hike east from the portage to the high cliffs overlooking Rose Lake and the Canadian wilderness.

Duncan Lake covers 630 acres and is 130 feet deep in spots. It has populations of all the usual boundary waters fish, such as walleye, smallmouth bass, lake trout, and northern pike. Duncan Lake has several campsites and is a good place to spend some time fishing and recovering from the trip. Next morning portage 73 rods to Bearskin Lake, cross the lake, and take out at the portage to Hungry Jack Lake.

Access: Start at U.S. Highway 61 at Grand Marais, and follow the Gunflint Trail 46 miles north to County Road 50. Turn right on CR 50 and follow it for 0.5 mile to the public landing on Gunflint Lake. South Lake is four lakes and two portages to the east.

Shuttle: 19 miles one way. About 45 minutes.

Camping: Iron Lake Campground. A fee is charged, and reservations are recommended.

Food, gas, lodging: Grand Marais.

For more information: Gunflint Ranger District (see appendix).

Daniels Lake Loop

Entry point: 60

Character: This trip heads north to the United States–Canadian border through some scenic and rugged terrain. It then bends east and follows the border to four lakes before heading south through four lakes. Then it bends west and finally returns to Flour Lake. Towering hills with picturesque palisades, scenic valleys, blue-water lakes, and deep forest scenes are enjoyed. There is fishing for lake trout, walleye, northern pike, and smallmouth bass. Motors are allowed on some of the lakes. Independence Day storm–affected area.

Length: 28 miles, if the complete route is finished.

Average run time: 4 to 6 days, with fishing and sightseeing.

Skill level: Beginner.

Hazards: Wind on the larger lakes, steep portages, storm-stressed trees (see introduction).

Maps: USGS: Hungry Jack, Crocodile Lake.

The paddling: If camped at Flour Lake Campground, portage 162 rods to the Hungry Jack Lake access. Paddle north from the access point to find the 35-rod portage to Bearskin Lake. Paddle to the northwest shore of Bearskin Lake to find the 60-rod portage to Daniels Lake (entry point 61). The canoe can also be transported by vehicle from the Flour Lake Campground to the Bearskin Lake access. Outfitters in this area will do this for a fee. Friends and campground hosts also sometimes can be coerced into supplying shuttle service. Head north on Daniels Lake to the 265-rod portage to Rove Lake. This portage is no piece of cake. Further be cautioned that the first part of this portage trail is used for both Rose Lake and Rove Lake. Be sure to turn east (right) when the trail forks. The right fork goes to Rove Lake.

Rove Lake is about 1 mile long and narrow. Steep hills border the south shore. It is 30 feet deep and holds smallmouth bass and northern pike. No portage is needed between Rove Lake and Watap Lake. Watap Lake is a larger sister of Rove Lake, about 2 miles long, 45 feet deep, bordered by steep hills, and hosting northern pike and smallmouth bass. Paddle the length of Watap Lake to find the 100-rod portage to Mountain Lake.

Mountain Lake has multiple campsites and is a good location for the first night layover. This lake covers almost 2,000 acres and is 210 feet deep in one place. It is known for good lake trout fishing. Try to camp at the west end. After camp is set up, find the portage to Clearwater Lake, and hike up it to the Border Route Hiking Trail. There are several locations along the Border Route Hiking Trail where a spectacular view of Mountain Lake can be enjoyed. Hike 1 mile west of the portage trail or a shorter distance east of the portage trail to look down on the length of Mountain Lake from hundreds of feet above. Of course this is the portage route for the next day, also, but it can be enjoyed more enthusiastically when unencumbered by the concerns of portaging.

When it is time to leave Mountain Lake, portage 90 rods over this route to Clearwater Lake. Clearwater Lake is over 5 miles long, narrow, and covers 1,537 acres. It is 130

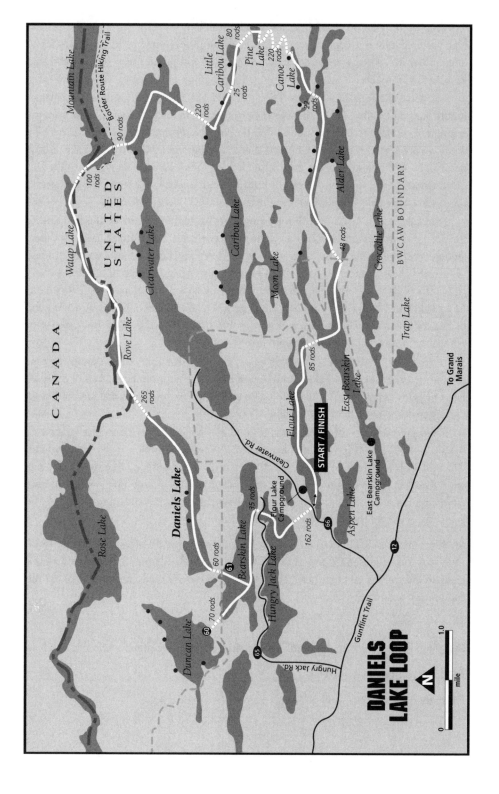

DANIELS LAKE LOOP

N

0 mile 1.0

feet deep in spots and has lake trout and smallmouth bass to tempt the angler. It, too, has high scenic banks and good fishing and several campsites. Some paddlers may want to linger a day or two. Leave Clearwater Lake by a 220-rod portage near the east end that leads to Caribou Lake.

Caribou Lake is shallow, covers 497 acres, and has fishing for northern pike, largemouth bass, and walleye. There are several campsites on this lake. Portage 25 rods from the east end of this lake to Little Caribou Lake. It also has largemouth bass and northern pike within its 85 acres of water. Leave Little Caribou, and portage 80 rods to Pine Lake. If time permits, be sure to visit Johnson Falls before leaving Pine Lake. The short trail to the falls is located at the west end of the lake. It leads through a rock gorge to a 25-foot waterfall on an unnamed creek flowing into Pine Lake.

Pine Lake is very large, over 6 miles long, but this route only crosses the west end to the 220-rod, zigzag portage from Pine Lake to Canoe Lake. This portage has been called, among other things, the worst portage in the BWCAW. It climbs almost steadily en route to Canoe Lake, except when going through a swamp. After completing this carry, many paddlers will be ready to stop for the day, either on Canoe Lake or adjoining Alder Lake. Alder Lake can be reached by a 22-rod portage. Each lake has several campsites and good fishing for walleye, northern pike, and smallmouth bass. Only Alder Lake has a lake trout population. Motors are allowed on both lakes.

Leave Alder Lake by the 48-rod portage to East Bearskin Lake. Then portage 85 rods to Flour Lake, where Flour Lake Campground is located. This can be the end of the journey, unless the trip vehicle is at the parking lot on Hungry Jack Lake. In that case, one more portage and one more hour of paddling will be needed.

There are two scenic overlooks to be enjoyed in this area. Honeymoon Bluff is accessed from County Road 66 at a trail that begins near the entrance to Flour Lake Campground. The trail leads to the top of a bluff, which offers a thrilling overlook of Hungry Jack Lake, with Bearskin Lake spreading out in the background. Caribou Rock offers another panoramic overlook of Bearskin Lake. This trail starts near the end of County Road 65 and is also the trailhead for the Caribou Rock Hiking Trail.

Access: Start at U.S. Highway 61 at Grand Marais and drive 30 miles north on the Gunflint Trail. Turn right on County Road 65 (Hungry Jack Road) and drive approximately 2 miles to the access for Hungry Jack Lake. Portage to Bearskin Lake and paddle to the 80-rod portage to Duncan Lake.

Shuttle: None.

Camping: Flour Lake Campground. A fee is charged and reservations are recommended.

Food, gas, lodging: Grand Marais.

For more information: Gunflint Ranger District (see appendix).

Daniels Lake to Clearwater Lake

Entry point: 61

Character: This is a semi–base camp trip where fishing and exploring are more important than the distance covered. The number of lakes is kept to a minimum, leaving time to explore the length and breadth of the few large lakes encountered. Two entry points are breached and a permit must be acquired for each one. For this reason this trip will usually be most available after September 15 when permits can be filled out right on the lakes from the boxes placed at the access points. Fishing opportunities abound, and campers at Flour Lake Campground or East Bearskin Lake Campground will be able to use their main campsite for one or more nights while on the trip. The portages north from East Bearskin Lake are steep and rugged.

Length: 18 miles minimum distance; several times longer if the lakes are thoroughly explored.

Average run time: 2 to 5 days, with fishing and sightseeing.

Skill level: Beginner.

Hazards: High wind and motorboats on some lakes.

Maps: USGS: Hungry Jack Lake, Clearwater Lake.

The paddling: Like many other access points in this region, Daniels Lake has no direct road access. Start two lakes and two portages away at Hungry Jack Lake. Paddle the length of Hungry Jack Lake and Bearskin Lake, find the 60-rod Daniels Lake Portage in the northwest corner, and finally enter your access point.

Daniels Lake is most often used as a gateway to Rose Lake or to Rove Lake and the Voyageurs route. On this trip, however, time will be spent just exploring the lake and fishing. Daniels Lake covers 529 acres, is 90 feet deep in spots, and is nearly 3 miles long. Lake trout like this deep, cool lake, as do northern pike and smallmouth bass. Find fish by trolling a spoon behind the canoe while paddling the lake. If a lake trout hits the spoon, stop and cast a while, letting the spoon sink for a minute or more before starting the retrieve. Northern pike and smallmouth bass are more apt to be in shallow water near the shoreline. Live bait and crank baits are often used in this lake for these two species.

The first day can be spent at Daniels Lake. Paddle to the north end along the west shoreline, cross the lake, and paddle back south again along the east shoreline. Then portage to Bearskin Lake and into Hungry Jack Lake, arriving just in time to camp at Flour Lake. This is especially convenient if you already have a camp set up.

The next day head south from Flour Lake to the 117-rod portage to Aspen Lake. Aspen Lake is a 95-rod portage from East Bearskin Lake. It has a campsite, also, and it is quite enjoyable to spend the second day fishing and exploring the three mentioned lakes. Then camp overnight at the East Bearskin Lake Campground. If there are no available sites that night, or after overnight camping, paddle approximately 3 miles to the east end of this lake and portage 115 rods to Moon Lake. Moon Lake has three campsites and is entirely inside the BWCAW. This lake covers 156 acres, is 30 feet deep, and has largemouth bass,

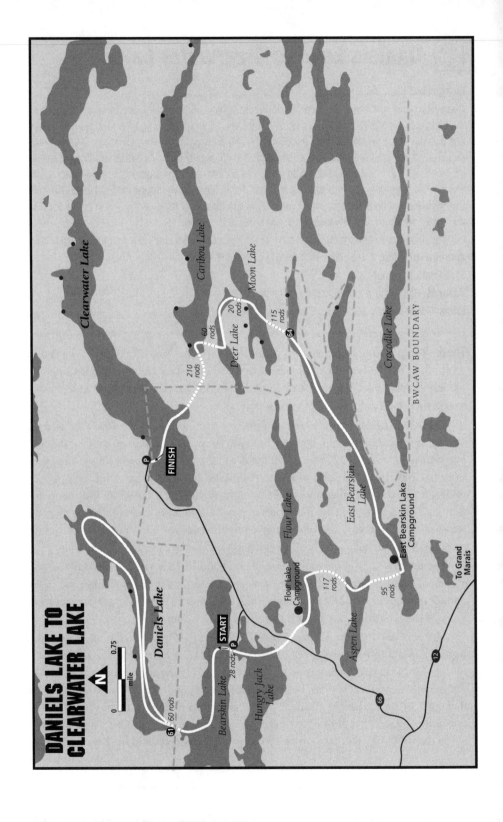

DANIELS LAKE TO CLEARWATER LAKE

N

0   0.75   mile

Clearwater Lake

Caribou Lake

Moon Lake

Deer Lake

20 rods

115 rods

64

60 rods

210 rods

P

FINISH

Daniels Lake

Crocodile Lake

BWCAW BOUNDARY

Flour Lake

East Bearskin Lake

Flour Lake Campground

East Bearskin Lake Campground

117 rods

95 rods

Aspen Lake

START

P

28 rods

Bearskin Lake

61   60 rods

Hungry Jack Lake

To Grand Marais

12

66

northern pike, walleye, and perch to offer the angler. It is worth some serious fishing effort. Leave Moon Lake by a 20-rod portage to Deer Lake. Deer Lake also has pike, largemouth bass, and walleye within its 83-acre basin.

Portage 60 rods from Deer Lake to narrow, 3.5-mile long Caribou Lake. Towering, picturesque bluffs backdrop the south bank. Northern pike, largemouth bass, and walleye live in this unusually shallow (six feet deep) lake. Five campsites are located on the north shore, none on the south shore. If time permits, a day or two can be spent fishing and exploring this beautiful waterway.

The next portage, from Caribou Lake to Clearwater Lake, is 210 rods. Clearwater Lake is the last lake of the trip. Any time remaining can be productively spent on these 1,537 acres of water, where lake trout enjoy the 130-foot depths and smallmouth bass are most likely to be along the rocky shoreline. The take-out point is at the west end, not far from the portage to Caribou Lake. Walk back to the trip vehicle, if necessary.

Access: Start at U.S. Highway 61 at Grand Marais, and drive 28 miles north on the Gunflint Trail. Turn right on County Road 66 (Clearwater Road), and drive approximately 3.5 miles to the access for Hungry Jack Lake. Portage to Bearskin Lake, and paddle to the 60-rod portage to Daniels Lake.

Shuttle: Approximately 2 miles.

Camping: Flour Lake Campground or East Bearskin Lake Campground. A fee is charged. Reservations are accepted at Flour Lake.

Food, gas, lodging: Grand Marais.

For more information: Gunflint Ranger District (see appendix).

41 Clearwater Lake Loop

Entry point: 62

Character: This region is probably the most scenic of the entire BWCAW. Deep blue-water lakes stretch for miles between spectacular bluffs. All the customary game fish can be caught, and one lake even has muskellunge. Most time will be spent paddling, but there are a few long portages. Motors are allowed on some of the lakes. Wind will probably be a consideration. Independence Day storm–affected area.

Length: 34 miles.

Average run time: 5 to 7 days, with fishing and sightseeing. Allow one day for a possible "wind day." Avid anglers might want 8 days or more for this trip.

Skill level: Beginner.

Hazards: Wind and motorboat wakes.

Maps: USGS: Hungry Jack Lake, Crocodile Lake, Pine Lake East, Pine Lake West.

The paddling: Launch the canoe at the public landing at the west end of 1,537-acre Clearwater Lake. Anglers will be interested in the lake trout that enjoy the 130-foot depths. Smallmouth bass are numerous, also, and most likely to be along the rocky shoreline. Fortunately, the canoe will be pointing east and will benefit from any prevailing westerly winds. Keep in mind that wind speeds are often diminished the first two hours of the morning. The early bird gets the wind-free trip.

If much fishing or sightseeing is done, the first day can be used up in just reaching the east end of the 6-mile-long lake. Fortunately, there is a campsite at the east end of the lake. It's a good place to rest up for the portage to be encountered the next morning.

The second day starts with a 215-rod, fairly rigorous portage to 715-acre, 120-foot-deep West Pike Lake. This lake is almost 4 miles long, and 500-foot bluffs bordering the lake make the paddling a memorable experience. Like Clearwater Lake, this long waterway has a good population of lake trout and smallmouth bass. There are several campsites along the north shore of West Pike Lake, if the lake is too good to leave immediately.

Exit West Pike Lake by a 177-rod portage to East Pike Lake. This is a fairly level portage, but don't be fooled into launching at the small pond about midway along the carry. It leads away from the portage trail. Initially, East Pike Lake is so narrow it resembles a river flowing between high bluffs. It widens out somewhat at the east end but is still characteristically narrow. It covers 496 acres, is 40 feet deep, and is one of the few lakes in the BWCAW that has a possible muskellunge population. Smallmouth bass also live here and are much more abundant. There are several campsites on this lake, and groups who didn't stop at West Pike Lake will probably want to stop here the second night.

Portage 180 rods to John Lake the next morning. This 169-acre, 20-foot-deep lake has walleyes, smallmouth bass, and northern pike to offer the angler. Leave John Lake by a short portage to Little John Lake, and then portage from Little John Lake to McFarland Lake. A stream connects these lakes, and in high water the canoe can be lined or paddled

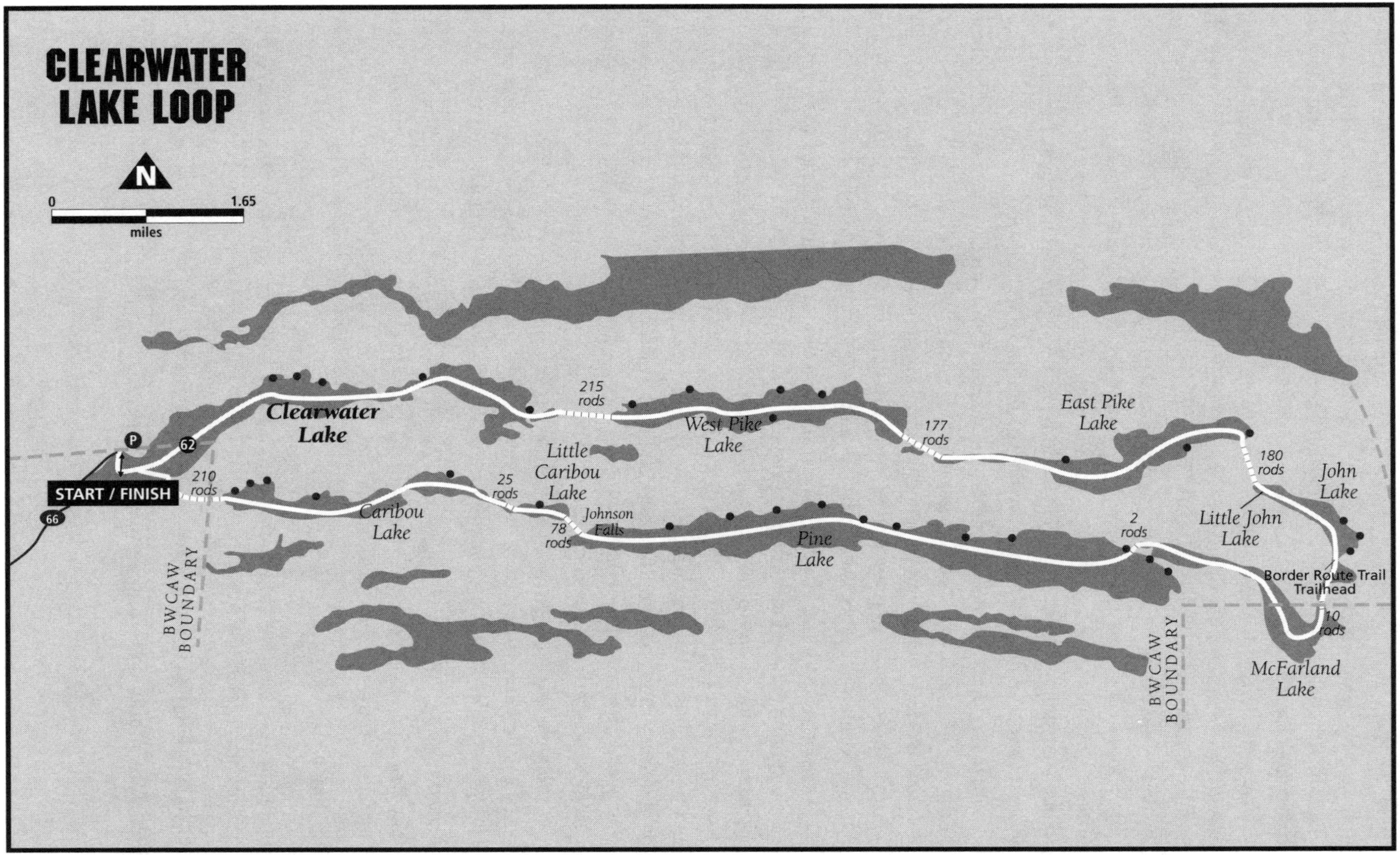

CLEARWATER LAKE LOOP

N

0   miles   1.65

P

62

66

START / FINISH

210 rods

Clearwater Lake

BWCAW BOUNDARY

Caribou Lake

25 rods

215 rods

Little Caribou Lake

Johnson Falls

78 rods

West Pike Lake

Pine Lake

177 rods

East Pike Lake

180 rods

2 rods

Little John Lake

John Lake

Border Route Trail Trailhead

10 rods

McFarland Lake

BWCAW BOUNDARY

down the short rapids connecting the lakes. McFarland Lake covers 384 acres, is 49 feet deep, and has good walleye fishing, along with a northern pike population. There are several campsites. The trailhead for the Border Route Trail starts at this lake, and there are three public boat accesses. People will probably be about.

Leave McFarland Lake by a short portage to imposing Pine Lake. This giant waterway covers 2,257 acres and has some water that is 113 feet deep. It will require approximately 8 miles of paddling from east to west. Pine Lake is well known for excellent walleye fishing and has lake trout and smallmouth bass, also. Most groups will want to stop over, possibly about halfway to the west end, to camp the third night. There are numerous campsites available. Most are located on the north shore, the south shore being too steep to provide enough platform area. High winds are a constant threat to canoeists, however, so keep close to shore. No motors are allowed on this lake.

Leave Pine Lake by the 78-rod portage to Little Caribou Lake, but take time to visit Johnson Falls first. It is one of the most impressive and unusual falls in the BWCAW. Find the small creek at the extreme west end of the lake, and follow the trail uphill to the falls. The falls spill cascades of white water 25 feet through a narrow rock gorge. After seeing it, no one considers the short walk to the falls and back a waste of their time.

The portage to Little Caribou Lake is mostly uphill and is considered to be rugged. The next portage from Little Caribou Lake to Caribou Lake is only 25 rods and fairly easy. There are several campsites on Caribou Lake, and it is an excellent place to camp and fish. Towering, picturesque bluffs backdrop the south bank. Northern pike, largemouth bass, and walleye live in this unusually shallow (five feet deep) lake. Five campsites are located on the north shore, none on the south shore. If time permits, a day or two can be spent fishing and exploring this beautiful waterway. See chapter 40, Daniels Lake to Clearwater Lake, for more information about these lakes.

Although two portages reach from Caribou Lake to Clearwater Lake, the west end portage is probably the easiest to negotiate. It is 210 rods long and fairly steep, however. Portage into Clearwater Lake, and head north across the lake to the take-out point.

Access: Start at Minnesota Highway 61 in Grand Marais, and drive north on the Gunflint Trail 28 miles to the intersection with County Road 66 (Clearwater Lake Road). Turn right and drive about 5 miles to the end of Clearwater Lake Road to Clearwater Lake.

Shuttle: None.

Camping: East Bearskin Lake Campground, Flour Lake Campground. Numerous campsites are along the canoe route.

Food, gas, lodging: Grand Marais.

For more information: Gunflint Ranger District (see appendix).

42 East Bearskin Lake Loop

Entry point: 64

Character: This route is intended for paddlers who enjoy a challenge. The longest portage in the eastern region of BWCAW, from Rove Lake to Rose Lake, is conquered. The majestic beauty of Rose Lake and its surroundings will heal any resentments about the difficulty of the portage from Rove Lake, however. Further, the other portages are not difficult, the scenery is magnificent, and fishing opportunities abound. After this trip nothing the boundary waters have to offer will be too rugged, and fond memories of the scenery and personal accomplishment will remain for many years. Independence Day storm–affected area.

Length: 26 miles.

Average run time: 3 to 7 days, depending on the experience and physical conditioning of the group, as well as the amount of time spent angling and sightseeing.

Skill level: Beginner.

Hazards: Wind, waves, storm-damaged trees (see introduction).

Maps: USGS: Hungry Jack Lake, Crocodile Lake.

The paddling: Carefully go over your gear and discard anything you positively don't need. On this route single-trip portages are almost mandatory. Put in at the public landing near the campground on East Bearskin Lake. Paddle along the north shoreline to find the bay that leads to the 115-rod portage to Moon Lake. Negotiate the north shoreline of Moon Lake to find the 20-rod portage to Deer Lake. The portage from Deer Lake to Caribou Lake is also found along the north shoreline. Caribou Lake is a convenient place to camp the first night. Paddle to the east end, and take one of the campgrounds near the 220-rod portage to Clearwater Lake. See chapter 40, Daniels Lake to Clearwater Lake for more information on these lakes.

Get a good night's rest because the portage to Clearwater Lake climbs over 150 feet before descending to Clearwater Lake. It starts as a steep slope, levels out somewhat, and descends another steep slope to the lakeshore. Head almost straight north from the Clearwater Lake access to find the 90-rod portage to Mountain Lake. While negotiating this portage, stop along the portage trail at the intersection of the Border Route Trail, leave the gear for awhile, and hike both north and south on the Border Trail to enjoy—and possibly photograph—some sensational overlooks of Mountain Lake.

Although it might be early in the day, consider stopping to camp on Mountain Lake to rest, fish, and enjoy the scenery. There are no more legal campsites until Rose Lake. Between Mountain Lake and Rose Lake lie 765 rods of portaging. Further, gigantic, 210-foot-deep Mountain Lake offers good fishing for lake trout. The dramatically steep shorelines above the deep blue water of the lake are captivating and relaxing. Rest well and gather your resources; tomorrow will bring the supreme challenge of the trip.

Portage 100 rods from Mountain Lake to Watap Lake, paddle this long, narrow lake to Rove Lake, conquer its length, and find the 665-rod "Long Portage" to Rose Lake. Even

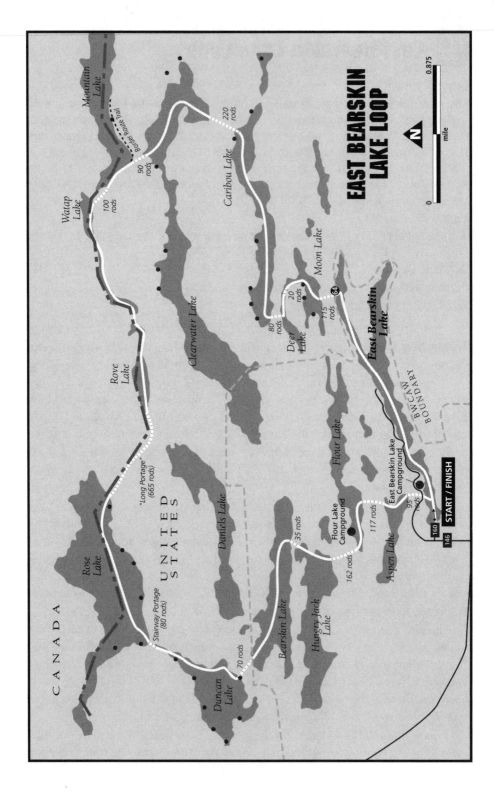

EAST BEARSKIN
LAKE LOOP

N

0   mile   0.875

CANADA

UNITED STATES

Mountain
Lake

Boat Route Trail

Watap
Lake

90
rods

100
rods

220
rods

Caribou Lake

Clearwater Lake

Moon Lake

Rove
Lake

Rose
Lake

"Long Portage"
(665 rods)

Stairway Portage
(80 rods)

Daniels Lake

Duncan
Lake

70 rods

Bearskin Lake

Hungry Jack
Lake

35 rods

Flour Lake

Flour Lake
Campground

162 rods

117 rods

Aspen Lake

95
rods

East Bearskin Lake
Campground

East Bearskin
Lake

64

20
rods

80
rods

115
rods

Deer
Lake

BWCAW
BOUNDARY

START / FINISH

160

146

though it is more than 2 miles long and starts out rough, most of it follows a smooth, ancient railroad bed on a downhill slope. Most groups can easily spend three to four hours on this portage, however.

After the Long Portage is behind, select one of the campsites on Rose Lake for rest, fishing, and sightseeing. Either of the campsites at the east end of the lake will be near the Border Lake Hiking Trail. Hiking along the trail will reveal dramatic overlooks of the lake. Photographers can shoot several rolls of film without duplicating a single exposure. Anglers can probably catch a few fish dinners from the walleye, smallmouth bass, and lake trout living in this 1,404-acre lake that has a maximum depth of 90 feet.

Leave Rose Lake by the 80-rod "Stairway Portage" to Duncan Lake. This has been called the most scenic portage in the BWCAW. It follows the creek connecting Rose Lake and Duncan Lake. A stairway has been built leading upward from Rose Lake to the Border Route Hiking Trail. Here, the Rose Lake Overlook looks down toward the Canadian shore of the lake. A beautiful waterfall is nearby. Farther along, the portage trail finally levels out somewhat and descends to Duncan Lake.

This can be the last day of the trip. Paddle and portage to Bearskin Lake, Hungry Jack Lake, Flour Lake, Aspen Lake, and end the trip at East Bearskin Lake. For more information about these lakes, see chapter 39, Daniels Lake Loop, and chapter 40, Daniels Lake to Clearwater Lake.

Access: Start at U.S. Highway 61 at Grand Marais, and drive approximately 26 miles north on the Gunflint Trail. Turn right on Forest Road 146, and drive to the East Bearskin Lake Campground. Follow the signs to the public boat landing or campsites.

Shuttle: None.

Camping: East Bearskin Lake Campground. A fee is charged. Numerous campsites are along the canoe route.

Food, gas, lodging: Grand Marais.

For more information: Gunflint Ranger District (see appendix).

Waterfall at Rose Lake.

43 Pine Lake Loop

Entry point: 68

Character: Pine Lake is an awesome sight. Its deep blue water stretches for almost 7 miles from east to west, and high bluffs line its shorelines. At the west end Johnson Falls, a 25-foot-high, boiling, smashing waterfall and white water chute, can be seen. This trip eventually leaves Pine Lake for a loop through several smaller, but unique, lakes and then returns to the west end again. Walleye fishing can be fantastic, and lake trout, northern pike, and smallmouth bass are available. Independence Day storm–affected area.

Length: 26 miles.

Average run time: 4 to 6 days, with time spent sightseeing and fishing.

Skill level: Beginner.

Hazards: Wind and waves.

Maps: USGS: Crocodile Lake, Pine Lake East, Pine Lake West.

The paddling: Launch the canoe from McFarland Lake and paddle west to the lift-over portage to Pine Lake. This giant waterway covers 2,257 acres and has some water that is 113 feet deep. It will require approximately 7.5 miles of paddling from east to west. Pine Lake is well known for excellent walleye fishing and has lake trout and smallmouth bass, also. There are numerous campsites available. Most are located on the north shore, the south shore being too steep to provide enough platform area. High winds are a constant threat to canoeists, however, so keep close to shore. No motors are allowed on this lake. Most groups will camp at the west end of Pine Lake the first night.

Leave Pine Lake by the 78-rod portage to Little Caribou Lake, but take time to visit Johnson Falls first. It is one of the most impressive and unusual falls in the BWCAW. Find the small creek at the extreme west end of the lake, and follow the trail uphill to the falls. The falls spill cascades of white water 25 feet through a narrow rock gorge. After seeing it, no one considers the short walk to the falls and back a waste of their time.

The portage to Little Caribou Lake is mostly uphill and is considered to be rugged. The next portage from Little Caribou Lake to Caribou Lake is only 25 rods and fairly easy. There are several campsites on Caribou Lake, and it is an excellent place to camp and fish. Towering, picturesque bluffs backdrop the south bank. Northern pike, largemouth bass, and walleye live in this unusually shallow lake. Five campsites are located on the north shore, none on the south shore. If time permits, a day or two can be spent fishing and exploring this beautiful waterway. See chapter 40, Daniels Lake to Clearwater Lake, for more information on these lakes.

Leave Caribou Lake at the 60-rod portage to Deer Lake. It is located at the extreme west end of the lake, along the south shore. Deer Lake has northern pike, largemouth bass, and walleye within its 83-acre basin. Leave Deer Lake by the 20-rod portage to Moon Lake. This portage is located at the east end of Deer Lake.

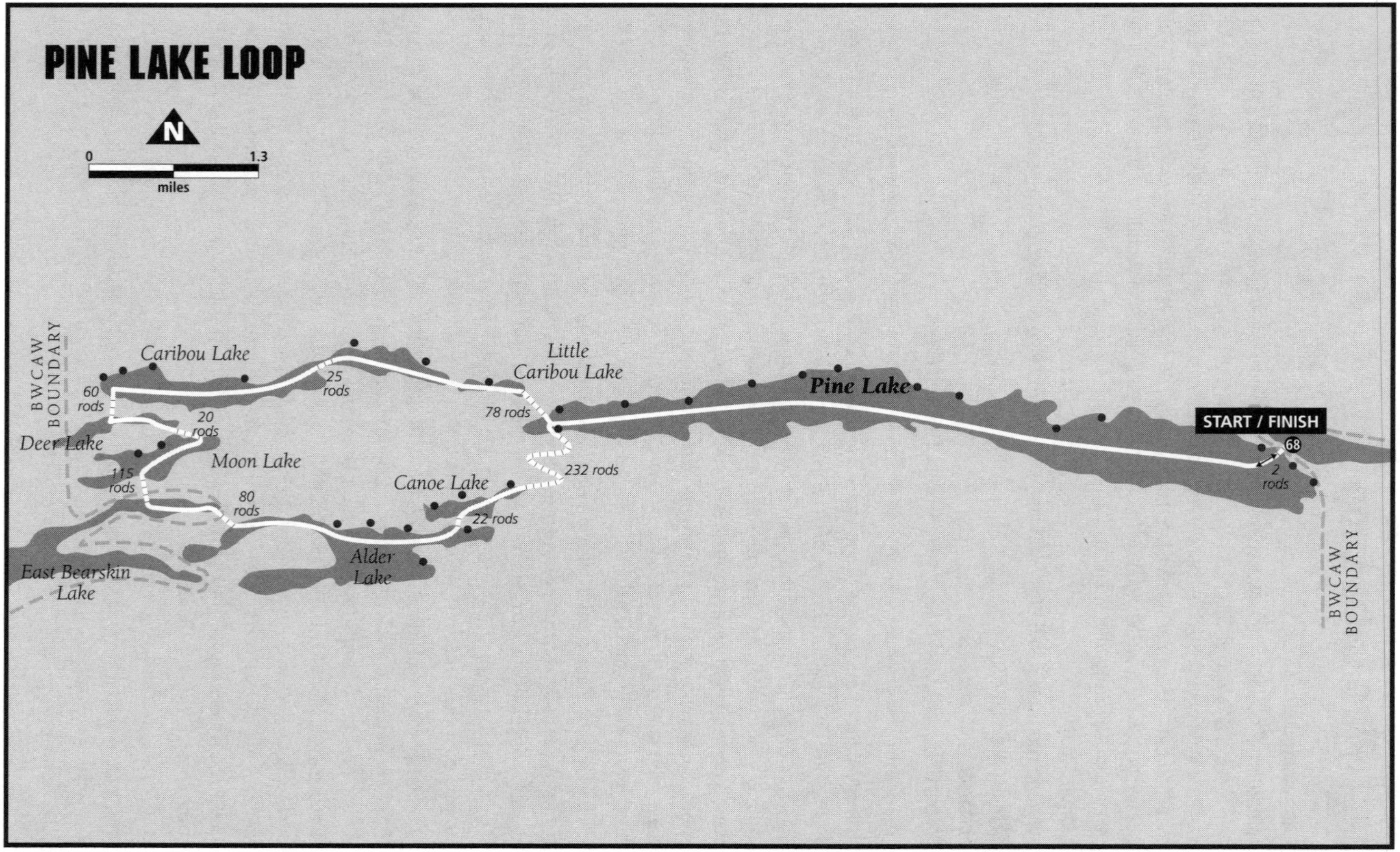

PINE LAKE LOOP

N

0 — 1.3
miles

BWCAW BOUNDARY

START / FINISH

68
2 rods

Pine Lake

Little
Caribou Lake

78 rods

232 rods

25
rods

Canoe Lake

22 rods

Alder
Lake

Caribou Lake

20
rods

Moon Lake

80
rods

60
rods

115
rods

Deer Lake

East Bearskin
Lake

BWCAW BOUNDARY

BWCAW
BOUNDARY

Moon Lake covers 156 acres, is 30 feet deep, and has largemouth bass, northern pike, walleye, and perch to offer the angler. It is worth some serious fishing effort. It has three campsites and is entirely inside the BWCAW.

Leave Moon Lake by the 115-rod portage to East Bearskin Lake. This large lake is an entry point and has East Bearskin Lake Campground situated at the west end. This run, however, just crosses the east end of the lake. After completing the portage to East Bearskin Lake, turn to the left (east) and paddle to the 80-rod portage to Alder Lake.

Alder Lake covers 342 acres, is 72 feet deep, and has excellent fishing. Walleye, northern pike, lake trout, and smallmouth bass live within its basin. Alder Lake is connected to Canoe Lake by a 22-rod portage from its north shore. Both lakes have several campsites and offer an excellent location for stopping over to get a good rest before starting the rigorous portage from Canoe Lake to Pine Lake.

The Canoe Lake to Pine Lake portage is 232 rods long and extremely steep and rugged. If it is taken at a slow pace, however, with no thought of completing it in an allotted time span, it isn't so bad. Figure on spending two to three hours on this portage and some strength will be left to set up camp somewhere on Pine Lake. Return to the put-in point on McFarland Lake by paddling along the opposite shore of Pine Lake from the outward bound journey. Each shoreline is distinctive and offers new vistas and fishing opportunities.

Access: Start at U.S. Highway 61 at Hovland, and follow the Arrowhead Trail (County Road 16) 18 miles north to McFarland Lake. Park at the McFarland Lake public landing. There is a short portage between McFarland Lake and Pine Lake.

Shuttle: None.

Camping: The McFarland Lake Camping Area. If this is full, camp at East Bearskin Lake or Flour Lake Campgrounds. A fee is charged and reservations are recommended.

Food, gas, lodging: Grand Marais.

For more information: Gunflint Ranger District (see appendix).

44 John Lake Loop

Entry point: 69

Character: This trip follows a section of the Voyageurs highway along the international border, retracing the route these hardy eighteenth-century French Canadians used as a highway to the rich fur trading territory in northwestern Canada. It leaves the Voyageurs highway at the west end of Mountain Lake and returns to the starting point through a series of waterways. Most of the lakes are long, narrow, and rimmed with high bluffs. Walleye and lake trout fishing could be superb, and the scenery is incomparable. Moose have been spotted on this trip. Independence Day storm–affected area.

Length: 27 miles.

Average run time: 4 to 6 days, with fishing and sightseeing.

Skill level: Beginner.

Hazards: High winds, motorboats on some lakes, storm-damaged trees (see introduction).

Maps: USGS: Hungry Jack Lake, Crocodile Lake, Pine Lake East, Pine Lake West.

The paddling: Launch on Little John Lake, and paddle north to the 10-rod portage to John Lake. Paddle along the east bank to the mouth of the Royal River, and turn right to enter it. Follow the river to Royal Lake.

Find the 160-rod portage from Royal Lake to North Fowl Lake and the Canadian border. North Fowl Lake covers 1,094 acres, is about 10 feet deep, and has walleye, northern pike, and smallmouth bass to interest the angler. Walleye fishing can be very productive in this bluff-lined border lake. Motors are permitted, so fishermen will probably be sighted.

Portage 132 rods from North Fowl Lake to Moose Lake. Moose Lake is divided almost equally by the international boundary. It covers 1,030 acres, is 118 feet deep, and shelters lake trout and walleye. Typical eastern BWCAW hill scenery surrounds this lake, also. Long portages at both ends of this lake discourage motor use, so it should be much quieter than North Fowl Lake. After almost 1 mile of portaging and more than 7 miles of paddling, most groups will be ready to camp on Moose Lake the first night. It has a half dozen campsites along the steep shoreline. Keep in mind it is against regulations to camp on the Canadian side of the lake, and fines are high for violations.

Avid angers or landscape photographers will probably want to spend a day or so on Moose Lake. Excellent lake trout fishing success has been recorded for this lake. Photographers can go home with stunning images. Leave Moose Lake by the 140-rod "Greater Cherry" Portage to Lower Lilly Lake. This portage is steep and rugged. From Lower Lilly Lake portage 40 rods to Upper Lilly Lake, and from this lake portage 90 rods to Mountain Lake.

Mountain Lake has multiple campsites and is a good location for a layover. This lake covers almost 2,000 acres and is 210 feet deep in one place. It is known for good lake trout fishing. Try to camp at the west end. After camp is set up, find the portage to Clearwater Lake, and hike up it to the Border Route Hiking Trail. There are several locations along the Border Route Hiking Trail where a spectacular view of Mountain Lake can be enjoyed.

JOHN LAKE LOOP

N

0   1.65
miles

CANADA

UNITED
STATES

Watap
Lake

Clearwater
Lake

Mountain Lake

Upper Lilly
Lake

90
rods

220
rods

Greater Cherry
Portage
(140 rods)

40
rods

90
rods

Border Route Hiking Trail

West Pike Lake

Moose Lake

132
rods

North Fowl Lake

South
Fowl Lake

160 rods

78 rods

Little
John
Lake

Royal
Lake

Arrowhead Trail

To Hovland

John Lake

START / FINISH

69

10 rods

2 rods

McFarland
Lake

Border Route Trail
Campground

BWCAW
BOUNDARY

East Pike Lake

Pine Lake

Little
Caribou Lake

80
rods

25
rods

Johnson Falls

Caribou
Lake

Hike 1 mile west of the portage trail or a shorter distance east of the portage trail to look down on the length of Mountain Lake from hundreds of feet above. Of course this is the portage route for next day, also, but it can be enjoyed more enthusiastically when unencumbered by the concerns of portaging.

Next morning portage 90 rods over the hill from Mountain Lake to Clearwater Lake. This lake has 1,537 acres of water. Lake trout hide in the 130-foot depths while smallmouth bass live mostly along the rocky shorelines. The west end of Clearwater Lake is outside the BWCAW, and motors are permitted on the entire lake. Paddle to the southeast shore of Clearwater Lake to find the 220-rod portage to Caribou Lake. If your energy level is low after clearing this portage, either Caribou Lake or Little Caribou Lake is an excellent location to camp and fish.

Caribou Lake is shallow, covers 497 acres, and has fishing for northern pike, largemouth bass, and walleye. There are several campsites available. When ready, portage from the east end of this lake to Little Caribou Lake. This lake also has largemouth bass and northern pike within its 85 acres of water. Leave little Caribou, and portage 80 rods to Pine Lake. If time permits, be sure to visit Johnson Falls. The short trail to the falls is located at the west end of the lake between the portage trails from Little Caribou Lake and Canoe Lake. Find the small creek at the extreme west end of the lake, and follow the trail uphill to the falls. It leads through a rock gorge to a 25-foot waterfall on an unnamed creek flowing into Pine Lake.

Pine Lake is a gigantic waterway, covering 2,257 acres. It has some water that is 113 feet deep. It will require approximately 7.5 miles of paddling from west to east. Pine Lake is well known for excellent walleye fishing and has lake trout and smallmouth bass, also. The trip could be ended this day but there are numerous campsites available if the fish are biting well enough to warrant another night on the trip. Most are located on the north shore, the south shore being too steep to provide enough platform area. High winds are a constant threat to canoeists; however, no motors are allowed.

Paddle to the east end of Pine Lake, find the portage to McFarland Lake, and follow this lake to the put-in point on Little John Lake.

Access: Start at U.S. Highway 61 at Hovland, and follow the Arrowhead Trail (County Road 16) 18 miles north to McFarland Lake. Park at the parking lot near the bridge on the stream connecting McFarland Lake and Little John Lake.

Shuttle: None.

Camping: McFarland Lake Camping Area (no fee), East Bearskin Lake Campground, Flour Lake Campground (a fee is charged). Reservations are allowed at Flour Lake. There are numerous campsites along the canoe route.

Food, gas, lodging: Grand Marais.

For more information: Gunflint Ranger District (see appendix).

45 North Fowl Lake to Bearskin Lake

Entry points: 69, 70

Character: This trip accesses the North Fowl Lake entry point through Little John Lake and John Lake. Then it heads west along the Voyageurs Trail. Most of the lakes are large; they are much longer than they are wide and have few or no islands. They look, one paddler remarked, like they were created for the canoe tripper to use. They are also kind to fishermen. All of the common Boundary Waters game fish are found in these lakes, and there is a stream trout lake just over the hill from Mountain Lake. This trip does not return to the put-in point, so a shuttle is necessary. Independence Day storm–affected area.

Length: 25 miles.

Average run time: 4 to 6 days, with fishing and sightseeing.

Skill level: Beginner.

Hazards: Wind, waves, and storm-damaged trees (see introduction).

Maps: USGS: Hungry Jack Lake, Crocodile Lake, Pine Lake East, Pine Lake West.

The paddling: Launch on Little John Lake, and paddle north to the 10-rod portage to John Lake. Continue to the mouth of the Royal River, and follow the river to Royal Lake.

Find and negotiate the 160-rod portage from Royal Lake to North Fowl Lake. North Fowl Lake covers 1,094 acres, is about 10 feet deep, and has walleye, northern pike, and smallmouth bass to interest the angler. Walleye fishing can be very productive in this bluff-lined border lake. Motors are permitted.

Portage 132 rods from North Fowl Lake to isolated and picturesque Moose Lake. It covers 1,030 acres, is 118 feet deep, and shelters lake trout and walleye. After almost 1 mile of portaging and more than 7 miles of paddling behind them, most groups will be ready to camp. Moose Lake has a half dozen campsites along the steep shoreline.

Avid angers or landscape photographers will probably want to spend a day or so on Moose Lake. Excellent lake trout fishing success has been recorded for this lake. Photographers can go home with stunning images. Leave Moose Lake by the 140-rod "Greater Cherry" Portage to Lower Lilly Lake. This portage is steep and rugged. From Lower Lilly Lake paddle into Upper Lilly Lake and portage 40 rods to Fan Lake, and from Fan Lake portage 90 rods to Mountain Lake.

Mountain Lake has multiple campsites and is a good location for a layover. There are no more designated campsites until Daniels Lake. This lake covers almost 2,000 acres and is 210 feet deep in one place. It is known for good lake trout fishing. Although not part of the trip, Pemmican Lake, a good brook trout lake, is a short hike or portage from the south bank, also. To see some spectacular scenery, find the portage trail to Clearwater Lake, and hike up to the Border Route Hiking Trail. There are several locations along the trail where overlooks of the Mountain Lake basin can be enjoyed.

NORTH FOWL LAKE
TO BEARSKIN LAKE

N

0 ___ 2.0
miles

North Fowl Lake

South Fowl Lake

Moose Portage (132 rods)

110 rods

Royal Lake

16

Moose Lake

10 rods

69 rods

CANADA

John Lake

START

McParland Lake

Little John Lake

UNITED STATES

90 rods

Lilly Lakes

Greater Cherry Portage (140 rods)

Fan Lake

Pemmican Lake

Pine Lake

West Pike Lake

Mountain Lake

Clearwater Lake Portage

100 rods

Watap Lake

Clearwater Lake

Rove Lake

264 rods

Daniels Lake

Bearskin Lake

FINISH

Portage 100 rods to Watap Lake to continue the trip. This lake is about 2 miles long, 45 feet deep, bordered by steep hills, and has northern pike and smallmouth bass fishing. Leave Watap Lake by paddling into Rove Lake. No portage is necessary.

Rove Lake is about 1 mile long. Steep hills border the south shore. It is 30 feet deep and holds smallmouth bass and northern pike.

At Rove Lake turn south on the 264-rod portage to Daniels Lake. This portage starts out as part of the "Long Portage" to Rose Lake. The trail forks and the right fork stretches to Rose Lake. Take the left fork. Daniels Lake covers 529 acres and is nearly 3 miles long and 90 feet deep. Lake trout inhabit this deep, cool lake, as do northern pike and smallmouth bass. The first campsite on Daniels Lake is found near the portage trail. Three others are situated on the west shoreline near the center of the lake.

Paddle the length of Daniels Lake to find the portage to Bearskin Lake at the south end. Take out at Bearskin Lake to end the trip.

Access: Start at U.S. Highway 61 at Hovland, and follow the Arrowhead Trail (County Road 16) 18 miles north to McFarland Lake. Park at the parking lot near the bridge on the stream connecting McFarland Lake and Little John Lake.

Shuttle: Approximately 60 miles one way. 3 hours.

Camping: McFarland Lake Camping Area, Flour Lake Campground. A fee is charged. Reservations are accepted.

Food, gas, lodging: Grand Marais.

For more information: Gunflint Ranger District (see appendix).

Introduction to the Park

Voyageurs National Park is found in northeastern Minnesota, near the town of International Falls. It stretches for 56 miles along the Canadian border. The park lies in the southern portion of the Canadian Shield and is composed of some of the oldest exposed rock formations in the world. At least four times in the past 1 million years, glaciers, 2 miles thick, plowed through the area. Their action exposed pockmarked rock formations 2.7 billion years old. Hundreds of ponds, lakes, and streams now nestle in these depressions.

Water dominates the Voyageurs National Park landscape. Within its boundaries more than thirty lakes fill glacier-carved lake basins. Four of the lakes—Rainy Lake, Kabetogama Lake, Namakan Lake, and Sand Point Lake—make up most of the park. The four big lakes are dotted with 500 rock islands that are mostly heavily forested. The Kabetogama Peninsula makes up most of the land mass in the park.

The Kabetogama Peninsula is almost 26 miles long and up to 7 miles wide. It is surrounded by the four large lakes of the park and contains dozens of inland ponds and lakes. Some of these inland lakes are a mile long.

Voyageurs National Park was named after the Voyageurs, French-Canadian canoemen who moved beaver and other pelts and trade goods between Montreal and the Canadian northwest. Some of the most colorful people in history, these men paddled 25-foot birchbark canoes along the Voyageurs Highway, carrying goods to trade with the Indians for fur pelts. The Voyageurs are reputed to have paddled fifteen to eighteen hours per day, hand-carrying 180 to 270 pounds per man, per carry, over the portages. Theirs was a highly profitable business, returning twenty fold on the investment for the fur companies. For several generations the fur trade was the continent's chief industry. The route the Voyageurs traveled became so established that a 1763 treaty ending the American Revolution specified that the boundary between the United States and Canada would follow their "customary waterway."

The Voyageurs' canoe is gone now, but it's been replaced by canoes, kayaks, motorboats, houseboats, and seaplanes, as thousands of visitors flock to Voyageurs National Park each year.

Voyageurs National Park is a relatively recent addition to the national park system, having been established on April 8, 1975. It is the only national park contained within the arctic watershed. The park, with fewer than 8 miles of paved roads in its 218,000 acres, boasts 83,789 acres of water.

History of Economic Activity in the Park

Logging began in the area in about 1870, after the white pine in Michigan and Wisconsin was depleted. By 1907 lumbermen began cutting the white pine in what is now the southern part of Voyageurs National Park. Within four years dams at the mouth of Rainy River,

Kettle Falls, and Squirrel Falls were completed, providing cheap power for sawmills. This inspired the logging companies to complete the cutting of the white pine on the Kabetogama Peninsula.

In 1893 gold prospector George W. Davis discovered traces of gold as he was panning quartz on Little American Island in Rainy Lake. After the news spread a gold rush was on, producing over a dozen mines on nearby islands, as well as a boomtown. Rainy Lake City was a classic tent city that evolved into a boomtown, with all the color and hazards of a Wild West counterpart. The gold fever only lasted for six years, but it brought people into the area. Some stayed and worked in the burgeoning logging industry and at other enterprises in the area.

Armstrong Fish Company, a Canadian firm, began commercial fishing in Rainy Lake in 1898. Originally the fishermen sought sturgeon. Six feet long with weights up to 250 pounds, the sturgeon supplied considerable fish flesh, but their eggs were even more valuable for caviar. The eggs were salted, placed in barrels, and shipped to processing firms in Europe and the eastern United States. At the height of the industry, in 1895, four million pounds of sturgeon were processed, producing 200,000 pounds of caviar. Commercial fishing for sturgeon continued until 1914, when most of the sturgeon had been taken out of the lakes.

Commercial fishing was still profitable, however, and about sixty fishermen netted walleye, northern pike, whitefish, cisco, and burbot from area waters. The catch was iced and sold in seventy-pound boxes at Kettle Falls to buyers who came to bid for them. About 350,000 pounds of fish were sold annually through this industry.

A blueberry industry also flourished for a short time. Local Indians would pick the berries and sell them to a store located on Dryweed Island.

The Depression all but halted the economic activity in the area, though, and the last log was sluiced through the Kettle Falls Dam in 1937. Logging, mining, and commercial fishing was gradually replaced by the tourist industry.

A serious attempt to establish the area as a national park began in the 1960s. Congress authorized the park in 1971, and it was established in 1975 after the state deeded its land to the park. Now emphasis is on preserving the park and restoring it to its original state. The logging roads are slowly disappearing into stands of aspen and existing structures are being reclaimed by nature. Nature is being allowed to reclaim the park.

Fishing

Hunting and trapping are illegal activities in the park but fishing is allowed, and most visitors expect to spend some time fishing, while many come primarily for fishing. Walleyes are the most sought after fish, but anglers also target lake trout, smallmouth bass, northern pike, and yellow perch. Muskies are found in the Shoepack Lakes in the interior of the Kabetogama Peninsula.

In demand more for their succulent fillets than a hard-sustained fight, walleyes are taken by jigging with leadhead jigs baited with minnows, leeches, or nightcrawlers. Minnows are used early and late in the season; nightcrawlers and leeches are most effective when the water is warmer. A slip sinker rig and bait is also widely used, and crankbaits can be effective in shallow-to-medium depths.

Early in the season walleyes are found in 5 to 15 feet of water, but as the water warms they work deeper. It is not unusual to find them in 30 to 40 feet of water in midsummer, although they are commonly in about 20 feet depths. Finding active fish is the most difficult part of catching a shore lunch of fillets. Many anglers slowly troll until they get a bite, and then they anchor and work the area thoroughly. Walleyes are schooling fish, and if one bites, others are probably located nearby.

Smallmouth bass are found in most lakes in the park. They are usually located along rocky banks in fairly shallow water and at the mouth of streams, coves, bays, and reefs. They can be caught with the same rigs used for walleyes but are also susceptible to artificial plugs and spinners cast against a shoreline or trolled over a weed bed.

Northern pike can be found almost anywhere, usually in shallow water and often near a weed bed. They can be taken with live bait, but bright colored spoons as well as spinners and crankbaits are also very effective.

Muskies share many characteristics with the northern pike, except they grow larger and don't seem to be so eager to bite. The best fishing for muskies is in the Shoepack Lakes far inland in the Kabetogama Peninsula. The Shoepacks can only be reached after an extremely long, bushwhacking portage following a compass heading—no portage trail is maintained—or by hiking in and using a Park Service boat or canoe kept on the lake just for this purpose. Muskies are usually caught on large bucktail spinners and spoons, although they also will bite on minnows and sometimes leeches and nightcrawlers.

Yellow perch are widespread and can be taken by fishing with live bait around weed beds.

Lake trout are found in some inland lakes. They are usually found in deep water and will bite on heavy jigs baited with strips of fish or plastic tails, fished vertically at depths from 35 to 100 feet or more. Spoons are vertically jigged in deep water to take lakers, also. In spring and fall, when they are in shallow water, lake trout can be taken by casting spoons or crankbaits.

Climate

Ice-out in Voyageurs National Park is usually complete around May 1. At that time daytime temperatures average 55° to 60° and nighttime temperatures fall to the high to mid 30s. Then temperatures rise steadily until in late July daytime temperatures are in the high 70s and nighttime temperatures average in the mid 50s. August temperatures are lower than July, and by September daytime temperatures can average in the mid 60s and nighttime in the mid 40s.

Camping

More than 215 campsites are scattered around the park, accessible only by air or water. The campsites are found on all of the four large lakes and several of the small lakes in the Kabetogama Peninsula. The campsites are marked with Voyageurs National Park signs and are classified as tent, houseboat, or day-use sites. No fee is charged and no reservations are needed.

All surface water in the park should be treated or boiled for 5 minutes before using for cooking or drinking. Use the pit toilets provided at the campsites, or bury all human waste in a shallow cat hole at least 150 feet from the lake.

There are two state campgrounds bordering the park. Chief Woodenfrog State Campground is located near the west end of Kabetogama Lake, while Ash River State Campground is located near the east end. Both have running water and toilet facilities and are accessible by road. A fee is charged.

There are also several private campgrounds and some resorts in the area that offer camping. Some are full-service campgrounds.

From May through August deerflies, mosquitoes, gnats, and blackflies can be a nuisance or—in extreme cases, for short periods—a health hazard to unprepared paddlers. Usually these insects aren't a factor when out on the lake. However, biting insects are almost sure to be a nuisance on trips to the inland lakes of the Kabetogama Peninsula. Be prepared with plenty of repellent and loose fitting clothing. Head nets and complete suits of mesh for warding off insects are available commercially and should be considered by people unusually sensitive to insect bites. In camp wear loose fitting, light colored clothing, and always have a container of insect repellent along. Head nets are easy to take along and can be helpful at times. Make sure the insect netting on the tent is in good repair.

Boating

Park visitors travel by motorboat, canoe, kayak, or houseboat. Each boater must comply with United States Coast Guard (USCG) regulations and have a wearable PFD (personal flotation device) aboard and readily accessible.

Along main travel routes a numbered buoy system guides boaters and marks navigational hazards. The red nun buoys are placed on the right side of the channel, and the green can buoys are placed on the left when going up stream or up lake. All of the lakes flow toward Kettle Falls except Rainy Lake, which flows away from the falls. Boats heading toward Kettle Falls on Rainy Lake should keep the nun buoys on the right. Boats heading to Kettle Falls from the other lakes should keep the nun buoys on the left. White rock markers with orange diamonds show where large rocks are. Outside the main travel routes most rocks and reefs are unmarked and therefore can be dangerous.

Maps of the park are available from McKenzie Map Company and Fisher Map Company (see appendix). USCG navigation maps are dispensed at the visitor centers. No one should attempt to navigate the park without a good map and compass.

A typical campsite in Voyageurs National Park.

The Park Service maintains boats and canoes on some interior lakes of the Kabetogama Peninsula. They are located on Locator Lake, Quill Lake, Cruiser Lake, Ek Lake, Little Shoepack Lake, Shoepack Lake, Brown Lake, and Peary Lake. The boats are available free of charge on a first come basis. Ask at the visitor centers for information on using the boats and arrangements for reaching the trailheads.

Public boat ramps and parking for vehicles are available at all of the park's visitor centers and at the two Minnesota State campgrounds, Chief Woodenfrog and Ash River. Watercraft can be rented or hired from private outfitters and resorts at the park's gateway communities: Ash River, Crane Lake, International Falls, and Kabetogama.

Visitor Centers and Contact Information

The park maintains three visitor centers. The Rainy Lake Visitor Center is open all year, while the Kabetogama Lake Visitor Center and Ash River Visitor Center are open seasonally. Information, maps, films, exhibits, and other visitor services are available at the visitor centers.

Superintendent
Voyageurs National Park
3131 Highway 53
International Falls, MN 56649-8904
(218) 283–9821

Rainy Lake Visitor Center
(218) 286–5258

Kabetogama Lake Visitor Center
(218) 875–2111

Ash River Visitor Center
(218) 374–3221

Crane Lake Ranger Station
(218) 993–2481

www.nps.gov/voya

Accommodations and Services

Overnight lodging, campgrounds, restaurants, boat rentals, and shuttle service are offered outside the park at private resorts on Rainy Lake, Kabetogama Lake, Ash River and Crane Lake. A park concessionaire at Kettle Falls offers lodging, a restaurant, boat rentals, boat fuel, and a mechanized portage between Rainy and Namakan Lakes for boats up to 21 feet. Facilities for special accessibility needs are offered at visitor centers. A cruise service runs daily from the Kabetogama Lake Visitor Center from mid-June to Labor Day.

Park Regulations

Hunting, archery, firearms, chainsaws, and fireworks are prohibited in the park. Off-road vehicles and personal watercraft are also prohibited. Pets must be on a leash no more than 6 feet long. Pets are not permitted on any trails or in the backcountry. All food, garbage, and cooking equipment must be in a secure place, safe from black bears. Only dead and downed wood may be used for campfires. Pack out all refuse. Cultural artifacts may not be disturbed or removed from the park. Do not trespass on private property in the park, stay at least 0.25 mile from bald eagle, osprey, and great blue heron nests. Quiet hours are from 10:00 P.M to 6:00 A.M.

National Park Service rangers enforce federal and state laws. U.S. Coast Guard boating regulations apply within the park, as do Minnesota state fishing and waterskiing regulations.

Getting to the Park

Voyageurs National Park is a six-hour drive from Minneapolis–Saint Paul, Minnesota, and a three-hour drive from Duluth, Minnesota. Most of the park's visitors arrive by way of U.S. Highway 53 from the south. Four roads lead to the park from US 53. County Road 23 heads north from Orr, joins County Road 24 at Buyck, and proceeds to the south shore of Crane Lake. North of County Road 23, County Road 129 (Ash River Trail) leaves US 53 and leads to the Kabetogama Narrows, where the Ash River Visitor Center is located. The Ash River State Campground is also accessible from this road. Three miles northwest of the Ash River turnoff on US 53, County Road 122 heads north. Chief Woodenfrog State Campground and the Kabetogama Lake Visitor Center are accessible from this road. US 53 continues north to International Falls, where the park headquarters is located. North of the park headquarters in downtown International Falls, US 53 intersects with Minnesota Highway 11. MN 11 leads 12 miles east to Island View and the Rainy Lake Visitor Center on Rainy Lake. Check with Canadian and U.S. Customs before crossing the international border. Custom services are available by water at Portage Bay on Sand Point Lake or Sand Bay on Rainy Lake. Custom services are available by road at the Crane Lake public landing or at the International Falls Bridge. Or contact:

U.S. Customs Service
Second Avenue
International Falls, MN 56649
(218) 283–2541

Revenue Canada
Customs, Trade & Administration
302 Scott Street
Fort Francis, Ontario P9A 1H1
(807) 274–3655

Circling the Kabetogama Peninsula

Character: This trip is all paddling on big water, except for two portages. Canoes must stay along the shoreline to avoid waves and motorboat wakes. Sea kayaks are more versatile on these waters. Explore islands and interconnected lakes. Visit historic and colorful Kettle Falls Hotel, accessible only by water or air. Tour gold mines from a short-lived 1890s gold rush. See a major herring gull/cormorant nesting area. The fishing is world class for walleye, northern pike, small-mouth bass, and crappies. Campsites are plentiful, and camping is allowed off designated campsites.

Length: 62 miles, minimum; much longer if exploring and fishing are part of the trip.

Average run time: 7 days.

Skill level: Beginner.

Hazards: Wind is a constant threat on the large stretches of open water. Motorboat wakes can be dangerously high, also.

Maps: Ash River NE, Cranberry Bay, Daley Bay, Island View, Kabetogama, Kempton Bay, Namakan Island, Soldier Point.

The paddling: Wind is a prime consideration on this route; the prevailing winds are from the northwest. This direction of travel takes advantage of the northwest wind by traveling in an easterly direction across Rainy Lake. It is the most windswept of the lakes traveled on this circuit. Study the map, then launch the canoe or kayak at Chief Woodenfrog State Campground and head north. Find the channel that leads to the 160-rod Gold Portage. Negotiate the portage and resume paddling on Black Bay to the vicinity of the Rainy Lake Visitor Center. Stop, if necessary, to get information or pop and resume paddling to the vicinity of Dryweed Island. About 12 miles have been covered. Stop for the night at one of several campsites. Walleye, northern pike, and bass can be caught around the shorelines and on the steep drop-offs in this area. Explore the gold mines on Little American Island; there is a rich history in the short-lived gold rush. Inquire at the visitors centers to learn about the history of the gold mines on Little American Island, or see the Rainy Lake chapter. There is also a gold mine shaft on Bushyhead Island, but the Park Service does not recommend exploring it.

After giving due consideration to the wind direction and speed, resume paddling the second morning in a southeasterly direction. Canoeists should follow the southern route between the islands, adjacent to the mainland. The northernmost route is most appropriate for sea kayaks. It is the shortest route, but apt to be hazardous if winds come up suddenly. The northern route is marked with buoys. Utilize the buoys as an aid to keeping oriented with your lake map. The can buoys are green and marked with uneven numbers. Can buoy #1 is located due south of Dryweed Island. The numbers get progressively larger as you move in an easterly, or upstream, direction. Can buoys are kept to the left-hand side of a canoe moving toward Kettle Falls. The nun buoys are red with even numbers. Nun buoys are placed on the right-hand side of a canoe heading uplake. This route heads uplake toward Kettle Falls.

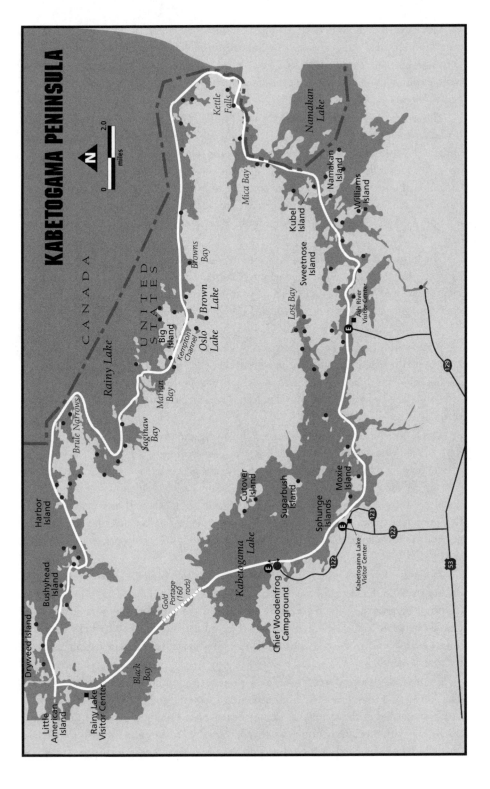

Move easterly among the islands to the vicinity of Harbor Island. There are several campsites. Lost Bay is the recommended overnight site for the second night. Some of the campsites have wooden boat docks. Islands can be explored, and the fishing is good for walleye and smallmouth bass. Eagles and loons are often seen. Fox Island is a busy herring gull/cormorant nesting area.

The second morning proceed east through Brule Narrows. Follow the buoys through Brule Narrows to nun buoy #32. Here, kayakers can proceed due south to Hitchcock Bay, but the canoeist should turn westerly and follow the south shore of Soldier Point into Saginaw Bay, especially if wind threatens. Turn due south at the first (unnamed) large bay encountered on Soldier Point. Proceed south to the vicinity of Marion Bay on the south shore of Saginaw Bay, and find a campsite. Campsites abound in this area, and suitable, unimproved sites are available. Fishing can be quite good for walleye, northern pike, or bass.

The third morning paddle east through Finlander Bay to Hitchcock Bay, and find the Kempton Channel. Follow the channel into Kempton Bay and continue east to the vicinity of Browns Bay and find a campsite. If your energy level is up, and time permits, consider portaging into Brown or Oslo Lake. The Park Service maintains a boat on Brown Lake. It can be reserved. Check at the Rainy Lake Visitor Center (see appendix).

While in this vicinity, be sure to explore Anderson Bay. It has been called the most scenic area on the peninsula. Smooth, bare bluffs that glow red and yellow in the setting sun rise 80 feet above the water. Picturesque rocky islands project from the water like frontier forts, and the water seems to be emerald green. There are no campgrounds in the bay, however.

The fourth morning continue easterly, following the mainland. Turn southerly into Kettle Channel and follow it to Kettle Falls Dam, where there is a portage. Most canoeists elect to do their own portaging to avoid delays, although a mechanical means of portaging is available, also. There is a fee for this service. Many paddlers enjoy staying overnight at the Kettle Falls Hotel, where all the luxuries of civilization can be enjoyed; there is a fee. Only two tent campsites are located close to the hotel. If they are occupied, it might be necessary to travel some distance to find a designated campsite, or camp at an undeveloped site.

Paddle south from Kettle Falls into Namakan Lake, following the channel indicated by the buoy system. Incidentally, the red buoys will still be located on the right-hand side of the canoe because the route is also upstream. Turn westerly (right) at nun buoy #14, and proceed between Namakan Island and Kubel Island past nun buoys #16 and #18. Continue to the vicinity of Sweetnose Island. Find a campsite and explore the fishing or any of the several islands.

The fifth day proceed westerly following the navigation buoys to Kabetogama Lake. The Ash River Visitor Center will be encountered near the end of the day. Several campsites are available in the vicinity of Round Bear Island. Fishing is good for walleye and perch. The sixth morning continue westerly toward the Kabetogama Lake Visitor Center. To avoid hazardous wind or motorboats, follow the south route, which passes south of

Deer Point Islands and Moxie Island. It will probably take most of the day to reach the vicinity of the visitor center. Consider camping on Sphunge Islands. The seventh morning follow the shoreline north to the Chief Woodenfrog Campground and the take-out point.

Access: Start at the junction of U.S. Highway 53 and County Road 122, 38 miles north of Orr, and follow CR 122 north for 5 miles to Chief Woodenfrog State Campground.

Shuttle: None.

Camping: Chief Woodenfrog State Campground.

Food, gas, lodging: Crane Lake.

For more information: Voyageurs National Park headquarters (see appendix).

Kabetogama Lake Loop

Character: Paddle a huge wilderness lake that is 15 miles long, 4 miles wide, covers 31 square miles, and has 78 miles of extremely irregular shoreline. Deep bays and 127 islands form an almost unending supply of new places to explore. The shoreline is heavily wooded; cliffs and rocky outcrops add visual interest. Visit a rock garden and the remains of historical commercial fishing ventures. Logging artifacts can be viewed. Fishing for walleyes should be first class, while northern pike, smallmouth bass, and perch are also abundant. The lake is usually busy with fishermen and sightseers from the resorts scattered along the west shore. Wind can be a factor in safe paddling.

Length: 33 miles, much longer if the bays are explored. This trip can be shortened—at most any point—by crossing to the opposite shore and heading back to the campground.

Average run time: 4 to 6 days. Allow more time for fishing and wind days.

Skill level: Beginner.

Hazards: High winds can come up suddenly. Stay close to islands or the mainland. Motorboat wakes can be powerful.

Maps: USGS: Kabetogama, Cranberry Bay, Daley Bay, Ash River.

The paddling: Get an early start and launch the canoe at the Chief Woodenfrog State Campground. Paddle north to pass west of Wood Duck Island and Bald Eagle Island. At Bald Eagle Island bend about 20 degrees northeast and continue this heading to the mainland of the Kabetogama Peninsula. Turn south to follow the shoreline and pass between Camel Back Island and the shoreline. Cutover Island will be straight ahead. This island was named as such because it was once completely logged off. It is the largest island in Kabetogama Lake. High cliffs on the northwest corner can be climbed for a good overview of the lake.

The largest natural rockslide in the lake is located off the northern shore on a small "island" connected to the main part of Cutover Island by a narrow arm of mud. The channel between the island and the mainland is an excellent walleye fishing location. Suitable campsites can be found on the west side; the east side shoreline is muddy and swampy. The small Shipwreck Islands directly west of Cutover Island are frequented by herring gulls and cormorants.

Clyde Creek tumbles down from the mainland in the channel between the island and the mainland. If time permits, it is worth exploring upstream to see a 4-foot-high balancing boulder left by a glacier, as well as beaver dams and houses. Perhaps the most unusual sight in this region, however, is the Ellsworth Rock Gardens. They are located on the mainland adjacent to Clyde Creek. This extensive rock garden was built by a Chicago contractor, Jack Ellsworth, for his own enjoyment between 1944 and 1965. It has statues and floral arrangements made from rocks, rock tables, and flower beds. A boat dock and marker leads to the maintained trail to the gardens.

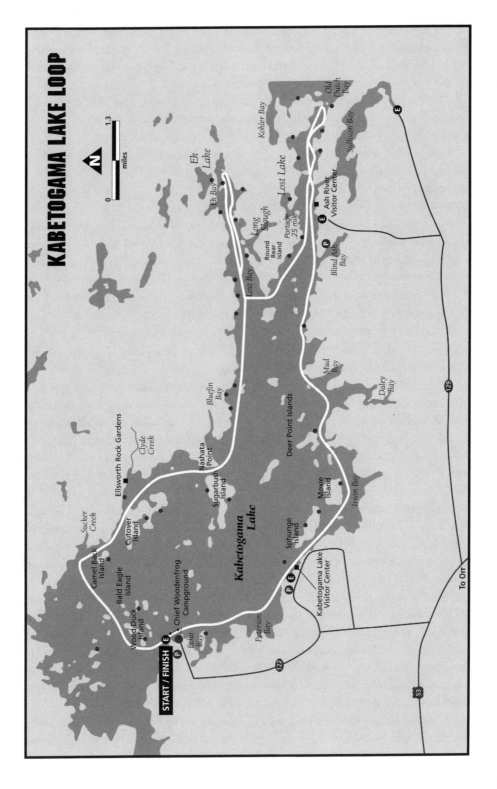

When it is time to leave this area, follow the shoreline south to Nashata Point and Sugarbush Island. Sugarbush Island was the site of an ancient Indian maple syrup making camp. This will be a good place to camp for the first night. The canoe campsite is located on the southwest shoreline. If your energy level is still up, consider exploring Nashata Point. It has remains of logging camps and hiking trails that lead inland. (The trip can be shortened to a weekend trip here by paddling west across the lake to the opposite shoreline, turning north, and returning to the Chief Woodenfrog Campground.)

Continue the trip by heading east, again following the shoreline. Bluefin Bay will be reached after paddling about 2 miles. This pretty little bay is a favorite of anglers, and fishermen may occupy the campsites. But it is an excellent place to wait out a wind day, because of the shorefishing opportunities.

Continue east into Lost Bay. Here in the bay's sheltered waters, exploring and fishing can be quite satisfying. The bay is about 3 miles long. Ek Bay is found near the tip of Lost Bay. Ek Bay and the adjoining Ek Lake were named after a commercial fisherman, Ed Ek, who netted fish here at one time.

Find a campsite for the second night. A campsite exists nearby on a peninsula in Lost Bay directly south of Ek Bay. In fact, all four of the developed canoe campsites in Lost Bay are located on the east shoreline, but there is a campsite on Ek Lake, also.

Consider negotiating the short portage into Ek Lake to find a quiet campground. The panfish in this lake are known to bite quite readily.

The third morning leave Lost Bay, paddle around Round Bear Island, and continue heading south. Round Bear Island got its name from a map error. It originally was named Round Bar Island because of a tavern that was located on the island. As an alternative to paddling around Round Bear Island, enter the mile-long Long Slough, paddle to its west end, and then portage about .25 mile to the open water of Kabetogama Lake. This will save about 3 miles of paddling and provide an opportunity to view several species of waterfowl.

Continue by heading south to the narrows between Dutch Island and the mainland. Can buoy #27 is placed here. This is the separation point between Kabetogama Lake and Namakan Lake. Reverse direction at can #27 and head north up the west shoreline. Find the campsite on the west shore about .75 mile north of can buoy #27. Another campsite is located on the east shore of Old Dutch Bay. Make camp and enjoy fishing for walleyes.

Next morning, the fourth morning of the trip, continue heading north. Sullivan Bay, which is the site of the mouth of the Ash River, offers a pleasant and interesting side trip, but it adds about 5 miles to the trip. If winds are at all favorable, the fourth day's trip can end at Deer Point Islands. The Ash River Visitor Center will be passed, and some paddlers may want to stop there for information. Boat traffic can be a real hazard from this location, back to the take-out point. Stay as far from the shoreline as safety considerations allow in order to avoid the traffic.

Camp on or near the Deer Point Islands, rise early the fifth morning, and easily reach the put-in point at Chief Woodenfrog Campground to end the trip. The Kabetogama collection of resorts and private cabins and the Kabetogama Lake Visitor Center are passed on the way to the campground. For protection from waves and wind, head west of Moxie Island through Irwin Bay and Duck Bay to pass though the channel between Sphunge Island and the mainland. End the trip at the Chief Woodenfrog Campground.

Access: Start at the junction of U.S. Highway 53 and County Road 122, 38 miles north of Orr, and follow CR 122 north for 5 miles to Chief Woodenfrog State Campground.

Shuttle: None.

Camping: Chief Woodenfrog State Campground.

Food, gas, lodging: Crane Lake, Orr, International Falls. Food and gas can be found at a general store at the corner of US 53 and CR 122. Resorts are in the area.

For more information: Voyageurs National Park headquarters (see appendix).

48 Rainy Lake

Character: Rainy Lake is a wild and scenic international waterway. More than a lake, it is an inland sea 60 miles long, 12 miles wide, and covering 350 square miles, with 2,500 miles of shoreline and 1,600 islands. The shoreline is wooded and rocky, and wooded islands are always in sight, jutting up from the deep blue water. From some of the bluffs and islands, the paddler can see the next day's destination, 8 to 10 miles away.

Rainy Lake has a capricious nature, mild and calm one minute, a white-water tempest the next. Danger, in the form of high winds and waves, is always a threat. It is safe enough, however, if the paddler stays close to shore, watches for the approach of storms or high winds, and is prepared to sit out windy days.

This route leads among the islands and bays of the south shore of the lake to Soldier Point, with a quick look at Saginaw Bay. A ghost town, gold mines, a point named after a military sortie, a fish camp, scenic bays, wildlife pastures, and a rookery can be seen. Fishing for walleye, northern pike, and smallmouth bass can be very successful. A short, 0.2-mile portage across Soldier Point is the only recommended portage, and it can be bypassed. Reverse the route to return to the put-in point.

Lengthen the trip by continuing to Kettle Falls or beyond. See chapter 46, Circling the Kabetogama Peninsula, for further information. Shuttle service is available to transport people and canoes from Kettle Falls to the Ash River Visitor Center on the mainland as an alternative to paddling back.

Length: 30 miles minimum for the round-trip; much longer if all the bays are explored.

Average run time: 4 days, longer with "wind days," fishing days, and intensive exploring days.

Skill level: Beginner.

Hazards: High winds and waves are always a possibility.

Maps: USGS: Soldier Point, Cranberry Bay, Island View.

The paddling: Wind is a prime consideration on this route; the prevailing winds are from the northwest. This direction of travel takes advantage of the northwest wind by traveling in an easterly direction across Rainy Lake. Study the map, consider the weather, and then launch the canoe or kayak at the Rainy Lake Visitor Center. Head due north through the Black Bay Narrows. Stop to explore and examine the remains of Rainy Lake City on the east shore of Black Bay Narrows. Then look west after passing Dove Island to locate Little American Island. A lookout tower is located on Dove Island. American Island is the nearest island northeast of this tower. Set a course to the south shore of this island. Circumnavigate the shoreline to the National Park Service dock. Land the canoe and find the improved walkway that leads to a gold mine.

George W. Davis, a prospector, discovered gold here in 1893. Word of the discovery spread like wildfire and by the spring of 1894 exploratory shafts and pits were excavated on all the nearby islands. At one time the area was called the Rainy Lake Gold Fields, and several hundred people created Rainy Lake City, with all the amenities and pitfalls of a Wild West town.

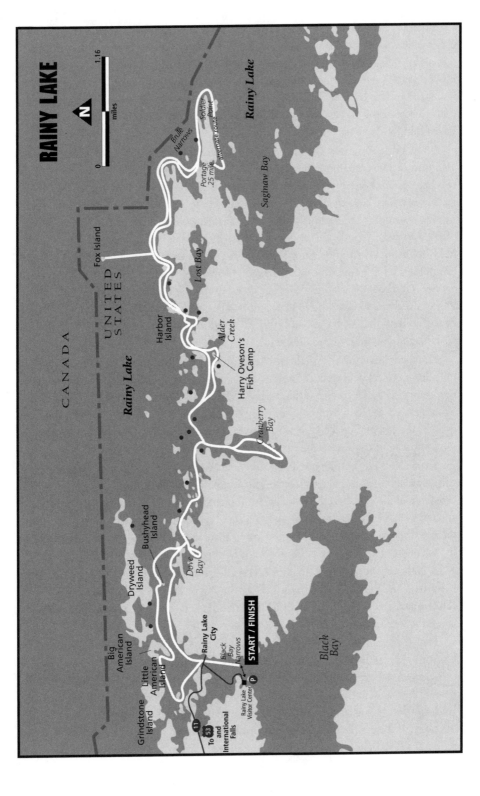

The Little American Island Mine was by far the most profitable, however. Even so, it only yielded about ten thousand dollars in gold bullion in seven years of stop-and-go production. A 0.25-mile improved walkway trail leads past the gold mine shafts and machinery and tailings piles. Plaques along the walkway keep visitors informed. Examine the mine shafts and machinery relics for an idea of what early gold mining was all about. A trail also leads to a bluff on the east shore of the island. It overlooks the other islands of the Rainy Lake Gold Fields.

Leave Little American Island and head northeast to Big American Island to see more gold mine activity. Examine the pits that are now mostly filled with dirt and water. If the weather is calm, head directly to the destination; it can be reached in twenty to thirty minutes. If waves are kicking up, head north to stay on the lee side of Grindstone Island before turning east to Big American Island. A green day marker sign is located on the south shore of Big American Island. The next stop is Bushyhead Island, where a prospector, "Bushy-head" Johnson, kept a mine going for two years, longer by far than any of the other mines, except for the Little American Island Mine. The shafts of this mine are visible, and the Park Service is in the process of restoring safe access to the mine and making it available to visitors. Bushyhead Island is more than a mile due east of Big American Island. On windy days stay along the south shore of Dryweed Island to get as close as possible to Bushyhead Island before heading south to reach it.

Head southeast from Bushyhead Island toward Dove Bay. Dove Bay is more than 0.5 mile deep. A long peninsula and three islands guard the entrance to this bay, making it a well-protected haven in case of high winds. The south shore is marshy, and feeding deer are often seen in the morning or evening. A Voyageurs National Park sign on the shore denotes the east end of the Black Bay Beaver Pond Hiking Trail. Fishing can be good for northern pike in the shallow bay.

From Dove Bay continue to head east. Stay between the islands and the mainland. If time is available for fishing, walleye and smallmouth bass hold around the drop-off on the shorelines of the islands and mainland. Continue this course to Cranberry Bay. Campsites abound in this area, but unless it is getting late, press on to the Alder Creek site to divide the trip distance evenly. After setting up camp there should be time for fishing and exploring Cranberry Bay. The bay offers good northern pike fishing.

A 200-ton, white, round, smooth boulder left by a glacier sits in the mouth of Cranberry Bay. The bay is also the site for the beginning of the Chain of Lakes route into the Kabetogama Peninsula. See chapter 51, Chain of Lakes, for more information on how to access the interior lakes.

Depart the campsite the second morning, and head east to find the island where Harry Oveson's fish camp buildings still stand; the bright green buildings can be readily seen. Oveson was one of the last commercial fishermen to work in the park. Watch along the marshy shorelines in this area for feeding whitetail deer. If it is windy, stay along the mainland shoreline. Cross the mouth of Lost Bay, and head between Harbor Island and the mainland. If there is time for exploring, Lost Bay is an interesting location. It is dotted with numerous islands, and the shoreline has extensive marshy areas. Eagles, ducks, geese, and herons congregate here. Fishermen work the bay for northern pike. It is ironic that the narrow strip of land between Lost Bay and Saginaw Bay is too wet and marshy to allow summer travel. Otherwise, it would be a quick portage to Saginaw Bay, saving many miles of paddling and bypassing the rough water usually found in the Brule Narrows and off the tip of Soldier Point.

Continue to follow the mainland shoreline toward the Brule Narrows. To avoid rough water follow the shoreline around the unnamed peninsula jutting out into Rainy Lake, and continue to follow it south into the first bay.

This bay is sheltered and, if need be, a good place to wait out windy weather. Otherwise continue forward to eventually enter the Brule Narrows. The narrows are usually rough; stay close to the shoreline in the event of a rollover. Eventually, Soldier Point will be reached.

Soldier Point is over 2 miles long and was a campsite for Canadian Colonel Garnet Wolseley and a force of 1,400 men who were sent here in 1870 to suppress a rebellion by Metis leader Louis Riel.

End the trip here, or continue around the tip of Soldier Point for the adventure of riding the waves on what is potentially the roughest water in Rainy Lake. Motorboats roar through here at top speed and huge houseboats chug through this narrow waterway, making the paddler feel very small and defenseless.

If these hazards are overwhelming, there is an alternative to paddling around the tip of Soldier Point. A seldom-used, short portage across the point can be used to gain the security of Saginaw Bay: It is located south of the first large island encountered after leaving the bay at the base of the point. Cross into Saginaw Bay, and find a campsite and rest up. This is the end of the trip. Reverse the route to return to the Rainy Lake Visitor Center.

On the way back, if the weather permits, consider paddling about 1.25 mile north of the Brule Narrows area to view the herring gull and cormorant nesting area on Fox Island.

Access: From the junction of U.S. Highway 53 and Minnesota Highway 11 in International Falls, turn east and follow MN 11 for 12 miles to the Rainy Lake Visitor Center.

Shuttle: None.

Camping: Chief Woodenfrog State Campground.

Food, gas, lodging: International Falls.

For more information: Voyageurs National Park headquarters (see appendix).

49 Namakan Lake

Character: Paddle on a huge, crescent-shaped lake that is 17 miles long and 3 miles wide but is less windswept than most lakes of Voyageurs National Park. Visit scenic islands with interesting historical significance. Enjoy the rugged beauty of forested rock islands. See a historical, thriving hotel that has no roads leading to it. Enjoy the rare, breathtaking beauty of Namakan Narrows. See Indian pictographs. The first and last days' paddling will be in a section of lake that resembles a river. During the rest of the trip the considerable size of the lake can be seen, most of it in Canada.

Length: 46 miles minimum, longer with side trips for exploring or fishing.

Average run time: 6 days, longer for "wind days," sightseeing, or fishing.

Skill level: Beginner.

Hazards: Wind and motorboats.

Maps: USGS: Hale Bay, Red Horse Bay, Namakan Island, Kettle Falls, Ash River.

The paddling: Launch the canoe at the Ash River Visitor Center and head west. Can buoy #31 lies directly north of the visitor center. Set the course directly east from this buoy to follow the channel past Sullivan Bay. Follow the buoys southeast to pass between the peninsula jutting from the Kabetogama Peninsula shore and the unnamed island lying just off-shore. Can buoy #27 is located at the mouth of Old Dutch Bay and is the division between Kabetogama Lake and the Namakan Lake basin. Turn northeast here to find nun (red) buoy #26 and set a course to Blind Indian Narrows passing between Sweetnose Island and the mainland. Sweetnose Island was the site of a former fish camp; reportedly workers used to discard their syrup pails on the island, hence the name (syrup is used to process fish).

Continue this course through Blind Indian Narrows. The long island directly ahead is Williams Island. Follow its west shoreline to Hoist Bay. Depending on the time of day and your energy level, find a campsite on the east shore of Williams Island or continue through Hoist Bay for about 2 more miles to the mouth of Junction Bay. Sheen Point, on the east shore of Junction Bay, has an excellent campsite; several others are located nearby on McManus Island and Wolf Pack Islands.

Leave the second morning by heading east, staying just offshore to pass between Wolf Pack and Jug Island and the mainland. The immensity of Namakan Lake can be seen here for the first time. On clear days islands and shorelines 4 or 5 miles away can be seen by looking north or east. Also, wind may begin to influence progress at this point. Just ahead is Randolph Bay. It is guarded by several islands and is a convenient place to slide into, to rest up from stressful winds. Continue to follow the mainland past the rocky shoreline. Bend south to see, fish, or just enjoy walleye rich Deep Slough.

The next landmark is a large unnamed bay that reaches south to the Grassy Bay Portage. Deer and waterfowl are frequently seen along the shorelines. Follow it to its deepest point to find the portage. This is an easy portage, located in a convenient spot. See chapter 50, Crane Lake and Sand Point Lake, for more information on Grassy Bay. Head back out of the bay and bend east toward the maze of islands around Hammer Bay.

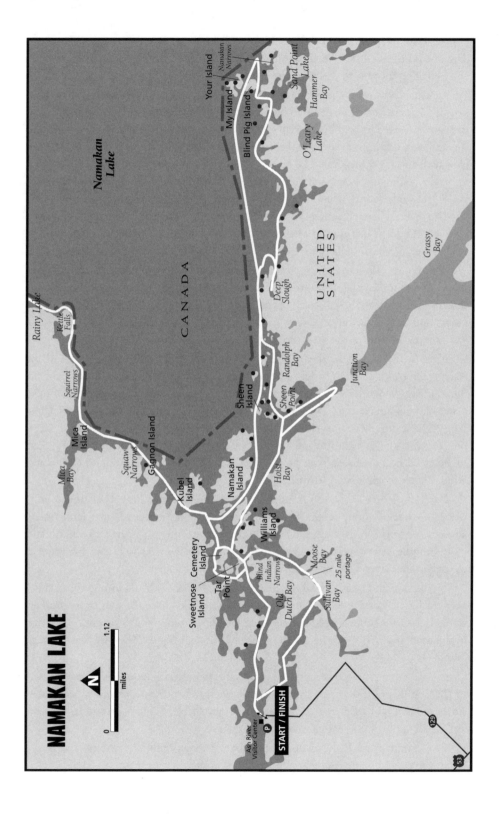

There are several excellent campsites here and two very interesting features to explore. The first is O'Leary Lake, which is found by paddling to the south end of Hammer Bay and portaging 0.1 mile to the lake. The lake is about 1 mile long and about 0.05 wide.

Namakan Narrows is the other feature close at hand and worth exploring. Many consider it the most scenic feature in Voyageurs National Park. Namakan Narrows is a narrow passageway framed by breathtaking cliffs and towering palisades of colored rock. When the sun sets, it reflects from the sides of the narrows and seems to set the rock cliffs on fire; they glow with a warm orange hue. The Narrows is located on the international boundary and forms the division between Sand Point Lake and Namakan Lake. In some places it is only about 100 yards wide, but in other places it is about 0.25 mile wide. It is so narrow and winding that travelers have entered it only to turn around and come back out thinking they were in a blind bay. Use caution when in the narrows: motorboats sometimes roar through at high rates of speed. Indian pictographs are found on the Canadian side of the narrows.

Both points of interest can be readily accessed from Depth Finder Island, Blind Pig Island, Windbreaker Island, Point Island, or the campsites on the unnamed peninsula in this area. Find a location, set up camp, and go exploring. Incidentally, My Island and Your Island, also located in this area, were named by a dispute the Canadians and Americans had over the location of the boundary line.

A day or two could be spent in this area sightseeing and fishing the drop-offs for walleyes. To continue on the original route, head west toward Pike Island. Set out early in the morning before the winds come up, and try to paddle a direct course to reach the peninsula wrapping around Deep Slough. This will save about 2 miles of paddling. Continue to head directly west to try to reach Twin Alligator or Namakan Island before stopping to camp for the night. If winds are too powerful, however, stay safe by paddling close to the mainland to the vicinity of Junction Bay. Then head north between McManus and Sheen Islands to reach Namakan Island.

Namakan Island has three campsites for canoe use and two houseboat sites. Unimproved sites are plentiful. Besides being the largest island in the group, Namakan Island is an interesting place to explore. Deer and bear live in its interior, a ridge runs north and south near the center, and a considerable wetland harboring extensive beaver ponds lies in its midsection. Sandy beaches invite sunbathing or swimming.

Break camp and head around the south shore of Namakan Island to find the channel between Kubel Island and the Kabetogama Peninsula. Continue the northward journey. Kettle Falls or the immediate area is the usual camping location for this night's sleep. Pass by Johnson Bay and continue up the shoreline through Squaw Narrows toward Mica Island.

Mica Island was named because two prospectors found a rich vein of mica on the island in 1895. At that time the clear, crystal rock was extensively utilized—among other uses, in stoves and electrical apparatus—and was extremely valuable. The prospectors sank a shaft and began mining but eventually abandoned the site.

Bend east at Mica Island, follow the channel through Squirrel Narrows, and finally reach Kettle Falls. Some paddlers camp out; others succumb to the temptations of civi-

The channel leading into Namakan Lake.

lization and rent a room for the night. Campsites are located on the shoreline of the Kabetogama Peninsula west of the Kettle Falls Hotel. Camping is allowed in the picnic area near the dam.

The Kettle Falls Hotel was built between 1910 and 1913 by a lumber baron and is on the National Register of Historic Places. It housed lumberjacks, gold prospectors, bootleggers, and sportsmen. John D. Rockefeller and Charles Lindbergh were among the notables who enjoyed the hospitality of the twelve room hotel. Over the years it had deteriorated but was rebuilt in 1988. Now it is open from May through September and from January through March. There is no access except by water or air. At Kettle Falls Dam water drops 10 feet from Namakan Lake to Rainy Lake. This can be viewed from a picnic area that features tables and pit toilets. See the Voyageurs National Park introduction for more information.

When it is time to leave the hotel area, head south on the return trip. If time permits, investigate Mica Bay for walleye fishing. It is often very good on the steep drop-offs along the south shoreline. Continue on the return trip passing between Kubel Island and the shoreline. Pick out a campsite in the vicinity of Sweetnose Island. An improved site is located on Day Marker 23 Island, but unimproved sites can be found on Tar Point, Cemetery Island, and Sweetnose Island.

The next day is the final day of the trip. To avoid retracing the outbound route, head west to Moose Bay, and paddle to the extreme west end of the bay. Avoid the finger of the bay that heads southwest and eventually leads to a creek. Portage from Moose Bay to

Sullivan Bay. This is a 0.25 mile portage along an old railroad grade. Paddle north on Sullivan Bay to the mouth of the bay and turn to the left. The put-in point at the Ash River Visitor Center is a twenty minute paddle west.

Access: Follow U.S. Highway 53 35 miles north from Orr to the junction with County Road 129. Turn east (right) on CR 129 and travel 10.5 miles to the Ash River Visitor Center.

Shuttle: None.

Camping: Ash River State Campground; numerous campsites are available along the route.

Food, gas, lodging: International Falls, Crane Lake, Orr.

For more information: Voyageurs National Park headquarters (see appendix).

50 Crane Lake and Sand Point Lake

Character: Launch the boat outside Voyageurs National Park, at Crane Lake. Head north to Sand Point Lake, the smallest of the four large lakes in the park. It is about 7.5 miles long and 2.5 miles wide at its widest point. Explore deep bays, visit the most scenic location in the park, one of the largest campgrounds, and portage to good fishing lakes. The outbound route could be busy with motorboat traffic, but the return route is planned to avoid traffic. Man-made structures are visible on this route. The fishing can be good, and comfortable campsites are plentiful.

Length: 30 miles, without side trips.

Average run time: 4 days, longer with fishing and sightseeing.

Skill level: Beginner.

Hazards: Wind and motorboat wakes.

Maps: USGS: Red Horse Bay, Crane Lake, Hale Bay.

The paddling: Launch the canoe at Crane Lake, where the Minnesota Department of Natural Resources has a boat landing with free parking. The Voyageurs National Park Ranger Station boat landing has a small fee. Many resorts in the area allow parking for a fee, also. Study the map, then head north to pass on the east side of Bear Island. Nun buoy #32 marks the correct location. Set a direct north course from this buoy to nun buoy #30, and pass the east shoreline of Indian Island. This route will lead into the southern boundary of the Voyageurs National Park and the King Williams Narrows.

The Narrows are very picturesque. High bluffs line the banks. Realize, however, that they restrict the motorboat traffic into a narrow passageway. Use caution, and stay out of the center of the waterway. The west shoreline is often the best choice for a paddling route. At the southern entrance to the Narrows is the King Williams Campground. This is one of only two group campgrounds in the Voyageurs National Park. This location also marks the boundary between Crane Lake and Sand Point Lake.

Exit from the Narrows and continue heading north. A waterway extending east is the entrance to the Little Vermilion Narrows, the western gateway to the Boundary Waters Canoe Area Wilderness. Continue heading north to Harrison Narrows. This passageway is much broader and shorter than the King Williams Narrows. Continue this course to nun buoy #22. About 8 miles have been run by this point, and it might be time to find a campsite for the night. Two improved sites are located on the peninsula north of buoy #22. Locations for camping can be found on the island adjacent to the buoy, also.

Next morning set a direct course for Burnt Island. From Burnt Island plot a route that passes just east of the peninsula jutting out from the west shoreline. Use the compass to set a course from N20 buoy to N14 buoy. By negotiating a direct course through the group of unnamed islands, much time can be saved over staying in the channel signified by nun buoys #20, 18, and 16.

Directly north of buoy N14 is the entrance to Namakan Narrows, considered by many to be the most scenic location in the park. Namakan Narrows is slightly more than 1 mile

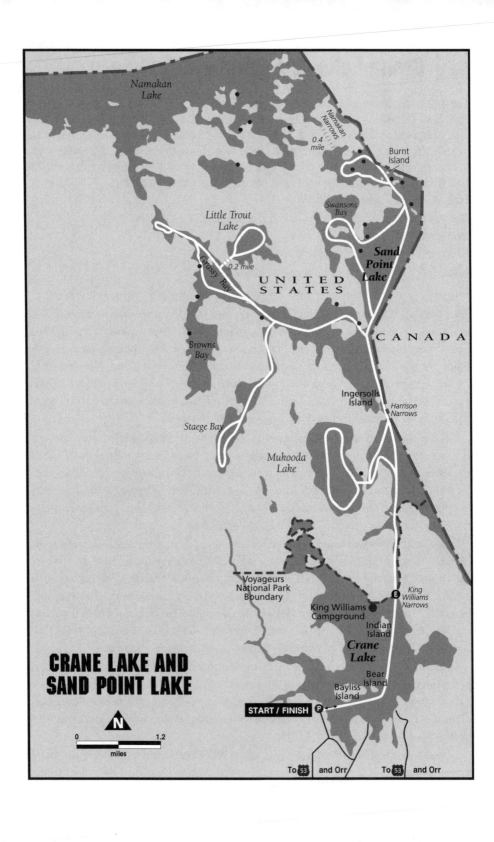

Namakan
Lake

Namakan
Narrows
0.4
mile

Burnt
Island

Swansons
Bay

**Sand
Point
Lake**

Little Trout
Lake

Grassy Bay

0.2 mile

UNITED
STATES

CANADA

Browns
Bay

Ingersolls
Island

Harrison
Narrows

Staege Bay

Mukooda
Lake

Voyageurs
National Park
Boundary

King
Williams
Narrows

King Williams
Campground

Indian
Island

**Crane
Lake**

Bear
Island

Bayliss
Island

START / FINISH

To 53 and Orr

To 53 and Orr

CRANE LAKE AND
SAND POINT LAKE

N

0   1.2
miles

long and is 0.25 mile wide at its widest point and about 100 yards wide at its narrowest point. High, scenic bluffs line its shoreline, and Indian pictographs are found on the Canadian side, about 0.3 mile from the south end. (See chapter 49, Namakan Lake, for more information.) Use caution in the Narrows to avoid problems with motorboats. The Narrows are the dividing point between Sand Point Lake and Namakan Lake. After viewing the Narrows reverse direction to return to Sand Point Lake.

Realize, also, that to avoid backtracking through the Narrows, a 0.4-mile portage back to Sand Point Lake is available. It is located in the first bay west of the north end of the Namakan Narrows and leads to the first bay west of the south end of the Narrows. It requires about 2 miles of additional paddling.

If time permits, explore along the shoreline of the first bay south of the Narrows and try casting for walleyes on the drop-offs. Watch carefully along the south shore of the bay for the portage that leads to Swansons Bay. This portage is about 0.3 mile long and is level and dry and has an easy rating. Take this portage to avoid retracing the previous route and avoid the occasionally busy motorboat passageway. This is also a good place to camp for the second night. A level camping area is located near the snow machine sign that marks the portage.

Next morning negotiate the portage to Swansons Bay. Explore Swansons Bay, if time and energy permit, but eventually paddle back out into Sand Point Lake and head south to the mouth of Grassy Bay. Turn west and paddle between the island at the mouth of the bay and the mainland. Head into the bay. Enter a water wonderland that includes Grassy Bay, Little Trout Lake, Browns Bay, and Staege Bay.

Grassy Bay is more than 0.25 mile wide and about 5 miles long. It is a very beautiful waterway. At the upper end, towering bluffs with stark pink and gray cliffs rise 100 feet above the water. The entrance to Staege Bay comes in to the south shoreline, about 2.5 miles west of the mouth of Grassy Bay. Staege Bay is about 3 miles long and very narrow at the mouth but opens up somewhat as it deepens. Towering bluffs line the east shoreline making it a very scenic part of the park.

After viewing Staege Bay head north on Grassy Bay. The next point of interest is the portage to Little Trout Lake. The portage is 0.2 mile long and rated easy. Little Trout Lake is about 1 mile long and 250 feet deep. It offers lake trout and smallmouth bass to the angler.

Continue north on Grassy Bay; Browns Bay is next. This 2 mile long bay is also lined with high, scenic cliffs and can offer good fishing. It is a good place to camp for the night. Next morning continue north on Grassy Bay to see more scenic shorelines. At the north end of the bay, the portage to Namakan Lake is found. Turn around here, paddle back to the mouth of Grassy Bay, and turn south.

Paddle along the west shoreline of Sand Point Lake, past Ingersolls Island. Stay along the shoreline to enter the bay that contains the 0.1-mile portage to Mukooda Lake. There is another portage, also. It is found north of Ingersolls Island and is longer and more difficult than the recommended portage. Negotiate the recommended portage over solid rock to find Mukooda Lake. The lake is more than 1.5 miles long, 1 mile wide, and 78 feet deep. Lake trout, smallmouth bass, perch, northern pike, and walleye are possible shore lunch entrees. If the fish are biting too good to leave, several improved campsites are available on the lake. The alternative is to paddle 4 miles south along the shoreline of Crane Lake to the King Williams Campground.

Return to the put-in point on Crane Lake the next day to end the trip.

Access: Start at the junction of U.S. Highway 53 and County Road 23 in Orr. Follow CR 23 to its junction with County Road 24 at Buyck (Bike), and turn onto CR 24 and continue to the shore of Crane Lake. The distance from Orr to Crane Lake is about 28 miles.

Shuttle: None.

Camping: Ash River State Campground.

Food, gas, lodging: International Falls, Crane Lake, Orr.

For more information: Voyageurs National Park headquarters (see appendix).

51 ⌁ Chain of Lakes

Character: Paddle across a section of Rainy Lake to the Kabetogama Peninsula. Find the creek that leads to Locator Lake. Continue to paddle and portage through the Chain of Lakes. Long portages must be negotiated. Enjoy fishing and sightseeing. Return by a route that leads to Kabetogama Lake.

Length: 32 miles.

Average run time: 4 to 6 days, longer with fishing and sightseeing.

Skill level: Beginner.

Hazards: Wind on the large access lakes and rough portages.

Maps: USGS: Daley Bay, Soldier Point, Ash River NE, Cranberry Bay, Island View, Kempton Bay, Kettle Falls, Rainy Lake, Kabetogama Lake.

The paddling: Study the map and then launch at the Rainy Lake Visitor Center or at Island View and head east to the Kabetogama Peninsula shoreline of Black Bay. Follow the shoreline closely enough to be safe from any sudden storms. Head for the Diamond Island area and camp for the first night. In calm weather this is an easy 6 miles of paddling. Improved campsites are found on Diamond Island, along the Peninsula shoreline, and on nearby Arden Island. Proceeding beyond this area the first day is not recommended. If the next improved campsite, Cranberry Creek, is occupied, 5 miles of paddling and a long, rugged portage lie between Diamond Island and Locator Lake, where other campsites are found.

Leave Diamond Island and head east to pass between Arden Island and the larger, unnamed island lying west of Arden Island. Topographical maps show a passageway between the island south of Diamond Island and the mainland, but it has been filled in with marsh grass and is impassable except in periods of high water. Enter Cranberry Bay and head to the southern tip of the bay to find Cranberry Creek.

The mouth of Cranberry Creek is noticeable because it has a lowland marshy area on the west side and a highland bluff on the east side. It can best be approached from the centerline of Cranberry Bay. The trip up Cranberry Creek is a rapid and pleasant journey. Cranberry Creek campsite is bypassed. The portage starts just downstream of the first set of rugged rapids. It leaves the west bank of the creek and meanders 1.3 miles through wetlands and up hills to the southern end of the portage. Cranberry Creek is deep and accommodating from there on to Locator Lake, with some sharp curves and possible beaver dams to work around.

Locator Lake is the largest of the Chain of Lakes and has high bluffs on three sides; it is almost 1 mile long and 0.5 mile wide. The lake is about 52 feet deep and hosts northern pike, yellow perch, and smallmouth bass. A campsite with two tent pads, fire ring, bear pole, table, and privy is located on the north shore, and a day use area is found on the south shore. Steep shorelines limit the unimproved campsite opportunities.

Paddle east on a short stream to find War Club Lake. War Club Lake is 40 feet deep and is not as long and slightly narrower than Locator Lake. Fishing opportunities are

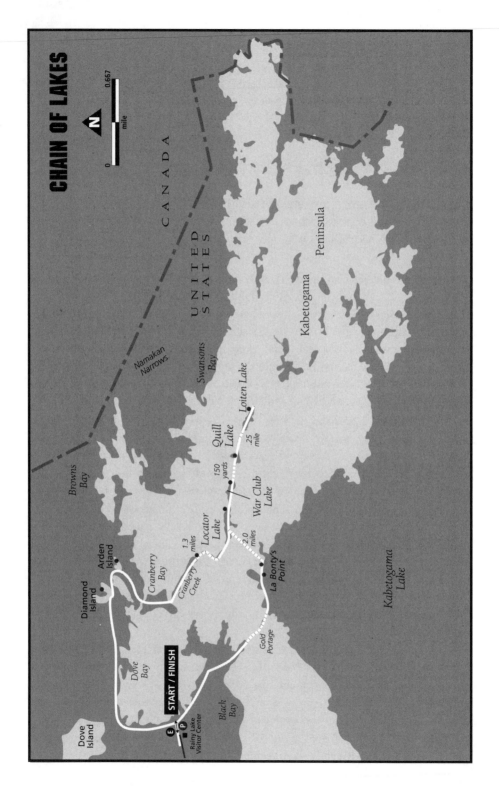

A large boulder in Cranberry Bay, polished almost smooth by the action of a glacier.

similar. An improved campsite with a fire ring, table, and privy is located on the north shore of the lake.

The next lake of the chain is Quill Lake. It requires a 150-yard portage from War Club Lake. The stream between the lakes is the site of several beaver dams that must be pulled over or bypassed. Quill Lake covers 92 acres, has a steep, heavily wooded shoreline, and is probably the most scenic of any of the lakes in the chain. It also might offer the best fishing. Northern pike and largemouth bass are found here, as are yellow perch and rock bass. A Voyageurs National Park campsite sits on an island in the center of the lake. It has a tent pad and fire ring. Paddle to the east end of this lake to cross a small pond and locate the stream from Loiten Lake. Negotiate the stream to the portage to Loiten Lake. This portage is rated as rugged. It crosses large boulders and fallen trees for 0.25 mile.

Loiten Lake is about a mile long and more than 0.25 mile wide. It covers 90 acres and is the highest in elevation of any of the chain of lakes. Northern pike can be found in its depths. The Loiten Lake campsite has a fire ring, a table, and a privy. This is a good area to spot deer, moose, or even a bear. Enjoy Loiten Lake for at least one day and then reverse direction to return to the put-in point. To avoid backtracking find the Locator Lake Trail and portage the canoe to Kabetogama Lake. The Locator Lake Trail ends on Locator Lake, adjacent to the day use area at the west end of the lake on the south shore. It is 2 miles long and climbs over ridges before reaching Kabetogama Lake 0.75 mile east of La Bonty's Point. At Kabetogama Lake a sign and dock mark the location for the trailhead. Paddling from Loiten Lake to the Locator Lake Trail and then portaging 2 miles to Kabetogama

Lake requires considerable energy, and most groups will be ready to find one of the two campsites nearest the trailhead and rest up.

On the final day paddle northwest to find the Gold River, which runs between Kabetogama Lake and Black Bay. Find and negotiate the 0.2 mile Gold Portage that bypasses rapids along the river. Continue north to the Rainy Lake Visitor Center and the end of the journey.

Access: From the junction of U.S. Highway 53 and Minnesota State Highway 11 in International Falls, turn east and follow MN 11 for 12 miles to the Rainy Lake Visitor Center.

Shuttle: None.

Camping: Chief Woodenfrog State Campground, Ash River State Campground. Several campsites on the trips.

Food, gas, lodging: Orr, International Falls.

For more information: Voyageurs National Park headquarters (see appendix).

52 Shoepack Lake

Character: This run will challenge your stamina and outdoor skills. Paddle across a short section of Kabetogama Lake, enter a bay, paddle to the end, and find a long portage. Portage and paddle to three interior connected lakes. Enjoy the solitude and the opportunity to fish for muskies on a remote lake. Take drinking water along or be prepared to boil and filter the lake water.

Length: 20 miles.

Average run time: 3 to 4 days.

Skill level: Beginner.

Hazards: Wind on Kabetogama Lake.

Maps: USGS: Daley Bay, Ash River.

The paddling: Shoepack Lake is the largest lake in the Kabetogama Peninsula. It is also one of the most difficult lakes to approach. Bring fishing tackle; this lake has a good musky population and the fish usually can be persuaded to bite. The lake water is heavily stained.

Although Shoepack Lake can be reached from Rainy Lake, the most expedient route starts at the Ash River Visitor Center and accesses the Peninsula at the east end of Lost Bay. Conditioned paddlers, traveling light, can make it to Shoepack Lake in one day. The route is about 5.5 miles long and requires two long portages; the longest is 1.4 miles.

Depart from the boat landing at the Ash River Visitor Center and paddle north around the west shore of Round Bear Island. Enter Lost Bay and paddle to Eks Bay. Find the portage/hiking trail. Head north from the Eks Bay campsite and negotiate the trail to Jorgens Lake. This is about 0.9 mile long. The trail has been improved by planking in the wet areas, but steep ridges are encountered. Watch for and bypass the spur to Quarter Line Lake.

The portage ends at the Voyageurs National Park campsite on the west shore of Jorgens Lake. This lake is about 1 mile long, covers 64 acres, and is 21 feet deep in places. Northern pike live in its stained water. Take any needed rest here at the campsite, then paddle to the north end to find the old logging road that leads to Little Shoepack Lake. A narrow bay along the west shoreline leads to the trail. Take out here and walk directly west through the grassy clearing. Little Shoepack Lake lies northwest of this point, at a compass reading (uncorrected) of 300 degrees. However, it is necessary to walk almost due west to find the old logging trail that leads to Little Shoepack. The logging trail reaches northwest to the east end of Little Shoepack Lake.

Little Shoepack Lake is about 1 mile long and 29 feet deep. Musky live here, and a campsite with a fire ring and table is located on the east shoreline. The 0.25-mile portage from Little Shoepack Lake to Shoepack Lake is found in the northeast corner of the lake. A stream connects the two, but it is usually impassable because of beaver dams and low water. The portage ends at the southernmost tip of Shoepack Lake.

Shoepack Lake is the largest lake in the Peninsula. It is 1.75 mile long, 1 mile wide, and 24 feet deep. It has an excellent musky population. The campsite is located on the

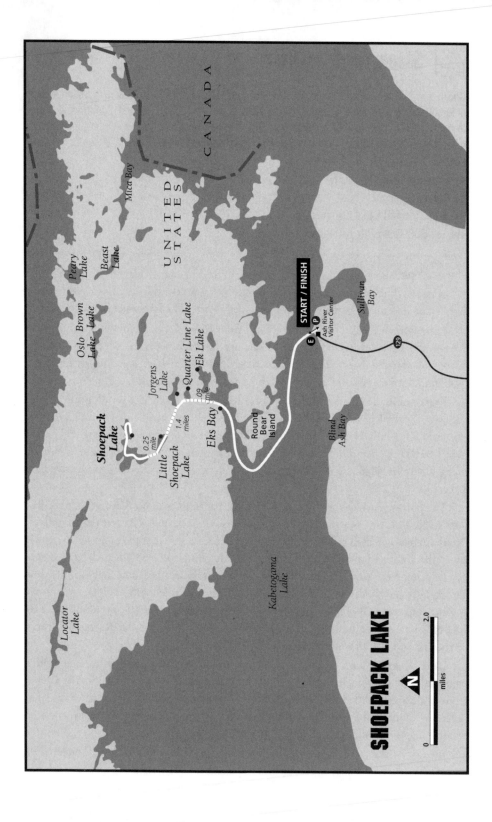

CANADA

UNITED STATES

Mica Bay

Peary Lake

Beast Lake

Oslo Brown Lake Lake

Jorgens Lake

Quarter Line Lake

Ek Lake

0.9 mile

0.25 mile

1.4 miles

Shoepack Lake

Little Shoepack Lake

Eks Bay

Round Bear Island

Locator Lake

Kabetogama Lake

Blind Ash Bay

Sullivan Bay

START / FINISH

E P

Ash River Visitor Center

129

SHOEPACK LAKE

N

0   2.0

miles

south shore and has a table and privy. Most of the shoreline is not suited for camping, but a grassy area near a cabin site in the southernmost arm of the lake is very useable. Shoepack Lake water should be boiled and strained to make it potable. A fire tower lookout that provides an excellent view of the peninsula is found along the Kabetogama Lake/Shoepack Lake Trail about 1 mile west of Shoepack Lake.

Enjoy Shoepack Lake and then reverse the route to return to the Ash River Visitor Center. On the return trip Quarter Line Lake and Ek Lake can also be explored.

Other interior lakes that are well worth the effort to visit are Cruiser Lake, Oslo Lake, Brown Lake, and Peary Lake—accessible from Rainy Lake—and Beast Lake, accessible from Namakan Lake. The Voyageurs National Park visitor centers can provide more information and also advise if the canoes kept on some of the lakes are available for those who don't want to portage in with their own equipment.

Access: Follow U.S. Highway 53 approximately 48 miles north from Orr to the junction with County Road 129. Turn east (right) on CR 129 and travel 10.5 miles to the Ash River Visitor Center.

Shuttle: None.

Camping: Ash River State Campground.

Food, gas, lodging: Orr, International Falls.

For more information: Superintendent, Voyageurs National Park (see introduction).

Appendix: Resources

U.S. Forest Service

Forest Supervisor's Office
Superior National Forest
8901 Grand Avenue Place
Duluth, MN 55808
(218) 626–4399
www.fs.fed.us/r9/superior

Laurentian Ranger Station
318 Forestry Road
Aurora, MN 55808
(218) 229–8800

Kawishiwi Ranger Station
118 S. 4th Avenue E
Ely, MN 55731
(218) 365–7600 (winter)
(218) 365–7561 (5/1–9/30)

Gunflint Ranger Station
P.O. Box 790
Grand Marais, MN 55604
(218) 387–1750

La Croix Ranger Station
320 N. Highway 53
Cook, MN 55723
(218) 666–0020

Tofte Ranger Station
Box 2159
Tofte, MN 55615
(218) 663–7280

Isabella Work Station
9420 Highway 1
Isabella, MN 55607
(218) 323–7722

BWCAW Reservations

BWCAW Reservation Center
P.O. Box 462
Ballston Spa, NY 12020
(877) 550–6777 (toll)
(518) 884–9951 (fax)
www.bwcaw.org

Canada
Quetico Provincial Park
District Manager
Ministry of Natural Resources
Atikokan, Ontario POT 1CO Canada
(807) 597–2735

Maps

Detailed canoe-route maps are available
from area outfitters and some Forest
Service offices. Or:

W.A. Fisher Company
123 Chestnut
P.O. Box 1107
Virginia, MN 55792
(218) 741–9544

McKenzie Maps
8479 Frye Road
Minong, WI 54859
(800) 749–2113

Superior National Forest ¼-mile maps are
available from Superior National Forest,
8901 Grand Avenue Place, Duluth, MN
55808.

Topographical quadrangle maps are dispensed by the USGS:

U.S. Geological Survey Map Distribution Center
Federal Center Building 41
P.O. Box 25286
Denver, CO 80225
(303) 236–7477
(800) USA–Maps

Emergency Phone Numbers

Cook County Sheriff
Grand Marais/Tofte Area
(218) 387–3030

Lake County Sheriff
Ely/Isabella Area
(218) 834–8385

St. Louis County Sheriff
Ely/Cook Area
(218) 749–6010

To Register a Canoe or Get a Fishing License by Mail

DNR License Center
500 Lafayette Road
Box 26
St. Paul, MN 55155-4026
(651) 296–2316

Minnesota State Publications and General Information

Minnesota Department of Natural Resources Information Center
500 Lafayette Road
St. Paul, MN 55155-4040
(621) 296–6157
info@dnr.state.mn.us

To Find Area Resorts and Outfitters:

Cook Chamber of Commerce
P.O. Box 59, Cook, MN 55723
(800) 648–5897

Ely Chamber of Commerce
1600 E. Sheridan Street, Ely, MN 55731
(218) 365–6123

Crane Lake Visitor and Tourism Bureau
Crane Lake, MN 55725
(800) 362–6405

Luften-Tofte Tourism Association
Box 2248, Tofte, MN 55615
(218) 663–7804

Grand Marais Reservation and Information Service
P.O. Box 1048, Grand Marais, MN 55604
(888) 922–5000

Gunflint Trail Association
P.O. Box 205, Grand Marais, MN 55604
(800) 338–6932

A free publications catalog listing BWCAW related material is available from:

Lake State Interpretive Association
3131 Highway 53
International Falls, MN 56649
(218) 283–2103

Other Numbers

U.S. Customs: (218) 720–5201
U.S. Immigration and Naturalization Service: (218) 720–5207
Canadian Customs: (807) 274–3655
Canadian Immigration: (807) 274–3815

About the Author

James Churchill and his wife spent two-and-a-half years researching and enjoying the vast and rugged Boundary Waters and Voyageurs National Park. Sadly, he passed away before seeing this book published.

Jim was an avid fisherman and nature enthusiast who spent much of his time paddling and exploring rivers and lakes. He grew up in a small town in southern Wisconsin, where his father taught him about fishing, hunting, and trapping while his mother educated him about life. After high school Jim enlisted in the navy and served in the Seabees during the Korean War. He married his wife, Joan, in 1952, and they had two children—Jim Jr. and Jolain. Jim worked in a factory by day, while at night he did freelance writing and studied photography. In 1974 he quit the job he had held for fifteen years, packed up his family, and moved north. For almost the next thirty years he lived his dream of being an outdoor writer and photographer.

In addition to *Paddling the Boundary Waters and Voyageurs National Park,* Jim wrote fourteen other books and nearly 1,000 magazine articles. He was a member of the Outdoor Writers Association of America since 1976.